GW01046560

Grumman F-14 Tomcat

Grumman F-14 Tomcat

David Baker

First published in 1998 by
The Crowood Press Ltd
Ramsbury, Marlborough
Wiltshire SN8 2HR

© David Baker 1998

All rights reserved. No part of this
publication may be reproduced or
transmitted in any form or by any means,
electronic or mechanical, including
photocopying, recording, or any
information storage and retrieval system,
without permission in writing from the
publishers.

**British Library
Cataloguing-in-Publication Data**

A catalogue record for this book is
available from the British Library.

ISBN 1 86126 094 6

This books is dedicated to Rachael who wears the Tomcat sweat shirt but, unlike her father, has yet to sample the delights of the 'feline swinger'.

Typeset by Phoenix Typesetting, Ilkley,
West Yorkshire

Printed and bound in Great Britain by
Butler & Tanner, Frome

Contents

Chronology

Because the F-14 emerged from the disastrous failure of General Dynamics' F-111B it has a less defined programme start date than most combat aircraft and the following chronology absorbs the key elements in the TFX requirement that preceded it so as to reflect this evolution.

1959

The Navy issued its Fleet Air Defense requirement defining a long-range perimeter patrol fighter equipped with very long-range missiles capable of autonomous flight control. Early in 1960 this resulted in the Douglas F6D-1 Missileer proposal equipped with Bendix AAM-10 Eagle missiles.

1960, 14 June

The USAF issued SOR-183 calling for a successor to the Republic F-105 Thunderchief capable of Mach 2.5 dash, rough field operation and treetop cruise for 500 miles (640 km) at supersonic speed.

1960, December

Outgoing Defense Secretary Thomas S. Gates cancelled the subsonic Missileer /Eagle combination as much to save money and balance the Federal budget books as for any technical reason. Work on the intercept radar and missile continued.

1960

During the year work began on the Phoenix missile as a replacement for the AIM-47A Falcon designed for the YF-12A.

1961, 16 February

Incoming Defense Secretary Robert S. McNamara officially endorsed a 'common' aircraft design to fit both Air Force SOR-183 and Navy FDF requirements with individual variants and using as great a number of common components as

possible. This became known as the Tactical Fighter Experimental (TFX) requirement. McNamara also asked the Army and the Marine Corps to obtain their future aircraft through TFX.

1961, June

The Army and the Navy refused to have anything to do with the TFX programme, saying that it was totally unsuitable for their requirements.

1961, July

Following a series of preliminary studies on a common aircraft for use by the Air Force and the Navy, Grumman came to an agreement with General Dynamics to join forces in the preparation of a design proposal. Seeing in the emerging requirement a lucrative production order for both the Air Force and the Navy, there were few industry critics of the 'commonality' concept.

1961, 22 August

Secretary of the Air Force Eugene M. Zuckert and Secretary of the Navy Paul Fay met the Secretary of Defense to assert that the TFX concept would not work and that it would compromise both variants.

1961, 1 September

McNamara flatly rejected the Secretaries of the Air Force and the Navy in their assertion that TFX would not work, ordering them to proceed with the programme. The Pentagon described its new TFX programme.

1961, 1 October

TFX Request for Proposals went out to industry following many months of work by contractors defining a compromise aircraft for the dual-service TFX requirement.

1961, 6 December

Six bids are entered for the TFX RFP and

GD/Grumman submit a joint proposal. None was found totally acceptable, but the Pentagon decided to enter the best two designs in a funded rework resulting in Boeing and GD/Grumman being asked to enter fresh designs.

1962, 19 January

The System Source Selection Board chose Boeing over GD/Grumman to receive the TFX contract, but the General Electric MF295 engine favoured by Boeing was changed to the Pratt & Whitney JTF10 and both companies entered a third round.

1962, 2 April

In the third round of the competition the Navy refused the proposed aircraft designs from Boeing and GD/Grumman, claiming their insufficient calculated loiter time, and when three weeks of tinkering failed to satisfy the Navy a fourth round was initiated on 29 June.

1962, August

Never a builder of aeroplanes, Hughes Aircraft received a contract for the development of the AIM-54 Phoenix missile assigned to the F-111B. Unguided flight tests began in 1965 followed by guided tests a year later and the first successful intercept in September 1966.

1962, 10 September

In the fourth and final submission of design proposals for the TFX requirement, Boeing again came out top and was the preferred choice of the Air Force and the Navy selection boards.

1962, 18 September

A tri-service agreement redefined nomenclature for US military aircraft, assigning sequential numbers for the USAF, the Navy and the Army. The VFX specification would result in the F-14, the first Navy fighter to receive a designation in the new system.

1962, 24 November

Against all technical and service advice and recommendation, Defense Secretary McNamara chose the GD/Grumman TFX proposal for the F-111 aircraft design. GD received a contract for eighteen Air Force (F-111A) and five Navy (F-111B) prototypes and pledged to get the first F-111A flying within twenty-five months. In an outcry from the Congress, hearings were held in early 1963 at which the GD/Grumman selection was scrutinized and the Defense Secretary called to explain his actions.

1963, March

General Dynamics rang the bell on serious technical problems with the F-111 design and NASA produced wind-tunnel studies that revealed flaws in the configuration. A serious overweight problem ensued and grew during the year.

1964, 3 February

After examining the design development of the F-111B, the Navy issued a detailed report condemning the aircraft as totally unsuitable for carrier-based operations in the FDF role. Eight days later the Chief of the Navy Weapons Bureau called for a total redesign.

1965, 21 December

The first F-111A took to the air ten days ahead of schedule. In flight tests over the next several months serious problems were experienced in engine stability, inlet flow control and base drag.

1965, 18 May

Seriously overweight but thirteen days ahead of schedule, the first F-111B flew at Grumman's Peconic Airfield, Long Island, at the start of a test programme during which compressor stalls similar to those afflicting the F-111A plagued the Navy version. The Pentagon agreed to a series of weight-reduction measures to be effective from the fourth Navy prototype but this eventually cut the 'commonality' of parts from 80 to 29 per cent and still left the aircraft below the performance requirements.

1965, 27 July

Capt D.C. Davis became the first Navy pilot to fly the F-111B when he took the first prototype aircraft into the air from Edwards Air Force Base in California.

1965, 24 October

The second Navy F-111B made its first flight from Peconic, seven days ahead of schedule.

1965, October

During the month the Navy conducted a Preliminary Evaluation on the F-111B and confirmed that the type was wholly unsuited to carrier work and that it would not fill the seaborne role for which it was funded.

1965, 21 December

The third F-111B flew at Peconic Airfield, the last of the grossly overweight prototypes.

1966, January

Preliminary Navy work began on the definition of a concept for the Fleet Defense Fighter role redefined in the wake of continuing problems with the F-111B design. This pre-concept phase allowed the mission and design engineers to look again at requirements to shape a completely new aircraft.

1966, 25 August

Secretary of Defense McNamara held the first in a series of weekly meetings in an attempt to solve serious technical problems with both versions of the F-111.

1967, March–April

A second Navy Preliminary Evaluation on the F-111B concentrated on the fourth and the fifth prototype, the first to get the weight improvement measures.

1967, September

Initial pre-concept definition of a new FDF was completed by the Navy and the VFX requirement emerged. Concept formulation now began in close association with Grumman, the engineering partner on the F-111 and long-established Navy aircraft builder.

1967, October

To ease funding curves and maximize the results of existing work, Grumman proposed a two-phase VFX programme: VFX 1 would use the engine from the F-111 while VFX-2 would adopt a high-technology engine and bring this superior version in at a later date.

1968, 1 January

The VFX concept was finalized and a contract definition was written for a replacement for the F-111B, which the Navy believed would be cancelled.

1968, January

Grumman consolidated work on a F-111B successor and defined a concept designated Design 303, eventually to become the basis for Grumman's winning entry in the VFX competition.

1968, May

Despite fierce lobbying by the F-111's proponents, including the Secretary of Defense, Armed Services Committees in both Houses of Congress refused to allow more money to go on the naval version, effectively cancelling the F-111B.

1968, 18 June

The Secretary of Defense authorized the release of the VFX RFP, putting the Navy back where it was in 1959, albeit with a much more advanced specification and in a better position to get the aircraft it wanted. With added years of evolving requirements, the VFX was intended to provide both an air superiority role – replacing the F-4 Phantom II – as well as the fundamental role of Fleet Defense Fighter.

1968, 21 June

The Department of Defense issued its RFP on the VFX requirement, attracting proposals from five prospective contractors. Under the terms of the Contract Definition Phase the Navy would review the submissions and select a single contractor by 15 January 1969. By this date Grumman had selected the 303E design as the optimum configuration among several evaluated in the first six months of the year.

1968, 10 July

In a historic but long overdue initiative after more than $377 million (in 1960s money) had been wasted, the Department of Defense cancelled work on the F-111B and began negotiations with GD and Grumman on contract termination. Agreement was reached on 14 December.

1968, 17 July

Five contractors were each awarded work packages for the VFX Contract Definition Phase: General Dynamics, McDonnell

Douglas, North American Rockwell, a LTV/Lockheed team and Grumman. Formal contract definition began and was completed on 1 October.

1968, 25 September
The Navy completed its Source Selection Plan and set up several investigating groups to evaluate the five VFX contract proposals due on 1 October.

1968, 1 October
The five CDP submissions were received from the competing contractors. Grumman submitted a refined variant of Design 303E, which at this date had a single fin but in other respects closely matched the definitive F-14.

1968, 13 December
Evaluation of the five CDP proposals was completed by the respective Navy boards and a decision made to encourage further work from Grumman and McDonnell Douglas. This was endorsed by the Chief of Naval Operations and the Secretary of Defense two days later.

1968, 17 December
The Department of Defense formally announced the rejection of VFX proposals from General Dynamics, North American Rockwell and the LTV/Lockheed team. Detailed analysis began on proposals from McDonnell Douglas and Grumman and the two companies were invited to make any desired alterations to enhance their chances.

1969, 5 January
Design teams from McDonnell Douglas and Grumman submitted their final proposals for the VFX contract.

1969, 14 January
The Department of Defense announced that Grumman was to be awarded a definitive research and development Fixed Price Incentive contract for the VFX, to be known in service as the F-14 Tomcat. A formal contract is signed on 3 February embracing six prototypes (later expanded to twelve) and 463 production aircraft (later changed to incorporate eight pre-production types). First flight is fixed for no later than 31 January 1971.

1969, 17 March
A radical step toward the future way of handling the Tomcat as a total weapon system was taken when the first Integrated Logistic Support Management Team (ILSMT) meeting was held in Bethpage.

1969, March
Design of the F-14 is frozen and Grumman changed the single-fin for a twin-fin configuration, making the last major shift in the external appearance.

1969, 8 May
The first engineering drawings of the F-14 were released to the jig sheds and detailed design was well under way.

1969, 23 May
The first Mock-Up Review was held at Grumman and detailed parts manufacture began during June.

1969, 18 August
The F-14 Management Systems Demonstration began and extended until 25 September, during which NASA verified the aerodynamic and aircraft performance characteristics.

1969, November
Construction began at Grumman of the F-14 Engineering Mock-up Manufacturing Aid (EMMA), a full-scale, three-dimensional metal model of the definitive design aiding systems fit-check and proximity evaluation as well as enhancing the subsystems layout definition. The wing pivot-bearing test article was completed.

1970, 21 January
The software and hardware Systems Integration Test Stand (SITS) arrived at Point Mugu, California, and was followed on 2 February by the AN/AWG-9 computer development test equipment for installation with the SITS.

1970, 27 February
Grumman submitted a proposal to the US Navy for the F-14B, designed to fill the advanced VFX-2 requirement. The aircraft differed from the F-14A primarily in an improved powerplant based on the JTF-22, the Pratt & Whitney F401-PW-400. Pratt & Whitney were awarded an advanced technology engine (ATE) development contract.

1970, February
The first AWG-9 radar for the F-14 was delivered to the Navy; the first integrated radar/missile tests began in April 1972.

1970, 2 March
Grumman completed fabrication of the boron horizontal stabilizer, a major feature of the weight-conscious design. Static tests were completed on 8 May.

1970, 15 April
LTV began test No. 9 of the wing pivot development programme. Tests were suspended on 2 June when two lower lugs experienced fatigue failure at 1.5 times the life cycle, equivalent to 9,000 as against the expected 12,000hr.

1970, 18 May
Considering the appalling mismatch between the engine and the inlet for the TF30 installed in the F-111, an important milestone was reached as inlet compatibility trials started on a XTF30-P-412 ground-test engine for the F-14. These tests finished with flying colours on 9 July, completely vindicating the new boxed inlet design.

1970, 23 July
Grumman successfully completed the final EMMA configuration and systems/subsystems integration demonstration for the Navy.

1970, 1 September
The boron stabilizer fatigue test was successfully completed with an equivalent life of 12,000hr, twice the expected time.

1970, 25 October
At 4:00am a large flatbed truck hauled the first prototype F-14 (BuAer No. 157980), shrouded for secrecy, from its assembly plant at Bethpage, NY, at the start of a journey that would take it to Plant 7 at Grumman's Calverton facility.

1970, 14 December
Engine runs were completed on the first F-14 prototype and taxi trials began at Calverton.

1970, 21 December
Piloted by Robert Smythe with William Miller in the back seat, the first F-14 prototype lifted off the runway at Calverton Field during the late afternoon for a first flight that lasted only a few minutes with two circuits of the area at 3,000ft.

1970, 30 December
As a result of massive hydraulic failure, the first prototype F-14 crashed at Calverton during the aircraft's second flight. Miller

and Smythe ejected within a second of impact.

1971, 29 January

An acceptance test on the Versatile Avionics Shop Test (VAST) station was successfully completed. Designated USM-247, it was built around a Univac 1240 computer for F-14 electronics tests.

1971, 1 February

Wing pivot test article 9A successfully demonstrated survivability at 7,000 test hours, equivalent to 15,120 flying hours, far beyond the specified equivalent 12,000 flying hours.

1971, 15 February

Grumman senior executives began a week-long briefing of Naval Air Systems Command on serious funding problems with the F-14, citing changes demanded by the Pentagon which increased the unit price.

1971, 5 March

The Pratt & Whitney TF30-P-412 engine completed qualification tests with performance ratings in excess of specification. On 28 April Pratt & Whitney demonstrated F401-P-400 installation and removal procedures, the engine specified for the F-14B.

1971, 31 March

In a letter to the Navy's Assistant Commander for Contracts, Grumman sought changes in the funding for future F-14 production lots to absorb increased costs and ease an impending financial crisis. The government refused to talk.

1971, 24 May

The No. 2 prototype F-14 (BuAer No. 157981) made its first flight from Calverton Field. Its flight test programme would explore high angle-of-attack characteristics and handling. Later it would be used for gun trials. The aircraft logged 454.4 flying hours before it was attrited on 13 May 1974.

1971, 27 July

Grumman made a commitment to Congress to build forty-eight F-14s in FY 1972 after seeking help with its financial problems by raising the funds it could not get from the government. This was only a short-term measure and did nothing to alleviate Grumman's long-term problems.

1971, 31 August

The third F-14 prototype to fly, aircraft No. 1X (BuAer No. 157991), made its first flight. It was officially the No. 12 aircraft assigned to replace No. 1 destroyed on 30 December 1970. It would explore the full performance envelope and perform high-speed tests. The first supersonic flight was logged on 16 September and it would exceed Mach 2.25 by the end of 1972. The aircraft completed 894.7 flying hours.

1971, 7 October

The F-14 prototype No. 4 (BuAer No. 157983) made its first flight and on 30 October commenced an avionics test programme when it arrived at Point Mugu, where the AWG-9 and the Phoenix missile system would be tested. After 1,375 flying hours the aircraft was mothballed.

1971, 26 November

F-14 prototype No. 5 (BuAer No. 157984) made its first flight from Calverton. On 12 December it was flown to Point Mugu where it was used for systems tests and mission feasibility trials. After 739.3 flying hours the aircraft was placed in storage.

1971, 2 December

Navy Preliminary Evaluation 1 (NPE-1) began during which a review of test data and flight information demonstrated that the aircraft was high on performance compared with the specification. NPE-1 was completed on 16 December.

1971, 10 December

F-14 No. 6 (BuAer No. 157985) made its first flight. This aircraft would conduct missile separation trials during its assignment at Point Mugu where it arrived on 15 January 1972. The aircraft was attrited on 20 June 1973 after 164 flying hours.

1971, 12 December

The wing carry-through box beam successfully completed fatigue tests equivalent to 12,000 flight hours or twice the life of the aircraft.

1971, 28 December

F-14 prototype No. 3 (BuAer No. 157982) and No. 9 (BuAer No. 1597988) made their first flights, becoming the seventh and the eighth aircraft to fly. No. 3 was assigned to test the structural limits of the aircraft and No. 9 was sent to Point Mugu for AWG-9 evaluation with Hughes

Aircraft engineers. It arrived on 10 January 1972. No. 3 was placed in storage after 752.4 flying hours and No. 9 was mothballed after 1,506.3 flying hours.

1971, 31 December

F-14 No. 8 (BuAer No. 157987) made its first flight before joining the flight test programme to gather aerodynamic data in several parts of the performance spectrum. The aircraft was attrited on 19 September 1974 after 456 flying hours.

1972, 20 January

Grumman informed the Navy that it could not honour original F-14 production quota from Lot 5 because of financial pressures on the company. The Navy took this to the Pentagon and the government began talks which lasted throughout the year.

1972, 29 February

F-14 No. 10 (BuAer No. 157989) made its first flight. It went for carrier trials and was ferried to Patuxent on 6 April where it was lifted aboard the USS *Forrestal*. It made the first catapult launch on 15 June and performed the first on-deck landing on 28 June. Two days later the aircraft was written off after completing only 88 flying hours when it crashed at the Naval Air Test Centre, Patuxent River, Maryland.

1971, 6 March

F-14 No. 11 (BuAer No. 157990) made its first flight. On 24 March it arrived at Point Mugu where it began a series of non-weapons systems tests. After 1,274 flying hours it was mothballed.

1972, 2 May

F-14 No. 13 (BuAer No. 158612) took to the air for the first time. It was assigned to the electromagnetic and radiation test programme and spent its early days in Grumman's anechoic chamber, arriving at the facility on 2 August.

1972, May

The Shah of Iran made it known to President Nixon that he was shopping for high-performance aircraft to counter Soviet intrusions of Iranian air space and requested details on a potential purchase of F-14 or F-15 fighters.

1972, 6 June

F-14 No. 14 (BuAer No. 158613) made its first flight. It was to be used by Grumman and the Navy for maintenance studies.

1972, 6 July
In the first in a series of critical pre-operational evaluations for the F-14. NPE-2/West began and was successfully completed on 23 July. On 10 July NPE-2/East began and was finished by 15 August. These important qualification and evaluation trials involved the active review of all flight data.

1972, 1 August
Considered the first production aircraft, F-14 No. 15 (BuAer No. 158614) made its first flight and on 23 October was delivered to Point Mugu for pilot training. After completing 1,231 flying hours it was mothballed on 23 November 1976.

1972, 11 August
F-14 No. 16 (BuAer No. 158615) made its first flight. Like its numerical predecessor it was assigned to pilot training at the Naval Air Station Miramar, where it arrived on 1 October to join VX-4.

1972, 12 September
F-14 No. 18 (BuAer No. 158617) took off for the first time, the sixteenth aircraft to fly. Assigned to pilot training it was delivered to VX-4 at Naval Air Station Miramar on 8 October.

1972, 8 October
The first Tomcat arrived with training squadron VF-124, the 'Evaluators', at Naval Air Station Miramar. Pilots would receive instruction in F-14 carrier operations and conversion to the aircraft and its Fleet Air Defense role.

1972, 13 October
F-14 No. 19 (BuAer No. 158618) made its first flight. Assigned to pilot training with VX-4 at NAS Miramar it was mothballed after 976.7 flight hours.

1972, 14 October
Naval squadrons VF-1 and VF-2 were assigned duty as the first front-line units to operate the F-14 and would receive their aircraft beginning on 1 July 1973.

1972, 24 October
F-14 No. 17 (BuAer No. 158616) made its first flight as the replacement aircraft for the No. 10 prototype which had crashed on 30 June 1972 (see 1972, 29 February). It continued with the carrier suitability trials slated for the No. 10 aircraft.

1972, 21 November
F-14 No. 20 (BuAer No. 158619) made its first flight. It was delivered to Point Mugu for weather testing and was attrited on 22 February 1977. This was the last of the eight Block 60 pre-production aircraft.

1972, 22 November
The first Pratt & Whitney F401 ground test engine (XD18) was delivered to Grumman for tests in association with the F-14B programme. The original plan had been to start F-14B production after sixty-seven F-14A had been built and aircraft No. 7 was scheduled to begin trials with the F401 in mid 1973.

1972, 27 November
The first Block 60 full production F-14, aircraft No. 21 (BuAer No. 158620) made its first flight.

1973, March
Following discussions about the funding difficulties which had plagued the F-14, it was agreed that the government would hold Grumman to the contracted price for the first 134 aircraft, forcing a 20 per cent loss on each aircraft, but renegotiate the remaining 256 F-14s the Navy planned to buy, enabling Grumman to make a profit.

1973, 20 June
The No. 6 F-14A prototype was lost during weapons firing trials when a AIM-7E Sparrow carried on the far aft centreline station tipped and struck the fuselage rupturing a fuel tank. The crew ejected and were recovered.

1973, August
The Shah of Iran notified the Pentagon that it would take up an offer to buy thirty Tomcats designated F-14A-GR. The agreement was signed in January 1974.

1973, 12 September
F-14 No. 7 (BuAer No. 157986) made its first flight powered by two Pratt & Whitney F401 engines. Regarded as the F-14B prototype, it had been held back for trials with the more powerful engine but difficulties were experienced which led to the cancellation of the original F-14B for the VFX-2 requirement.

1973, 21 November
For the first time, six AIM-54A Phoenix missiles were fired during simultaneous tracking and attack on diverse targets.

Four of the six hit their intended targets, one drone malfunctioned and one missile failed.

1974, June
Iran placed an order for an additional fifty Tomcats bringing the total to eighty F-14A-GRs.

1974, August
Congress voted to chop loan money for losses incurred on the F-14 contract, claiming the misuse of government funds after Grumman used them to buy government securities to offset loan interest rates far above commercial levels. Grumman put together a private loan package, headed by Iran's Bank Melli, came out of the red and triumphed.

1974, 17 September
VF-1 and VF-2 set sail aboard the USS *Enterprise* on the Tomcat's first long-duration patrol, a cruise to the western Pacific during which F-14s flew CAP over the American withdrawal from South Vietnam. The cruise ended on 19 May 1975.

1975, 2 January
The forty-third F-14A (BuAer no. 158982) from VF-1 aboard the USS *Enterprise* was destroyed when a fan blade broke free and severed critical lines in the aft fuselage. On 14 January a second aircraft from this unit (BuAer No. 159001) was lost from a similar cause.

1975, 28 June
The USS *Kennedy* set sail with VF-14 and VF-32 for the Tomcats' first Mediterranean patrol, exercising with NATO forces *en route*. The cruise ended on 27 January 1976.

1975, July
A decision to deploy the Tomcat with four Marine Corps squadrons was revoked in favour of four squadrons of F-18 air combat fighters.

1976, 27 January
The first Tomcat ordered by the Shah arrived at Mehrabad Air Base. The full complement of aircraft would equip four squadrons based at Khatami and Shiraz. Deliveries were completed in 1978, with one of the eighty aircraft retained in the US for tests on modifications ordered by Iran.

1976, 24 June
A Tomcat from VF-143 aboard the USS *America* experienced an engine fire caused by a broken fan blade in the port engine, which ruptured the compressor casing. Fan blade problems were solved through a major modification programme for engine damage containment.

1976, 2 September
An F-14A and its Phoenix missiles from VF-32 (BuAer No. 159588) aboard the *Kennedy* was lost overboard when it rolled off the deck off the coast of Scotland. A lengthy retrieval operation involving recovery boats from the US, West Germany and the UK finally pulled the remains of the aircraft ashore on 11 November.

1976, October
Development work began on the AIM-54C Phoenix missile, providing improved guidance, inertial reference unit, digital autopilot and other enhancements and upgrades. The first development rounds were available in August 1979 and qualification trials began during 1980. Production missiles were delivered to the Navy in early 1982.

1979, 16 January
The Shah left his country and abandoned it to the Islamic revolutionary movement. On 1 February Ayatollah Khomeini returned from exile and a republic was proclaimed on 1 April. All links with Iran rapidly disappeared and US personnel evacuated the country, leaving seventy-nine Tomcats behind.

1979, March
The Defense Department issued a contract to General Electric for the development of the F101-DFE powerplant, an engine that generically would lead to the F110.

1980, 22 September
War between Iran and Iraq broke out. In a conflict that would last more than eight years, Iranian F-14s were to see action against Iraq and several were to be shot down, others claiming unsubstantiated kills.

1981, 26 May
An EA-6B crashed on deck while attempting a landing on the carrier *Nimitz* destroying three Tomcats from VF-41 and VF-84.

1981, 14 July
The No. 7 F-14 (BuAer No. 157986) took to the air powered by two General Electric F101-DFE engines. Unrelated to the cancelled F-14B programme designed to meet the original VFX-2 specification, the No. 7 aircraft used the same designation (F-14B) for its new role as a test-bed for the F101. Flight trials lasted only a few weeks.

1981, 19 August
Two Libyan Su-22 fighters were shot down by F-14As from VF-41 operating off the carrier *Nimitz* when they refused to turn away and fired a AA-2 Atoll at the Tomcats. This was the first hot-fire engagement between US Navy F-14s and intruders.

1982, 9 September
Equipped with TARPS pods, F-14As from VF-143 aboard the carrier *Eisenhower* flew reconnaissance missions over hills near Beirut to provide damage assessment after US warships shelled terrorist groups. Ten days later the Tomcats flew similar missions over Beirut itself and on 11 September operated over the mountains when Syrian MiGs flew up the Bakaa Valley.

1982, October
Full-scale development of the F110 began on the results of the testing and evaluation of the F101-DFE. It was this engine that would be installed in the F-14D.

1982, 3 December
AAA and SAM sites operated by terrorists in the hills above Beirut opened up on F-14As from the carrier *Independence* as they flew reconnaissance missions, provoking the rebels into a response. The CIA director Admiral Stansfield Turner protested against the use of high-value aircraft in this way. Begun in September, penetrations continued for a further three months.

1983, 18 January
Tomcat training squadron VF-124 achieved a remarkable record for this Navy aircraft by chalking up 25,000 F-14 flying hours without an accident. In March the squadron completed three full years of F-14 operation without major accidents during which they completed 18,150 sorties and 2,700 arrested landings.

1983, 18 May
The US Air Force asked Pratt & Whitney and General Electric to provide competing engines for F-15 and F-16 fighters. On 3 February 1984 the USAF decided on the F110 for the F-16s and in July of the same year the Navy decided to adopt this power-plant for the F-14D.

1984, 25 July
Using them to press home a message of military intent, the US Defense Department ordered F-14As to overfly Libya's territorial boundary without warning, using a similar tactic to that which had successfully been exploited over Lebanon in 1982.

1984, 18 October
The last permanent Tomcat squadron to deploy, VF-154, went to sea with its F-14s on a short cruise aboard the USS *Constellation*, together with its sister squadron VF-21, returning to port on 15 November. It survived the cutbacks and remains operational.

1984, 2 December
An F-14A from VF-51 aboard the carrier *Carl Vinson* intercepted a Soviet Tu-22 Blinder, the first time an aircraft of this type had been 'escorted' by a Tomcat. The Tomcat was equipped with TCS.

1985, 9 January
US customs officers arrested intermediaries attempting to steal F-14 parts for Iran. Since the revolution in 1979 Iran had been cut off from its suppliers and the Revolutionary Air Force wanted as many F-14s operational as possible.

1985
During the year aircraft from VF-51 starred in the making of the feature film *Top Gun*, a fictitious and dramatized account of life at Naval Air Station Miramar, featuring Tom Cruise and Kelly McGillis.

1986, 24 March
F-14A Tomcats turned back Libyan MiG-25 Foxbats from the Gulf of Sidra off the North African coastline. Tomcats flew cover for A-6 strikes on AAA and SAM sites which had fired on US Navy aircraft in international air space.

1986, 14 April
Tomcats from the carriers *America* and *Coral Sea* based in the Mediterranean flew cover for F-111F fighter bombers and EF-111 Ravens during overnight strikes on Libya.

1986, 29 September
Having already flown with Pratt & Whitney F401 and General Electric F101 engines in 1973 and 1981 respectively, the No. 7 F-14 prototype took to the air again powered by two F110-GE-400 engines derived from the F101. Piloted by Joe Burke, it served as the prototype for the F-14A+, redesignated F-14B on 1 May 1991 in yet another application of that suffix.

1986, 1 December
In one of the shortest commissions in the history of naval aviation, VF-194 was formed as the first of a pair of squadrons to operate Tomcats aboard the carrier *Independence* with Air Wing 10. VF-191 was formed up on 4 December. Both squadrons conducted a brief cruise between 24 July and 5 August 1987 but were disbanded on 30 April 1988.

1987, 15 February
General Electric was awarded a full production order for the F110 to power F-14A+ and F-14D Tomcats. The first engine was delivered on 30 June and the first aircraft with this engine took off on 14 November.

1987, 14 November
The first full production F-14A+ (later designated F-14B) made its first flight. A total thirty-eight F-14A+s were newly built between FY 1986 and FY 1988.

1987, 23 November
The first of four F-14A Tomcats converted to F-14D prototypes made its first flight, designated PA-1 (BuAer No. 161865). It had standard TF30 engines but APG-71 radar and digital avionics with some cockpit modifications and was delivered to VX-4 in May 1990.

1988, 29 April
The second of four F-14A Tomcats converted to F-14D prototypes made its first flight. Designated PA-2 (BuAer No. 161867), this aircraft was the only one of the four to have the F110-GE-400 engines.

It was an integrated test vehicle for avionics, radar, environmental systems and TARPS.

1988, 31 May
The third of four F-14A Tomcats converted to F-14D prototypes took to the air for the first time powered by two TF30 engines. As PA-3 (BuAer No. 162595) it would be used for weapons systems integration, live firing trials and IRST/TCS integration.

1988, 3 July
Mistaking it for an Iranian Air Force F-14 coming to attack the US fleet, an Iranian Airbus A300 was shot down between Bandar Abbas and Dubai. Retribution came when a Pan American Boeing 747 was blown up over Lockerbie on 21 December.

1988, 21 September
The last of four F-14A Tomcats converted to F-14D prototypes made its first flight powered by two TF30 turbofans. PA-4 (BuAer no. 161623) was assigned to JTIDS integration and verification and systems integration.

1989, 4 January
Two Libyan MiG-23 Floggers were shot down by two F-14As from Air Wing 3 on the carrier *Kennedy* when they provoked an incident north of the Libyan city of Tobruk. Both pilots were recovered after they had ejected.

1989, 26 May
The first F-14B Tomcats equipped with TARPS pods arrived at VF-143 before a Mediterranean patrol beginning on 8 March 1990. By that time the squadron had been joined by its sister-squadron VF-142.

1990, 8 March
The first F-14B Tomcats to achieve operational deployment sailed with VF-142 aboard the carrier *Eisenhower* when it departed for the Mediterranean on a cruise that ended on 12 September.

1990, 23 March
The first F-14D was rolled out by Grumman. Of a planned 127 only thirty-seven F-14s were built. A further eighteen F-14s were converted to F-14D standard and designated F-14D(R). These fifty-five

aircraft were used to supply three operational squadrons (VF-2, VF-11 and VF-31) as well as the training unit VF-124.

1990, June
The first aircraft in a planned rebuild of 400 F-14A Tomcats into F-14D standard arrived at Grumman. Budget cuts savaged this plan with only eighteen aircraft being reworked and designated F-14D(R).

1990, 12 September
The Navy Tomcat training squadron VF-101 became the first to drop a bomb from an F-14 and signal its new role as a multi-mission aircraft, although it would be two years before that role was declared operational.

1991, 17 January
On the first day of Operation 'Desert Storm', the operation to evict Saddam Hussein from Kuwait, F-14s operated CAP missions and MiG sweeps without engaging the enemy in combat.

1991, 21 January
An F-14A from VF-103 based on the carrier *Saratoga* was shot down by a Soviet built SA-2. The aircraft (BuAer No. 161430) was equipped with TARPS for reconnaissance duties. After ejecting the pilot was retrieved but the NFO was taken prisoner by the Iraqis.

1991, 6 February
The only air victory achieved by an F-14 during the Gulf War was claimed when a Tomcat from VF-1 based on the carrier *Ranger* shot down a Mil Mi-8 helicopter using a single Sidewinder.

1991, 21 April
Grumman chairman Renso Caporali sent a letter to Defense Secretary Richard B. Cheney extolling the wisdom of buying upgraded Quick Strike Tomcats rather than the F/A-18 for the Navy's combined fleet fighter and attack aircraft requirement. Cheney was determined to close down the F-14 production line and opted for the F/A-18 instead.

1991, 1 May
All F-14A+ aircraft were allocated the designation F-14B. Although it had always been supposed that the definitive Tomcat

would need a more powerful engine to replace the TF30, the original F-14B had been planned to carry the F401 which, when cancelled, had been supplanted by the F110-GE-400.

1992, 20 July

The last of 718 Tomcats was delivered by Grumman, the last of thirty-seven F-14D variants. Of the total, seventy-nine were delivered to Iran, the remainder being assigned as prototypes or as production aircraft for the US Navy. The production line for operational aircraft had been open more than twenty years.

1992, July

The Navy began to receive new bomb rack adapters, enabling the F-14 to carry ground-attack weapons. Later in the year drop tests were conducted at the Navy Strike Aircraft Test Directorate, Patuxent.

1992, October

The carrier *Kitty Hawk* set sail with Tomcat squadron VF-14 on board, its aircraft now known as 'Bombcats' due to the newly-added role of ground attack. After several months in the Mediterranean providing practice for the F-14s, *Kitty Hawk* returned to port on 7 April 1993.

1993, 30 September

The first operational Tomcat squadron VF-1, was disbanded and some of its crew moved to sister squadron VF-2. This was part of a shift in Navy deployment policy and reduced F-14 carrier complement from two squadrons to one. A succession of disbandings followed.

1994

The carrier *Saratoga* was retired from service and, as one of its two Tomcat squadrons was now without a flat-top, VF-103 was assigned as the first F-14 unit to deliver precision-guided munitions.

1994, September

With the disbanding of VF-124, VF-101 became the sole F-14 training squadron and signalled new slimmed-down inventories.

1996, 26 April

Joint fleet exercises began to demonstrate the operability of Tomcats equipped with precision-guided munitions. They ended on 17 May having qualified the equipment and the mission capability.

1996, June

The carrier *Enterprise* set sail with F-14 Strike Fighters from VF-103. Nine of the fourteen aircraft were equipped with greatly improved Lantirn pods, modified for GPS and a new IMU. The Navy pods receive data from the AWG-9 radar and AWG-15 weapon control system. The Navy expected to adapt 212 Tomcats for this role.

Glossary

AAM	air-to-air missile	LM	Lunar Module
AEW	airborne early warning	MCO	missile control officer
AMRAAM	Advanced Medium Range Air-to-Air Missile	MSP	Mach Sweep Program
AMSA	Advanced Manned Strategic Aircraft	MTBF	mean-time-between-failure
AoA	angle of attack	N	newton; SI unit of force (= 0.225 pounds force)
BARCAP	barrier combat air patrol	NACA	National Advisory Committee for Aeronautics
BIDE	blow-in door ejector	NASC	Naval Air Systems Command
BIS	Board of Inspection and Survey	NBC	nuclear, biological and chemical [weapons]
BITE	built-in test equipment	NFO	Naval flight officer
BuAer	Bureau of Aeronautics	NPE	Navy Preliminary Evaluation
BVR	beyond-visual-range	Pa	pascal; SI derived unit of pressure (= 1 newton/sq m)
CAP	combat air patrol		
CDP	contract definition phase	PCM	pulse-code-modulation
CWIP	Colossal Weight Improvement Program	RCS	radar cross-section
DLI	deck launch intercept	RDF	Rapid Deployment Force
DoD	Department of Defense	RFP	request for proposals
ECM	electronic countermeasures	RIO	radar intercept officer
EMMA	engineering manufacturing mock-up aid	SAM	surface-to-air missile
EW	early warning	SCW	supercritical wing
FADF	Fleet Air Defense Fighter	SFC	specific fuel consumption
FLIR	forward-looking infra-red	SLEP	Service Life Extension Program
FPI	fixed price incentive	SOR	Specific Operational Requirement
FY	Fiscal Year	SWIP	Super-Weight-Improvement Program
GCI	ground-controlled interception	TAC	Tactical Air Command
GPS	Global Positioning System	TACAN	TACtical Aid to Navigation
HARM	high-speed anti-radiation missile	TARCAP	target combat air patrol
HDI	horizontal display indicator	TARPS	Tactical Air Reconnaissance Pod System
HUD	head-up display	TCS	Television Camera Sight
IFF	identification friend or foe	TFX	Tactical Fighter Experimental
IMI	Improved Manned Interceptor	UHF	ultra-high frequency
IMU	inertial measurement unit	VDI	vertical display indicator
INS	inertial navigation system	VFE	variable-flap ejector
IRST	infra-red search and track	VHSIC	very-high-speed-integrated-circuit
JTIDS	Joint Tactical Information Distribution System	VP	variable plug
Lantirn	Low Altitude Navigation and Targeting Infra-red system for Night	VSTOL	vertical or short take-off and landing
		WRA	weapons replaceable assemblies

Introduction

Unlike most aircraft of the post-World War II period, the F-14 Tomcat was developed from the failure of another aircraft. It was not designed as the successor to anything but arose from the need for an air superiority fighter and evolved from engines, radar and weapon systems conceived for earlier types that had not made the grade. In the end it became an air superiority fighter as well. The general operational requirement stemmed from the need to replace the F-4 Phantom II and absorb broader mission roles then not filled by any other fighter. In that regard it wrote its own specification to a mandate stipulated by the US Navy. But more than that, it arose through the genius of people at Grumman and their long line of Navy fighters incorporating creative engineering and radical production concepts embracing new materials and innovative means of putting them together.

The F-14 was the last in Grumman's feline family and the last great product of that company's long and prestigious range of aircraft and spacecraft. The latter cannot be stressed too highly for it contributed in no small measure to the success of the company and its unique way of doing things. Of those products that may be mentioned, the Lunar Module, which put twelve astronauts on the moon during six flights between July 1969 and December 1972, represented in many ways the peak of Grumman's engineering excellence. Less dramatic in world news, the F-14 adopted many of the management, design and engineering practices forged by Grumman through NASA's leadership in space projects.

Professionally I first came across Grumman in 1962 when it received the contract for the Lunar Module. First among nine contenders for the job of realizing America's hopes to reach the moon, Grumman was to have the job of fulfilling John F. Kennedy's dream that NASA astronauts would perform the ultimate demonstration of technical prowess. It did, less than seven years later, a period during which numerous problems and seemingly intractable obstacles were overcome. It was that spirit and the determination to get the job done that characterized Grumman, in many ways an old-fashioned company that put people in the forefront of corporate concern. Later, when Grumman gave the Navy the most powerful carrier-based air superiority fighter yet built, it applied that character to the daunting job of building a replacement for the failed F-111B. All eyes were on the VFX winner, the more so because a major industry player – General Dynamics – had been unable to match an impossible demand for a common design to serve both the Air Force's and the Navy's requirements.

Throughout the period when Grumman laboured to build the VFX winner, relations with the Soviet Union acquired a new sophistication: President Nixon wanted *détente* and the Soviets began to talk about arms reductions, only later using protocols to evade the intent of the SALT-1 and the SALT-2 agreement signed in the 1970s. A product of the Cold War, the Tomcat gave flat-top aviators protection from an expanding Soviet Navy and advancing technologies that threatened the integrity of carrier battle groups and free passage of cargo on the world's sea lanes.

Through the final period of Soviet imperialism the Tomcat policed the seas, providing cover and protection for the carrier battle group. In the aftermath of the Soviet collapse the F-14 continues to maintain the edge over an opposition which now comprises many separate states no longer under a single government.

All types of aircraft are subject to the Darwinist law: adapt or die. There has never been a more blatant application of that law than in the post-Cold War age in which many separate states vie for influence and power. In the bipolar world of communism and capitalism the choices were clear. Now, with neither side prepared to wage global nuclear war over the survival of a minor client state those disparate countries are abandoned to the biggest bully in the region. From the former Soviet Union a veritable flood of high-quality arms fuels concern about the technical toys now at the disposal of despots and anarchists. Terrorist groups with spending powers greater than some countries arm sad people with weapons for extremist ideology.

In this 'new world order' increasing numbers of states possess, or seek to possess, weapons of mass destruction, or otherwise threaten to destabilize the post-Cold War world. The need therefore remains for, in the words of Harry S. Truman, the 'big stick', and there is nothing to equal the psychological value of a carrier battle group looming on the horizon. It has worked well in the Mediterranean and when lack of restraint ensues, the firepower is there to neutralize the aggressor's assets. In protecting the carrier battle group, the F-14 will continue to play its part in carrying out that threat of retaliation or punishment to whomsoever threatens peace.

As defense budgets fall in response to demands for a 'peace dividend' following the end of the Cold War, a shrinking defence dollar has had to buy considerably more 'bang for the buck' than it ever did in the past. It is no longer acceptable for individual aircraft types to perform one role and the age of the multi-mission warplane is firmly entrenched in procurement policies for the next generation of combat aircraft. Designed and built for a specific purpose, the F-14 has had to change with the times, and the fact that it can with relative ease broaden its mission base aboard the carrier is testimony to a flexibility not anticipated when the aircraft was put together. Plying the skies of the new century, carrying reconnaissance pods or bombs, the Tomcat has displayed adaptability in true Darwinian style. But the roles of aircraft and type models that change for different defence needs are paralleled by corporate structures that are themselves subject to mergers and takeovers.

In some respects the Grumman company was well set up to adapt to the post-Cold War drawdown, but in others it was poorly equipped. While slimmer than the giants (Boeing or McDonnell Douglas), Grumman was depleted of reserves it once had and was not in a good position to resist takeover bids. In fact, it succumbed to just such an amalgamation when Northrop bought out the New York planemaker on 18 May 1994. In some respects the two companies were similar, both having been formed within a year of each other in 1928 (Northrop) and in 1929 (Grumman) and each being hampered by small production runs and low capitalization. But the takeover was the only way for Grumman to survive and it served government interests to bolster Northrop's corporate base and insulate it from the predatory tactics of the aerospace giants. Northrop had grown from being a relatively small builder and the B-2 made it a vital element in the US manufacturing base.

So it is that the Tomcat became the last of the Navy's Grumman felines, a product of a company that for sixty-five years maintained its place as a predominantly flat-top flyer. In the late 1960s the Tomcat had stimulated the introduction of new manufacturing techniques and new materials and resulted in a much copied design that would serve as a hallmark for front-line aviation in the last three decades of the twentieth century. It is likely that the F-14 will survive as a front-line combat aircraft well into the second decade of the next century, giving the type an operational age of at least forty years. This is fitting tribute indeed to the brave new ways of designing, building and operating an aeroplane for the fleet air defence role which characterized the genesis of the Tomcat. To those who have held guard against great danger from the two seats of a Tomcat, well done; to those who will continue to do so for the next several years, God speed.

CHAPTER ONE

From TFX to VFX

Emergence of the Carrier Task Force

Two decisions made by senior political and military leaders were crucial to development of the F-14 and both were made in Moscow. The first was to expand the inventory of turboprop Badger and jet-powered Blinder long-range bombers operated by Soviet maritime aviation units. The second decision came out of the Cuban missile crisis of 1962 when Admiral Gorshkov convinced Premier Khrushchev to expand Soviet naval power massively and put long-range, surface-to-surface missiles on ships and submarines. The resulting threat to US Navy carrier battle groups was profound and, from the American viewpoint, unacceptable. It was to counter those stand-off threats that the Navy sought, and eventually obtained, what many have regarded as the world's best long-range interceptor and fleet defence fighter, a heavyweight in every sense but one with a remarkable dogfighting capability. To understand the tortuous genesis of the F-14 it helps to set events within the evolution of the carrier task force.

It had been the large carrier battle groups that fought the Pacific sea war of 1942–45 that led to the US global maritime power projection of the Cold War; what was good for beating an aggressive enemy on the high seas was good as a deterrent against hegemony in distant places, and it was the invested value of America's most expensive defence resource – the carrier battle group – that resulted in a unique aeroplane to protect it. Because the global carrier force was immensely flexible it was a serious military threat to adversaries intent on political or territorial ambitions. Primarily British inventions, new technologies including the angled flight deck, the steam catapult

and improved landing aids enhanced carrier operability and efficiency, adding an awesome capability to an already effective force. Of American invention, nuclear propulsion gave the carrier virtually unlimited range while a revolutionary breakthrough in small-scale nuclear weapons during the 1950s provided shipboard aircraft with unprecedented hitting power.

Together, these refinements and capabilities multiplied greatly the effectiveness of the carrier task force in the 1960s. Now added to a constellation of Air Force bases in friendly countries, US firepower could be delivered through massive naval forces that could themselves be protected by seaborne air umbrellas. But getting to that point had been a long, hard road. When the Japanese attacked Pearl Harbor in

December 1941 the US Navy had nine carriers. At the end of the Pacific War in 1945 it had 99 flat-tops equipped with more than 5,000 aircraft, including fighters near to the theoretical limit of piston-engine performance. At the peak of wartime fleet carrier design, the three USS *Midway* class ships launched in 1945 and 1946 represented the best the Navy would get for a decade. With a displacement of 48,145 tonnes and a complement of 2,510, each could accommodate around 130 aircraft and sail half way round the world without touching land. They would carry the flag in the immediate post-war period.

Following major demobilization at the end of the Pacific War the US Navy found its capital ships without an obvious role and considerable opposition was raised to

Epitomizing the large carrier battle groups that won the Pacific War, this latter-day view of the USS Coral Sea reflects a bridge between eras. Laid down in 1944, it was commissioned in 1947 and would see more than four decades of service. On its deck are A-6 Intruders, F/A-18A Hornets and two E-2C Hawkeyes.

maintaining such an expensive capability. Only Britain remained as a world-class power with carriers and no one seriously contemplated conflict with her. Only the Soviet Union posed an immediate threat to the US and it had neither an ocean-going navy nor a warm-water port. To many the US carrier seemed an anachronism compounded by the strategic firepower of the newly formed US Air Force, which some believed made the slow moving capital ship as obsolete as the Dreadnoughts. After all, had not Billy Mitchell proved that point when his bombers sank the German battleship *Ostfriesland* in 1921 during a show of air strength with canvas-covered biplanes? Many thought not: Mitchell's target had been defenceless and the bombers faced no challenge from the sea or the air; Pearl Harbor showed the vulnerability of

warships at anchor, but a series of linked engagements in the battle of Midway neutralized the Japanese Navy through the use of carrier-based strike power.

Midway was the first battle in which a major naval engagement was fought without any two ships engaging each other in direct fire. It was the first sea battle in which the fate of navies hinged on a conflict fought out in the air. But was it relevant in an age when long-range bombers could destroy cities and large ships? When in 1947 the US Navy became one of three services under the Department of Defense the Air Force staked high claim for the strategic punch. It alone had the means to deliver the atomic weapon and it alone could bridge continental distances within a few hours. Moreover, it had on the drawing boards a bomber capable of flying to the industrial

manufacturing facilities of the Soviet Union and back to wage atomic war in the heart of enemy territory. Known as the B-36, it was central to a controversy fought over these fundamental questions: was the carrier effective in the nuclear age and would it survive to carry out its mission? But that begged another question: just what was the carrier's role?

The purpose of a modern navy is not merely to wage war. It is there in peacetime to protect vital national interests, which include the free passage of merchant fleets bringing commodities, raw materials and manufactured products. It is also there to strike deep into the heart of aggressors and states that directly or indirectly threaten the welfare of others. Naval air power is a vital part of that mission. Added to this, the US Navy was at the disposal of NATO and formed a central plank for consoli-

'Talk softly but carry a big stick' said President Truman, an injunction expressed through the Convair B-36, a hemispheric bomber which competed for funds which the Navy wanted to maintain a global carrier force.

Refusing to allow the Air Force to monopolize nuclear weapons, the Navy introduced the Douglas A-3 Skywarrior strategic nuclear bomber in 1956, here seen on the Coral Sea close by the Soviet spy trawler Gidrofon. The version here is the A3D-2 reconnaissance type.

dated deterrence. Most important of all, the Americas are isolated from the rest of the world by vast oceans, ice and deep waters in which hostile forces can roam at will. It is not in any nation's interest to leave those waters unprotected. These seemingly disparate defence functions were combined into two carrier roles: defensive anti-submarine and offensive strike, be that against incoming air threats or hostile land or naval forces. Immediately after World War II air threats were not seen as a major challenge to the USA. With Japan and most of Europe in ruins, only the Soviet Union posed a serious threat and it had few aircraft that could reach the North American continent. But

it was a threat that would grow in unforeseen ways.

The integration of national defence forces under the Pentagon umbrella brought competition and at times bitter controversy about which force should be responsible for what. The Air Force had considerable leverage in seizing the high ground and applied the doctrine of the 'indivisibility of the air' to all military activities not conducted by land or sea forces, thus seriously questioning the Navy's air role. Out of the big strategic air forces of 1942–45 came the Strategic Air Command tasked with dominating the offensive and, as the Joint Chiefs of Staff defined it, 'savaging the aggressor at will'. Quite

simply, it interpreted its mandate implicitly to embrace all aspects of air and space related to matters of defence. Under the new defence structure Army, Navy and Marine air forces would be constrained, limited by a specific definition relating to their primary roles. But the Navy wanted more and saw in the atomic bomb a lever of its own with which to secure an expanded role. It too sought a strategic mission, one which would require new carriers of immense size and unprecedented capacity.

The first atomic bombs were big and heavy, weighing about 10,000lb (4,545.5kg) with a diameter of 5ft (1.52m) and a length of 11ft (3.33m). To give itself

The A3D-2 Skywarrior was developed into a fully equipped reconnaissance version, the RA-3B, with fully pressurized fuselage and as many as twelve cameras. This derivative served with the Heavy Photographic Squadrons VAP-61 and VAP-62.

a strategic nuclear capability, in June 1946, before the Department of Defense Act was signed, the Navy ordered North American to build three prototype, high-performance, carrier-based, nuclear bombers. Known as the AJ Savage, the aircraft was to be powered by two 2,400hp Pratt & Whitney R-2800-44W radial engines attached to the high mounted wing and one 4,600lb (20.46kN) thrust Allison J33-A-19 turbojet in the tail for assisted take-off. The Savage had a wing span of 75ft (22.72m), a length of 63ft (19.09m) and a gross weight of almost 53,000lb (24,091kg), making it one of biggest aeroplanes then envisaged for carrier operations. The Navy went a step further in 1947 and persuaded President Truman to request funds in Fiscal Year 1949 (a twelve-months period beginning 1 July 1948) budget proposal for a super-carrier. At the same time, the Navy Bureau of Aeronautics completed the initial studies to define a jet-powered nuclear bomber requirement.

The super-carrier was coded CVA-58, but referred to under the designation CVB-58, and given the name *United States*.

Operating off conventional carriers in the late 1950s and the early 1960s, the Skywarrior represented the last of an era when specialized aircraft were developed for dedicated tasks.

With a fully loaded displacement of 80,000 tons and an overall length of 1,089ft (330m) it would have had a maximum flight deck width of 190ft (57.58m). A unique feature of the design gave up the characteristic fixed island from one side of the flight deck, which was clean along the entire length and width of the ship, for a telescopic bridge on the forward starboard deck edge. Four large lifts linked the flight deck to the hangar deck and the air complement comprised fifty-four AJ Savages for nuclear strike. The *United States* would also carry the new Navy jet nuclear bomber on which Douglas began design studies in 1947. This work would result in the A3D Skywarrior, for which Douglas received a contract in March 1949; it was first flown in October 1952 and deployed in 1956. At 82,000lb (37,273kg) gross weight it was the Navy's heaviest aircraft.

The vision of a strategic US Naval force was, however, short-lived and just days after the keel of CVB-58 was laid in early 1950 the project was cancelled and the money thus saved was diverted to the B-36. Yet this reversal was itself a temporary halt in the inevitable development of an ocean-going, nuclear capability. A sequence of events that began with the testing of the Soviet Union's atom bomb in August 1949 would give the Navy added responsibility. The most potent threat to the US had come a step closer to posing an unacceptable challenge to the country and this would trigger approval by President Truman for the development of thermonuclear weapons – the misnamed 'hydrogen' bomb. Within a matter of months the Communists in northern Korea made a bad mistake and invaded the south, triggering a United Nations response and bringing US forces back to the region in large numbers.

The Korean War and America's role through the United Nations brought a renewed vigour about the need for a global capability. The massive confrontation of superpower states in total war was no longer the only threat. Regional conflict was seen to be as great a threat to peace, perhaps more so, and the rapid movement of response forces a prerequisite for timely reaction to unprovoked aggression. Congressional opposition to an expansion in naval capability evaporated. Research on reducing the size of atomic and thermonuclear weapons was accelerated and a new concept of carrier battle

Flagship for the world's first class of carrier designed for jet aircraft, the USS Forrestal **drew heavily on the cancelled super-carrier the** United States**. She was laid down in 1952, commissioned three years later and would see thirty-eight years of service before retiring in 1993, leaving three more of her class –** Saratoga, Ranger **and** Independence **– all of which had gone by 1998.**

The Grumman Story

In its 12 June 1971 edition, that prestigious beacon of American corporate activity *Business Week* declared that the Grumman Corporation 'has an old-fashioned aura: paternalistic, inbred and cautious. Its workers remain steadfastly non-union. Each one still receives a turkey at Christmas as a gift from the management. Its top executives come up through the ranks and few defect. Consistently profitable, Grumman has never failed to pay a dividend in the 41 years it has operated in the precarious business of defense contracting.'

All this and more is true of one of the most remarkable American aircraft manufacturers, which began life as Grumman Aircraft Engineering when Leroy Grumman and two friends set up their own business in 1929.

Born in 1895 and brought up in Long Island, New York, a mecca for American flyers, Leroy Randle Grumman was an early convert to aviation and graduated as a Navy pilot in September 1918. After a brief period as an engineer and test pilot at the League Island Navy Yard he resigned his commission to join the Loening Aeronautical Engineering Corporation, a company building beautifully designed and exquisitely crafted seaplanes and amphibious aircraft for the Navy and the Army. In the gold rush to build aeroplanes that followed the popularization of air travel and the interest of Wall Street in mopping up small companies, Loening was gobbled up by bankers and merged with Keystone. But Keystone and its acquisitions were harnessed to other companies in the expanding holding operation known as North American Aviation, Inc.

When Loening employees were told that they would have to move to Pennsylvania, Grumman, Bill Schwendler and Jake Swirbul formed Grumman Aircraft Engineering and set up shop at Baldwin, Long Island, in December 1929. They turned a profit of just $5,500 in the first year, subsidizing development of the FF-1 two-seater biplane fighter by repairing aircraft. It was the first Navy fighter to achieve 200 mph (322kph) in level flight and incorporated an enclosed cockpit and retractable main landing gear. By the time it entered service in 1933 the Navy had lost interest in the two-seater fighter concept, which cleared the way for the F2F and the improved version, the F3F. Before that, utilizing the semi-monocoque fuselage of the FF-1, Grumman produced the JF floatplane. This eventually led to the J2F Duck of which almost 1,000 were built between 1933 and 1945.

However, it was the Grumman F2F and the F3F that gave the Navy a fighter that would seriously eclipse the Army's Boeing F4B. More than just a refined, single-seat version of the FF-1, the Grumman biplanes incorporated fully retractable landing gear with a fully streamlined fuselage and a closely cowled twin-row Wasp Jr radial engine. But production numbers were small – only 169 were built – and it fell the way of all the good biplane designs of the mid-1930s in that it was outclassed by a new generation of monoplane technology that Grumman itself would bring to the carrier deck. Before that, Grumman's last biplane appeared in 1934 when the company wheeled out the unsuccessful XSBF-1 two-seater scout bomber; this failed against the Curtiss XSBC-2 which entered service in 1939 as the Helldiver, the US Navy's last combat biplane.

Easily recognized by their island structure farther aft than on the four Forrestal class carriers, the four Kitty Hawk **class carriers, represented here by the flagship, were built to an improved** Forrestal **design. They included the** Constellation, America **and** John F. Kennedy. **The** America **was retired in 1996 but the remainder will serve into the next century.**

carriers and some would remain operational for more than forty years. Their contribution was enormous and helped build procedures and experience for the new and expanded roles of the present US Navy.

Shortly after the first *Forrestal* class vessel began sea trials, approval was given to build the first nuclear-powered carrier, the USS *Enterprise*. With a displacement of almost 77,000 tonnes this giant super-carrier was more than 1,100ft (333.33m) long, carried a complement of 5,300 and could cruise a distance equal to a trip to the moon and back. Launched in 1960 and commissioned a year later, *Enterprise* was a quantum leap toward the twenty-first century and was followed by a succession of *Nimitz* class carriers each with a complement of up to 6,400. *Nimitz* was launched in 1972 and commissioned in 1975 and was followed by six more carriers commissioned between 1977 and 1996. Two more will follow: *Truman* in 1998 and *Reagan* in 2002, thus maintaining eleven active vessels.

groups patrolling the world as a UN peace force grew. New carriers would be needed after all, and the Navy was ready with designs for a new *Forrestal* class carrier incorporating an angled deck 230ft (69.7m) wide at its maximum. These carriers would convey a naval nuclear strike capability through a selection of tactical nuclear weapons as well as an inventory of conventional munitions. The awesome horror of unconstrained nuclear war was not yet quite as limiting a factor as it would come to be regarded in the next decade. Atomic weapons had been seriously considered for use in Korea and their deployment by carrier air groups was only a logical step.

Laid down in 1952, the first of four *Forrestal* type carriers was commissioned in 1955. It had a displacement of 61,637 tonnes (79,248 tonnes deep load), a complement of 4,142 and capacity for almost a hundred aircraft. Dispensing with gun armament and adopting missiles for close defence, four improved *Forrestal* class carriers were laid down between 1956 and 1964. Although adapted from the *Forrestal* design, they were sufficiently different to be designated *Kitty Hawk* class carriers (the name of the first of the four laid down) and the last, the USS *John F. Kennedy*, was so different again as to justify a separate class by itself. Launched over a period of thir-

teen years (1954–67), these eight carriers spanned the changes from the post-World War II designs to the modern era in flat-top design. Representing the peak of conventional carrier technology of their day, they were the last non-nuclear US

Fighters for the Carriers

The influence of this evolution on fighter design was profound and reflects the changing patterns of aircraft size and capa-

Distinct from others in the Kitty Hawk **class, the** John F. Kennedy **was one of the first carriers to carry the F-14, going to sea with VF-14 and VF-32 in September 1976.** Kennedy **was unique in that construction was delayed while debate continued on whether to build it as a nuclear-powered ship.**

The world's second nuclear-powered carrier, Nimitz was laid down in 1968 and commissioned just under seven years later. Followed by five more in her class, the Nimitz is now in overhaul and will rejoin the fleet in 2001. Each ship is powered by four geared steam turbines driven by two pressurized water-cooled reactors.

bility which, together with an emerging threat from stand-off weapons, forged the requirement that led to the F-14. The long and tortuous path would result in fighters weighing as much as the heaviest strike aircraft, a situation unforeseen when the evolution began. In 1945 carrier fighters such as the Hellcat and the Corsair and attack aircraft such as the Grumman Avenger had gross weights of 15,000 to16,000lb (6,818 to 7,273kg) and first-generation Navy jet fighters such as the McDonnell FD-1 were no heavier. By the time the Korean War began in 1950, Navy fighters had begun to grow in weight. The Grumman Panther grossed 18,700lb (8,500kg) while the McDonnell F2H Banshee weighed 22,300lb (10,136kg) and the Douglas F3D Skyknight reached a maximum 26,850lb (12,205kg).

Just five years later the need for an effective fleet defence fighter to reach further out from the carriers they were designed to protect added to weight and expanded roles did little to help keep the weight down. Designed as an all-weather fighter, the swept-wing McDonnell F3H Demon had a gross weight of almost 30,000lb (13,636kg). The Vought F7U Cutlass hit almost 32,000lb (14,545kg) and the Vought F-8 Crusader weighed a maximum 34,000lb (15,455kg). It was the loss of a production order for the next generation Navy fighter after Vought's F-8 Crusader that prompted McDonnell to come up with the heaviest fighter yet, the F4H (later the F-4) Phantom II. This was conceived in 1953 as a twin-engine successor to the Demon all-weather night fighter and changed by the Navy a year later to an attack role. It was ordered to prototype stage in 1955 as an all-weather interceptor but had all the potential for being a failure. For three successive years it was made to change roles on an annual basis and even in its design it reflected brute-force solutions. Nothing about the F4H was refined. Its engineers did not subsribe to the 'blended aerodynamic profiling' nor 'integrated airframe and engine design' so lauded today. Each fought for his corner.

The F4H had been designed from the outset to have two engines. Just as the new fighter was being designed, failures with the Demon's single Westinghouse J40 turbojet brought near disaster to the early phase of the programme and all but destroyed any chances of getting the F3H into production. Only when McDonnell switched to the Allison J71 did the programme and the Demon's loss record improve. The lesson had been learned. From this point forward, all Navy aircraft would have at least two engines; carrier take-offs were denied the option of aborting and engine failures in flight could leave an aircraft far from its carrier and doomed to a watery grave. The twin-engine philosophy paid dividends in aircraft performance and gave the F4H extra capability which, eventually, it and its operators would exploit to the full. But the decision to put in two engines was only the first of several major decisions.

When the Navy stipulated an all-weather role for the F4H the complex radar, radio and weapons-control systems called for a second crew member, keeping the pilot free from overload. Then when tunnel tests showed that the preferred thin wing, already well along into detailed design, would cause serious stability problems, engineers gave the tip a 12 degree dihedral. This provided the 'averaged' 5 degree dihedral to get the tips at the correct place without having to redesign the main structure completely.

To get the horizontal stabilizers into the correct position for optimum stability, they were given 23 degreees of anhedral. Thus the unusual arrangement of wing and tail angles created the now familiar profile. Each body zone was designed by its own team to the complete disregard of the others.

But the F4H was more than a role-shuffler redesigned on the run. It was the world's first fighter to abandon the gun in favour of missiles at a time when many believed that the days of the dogfight were gone, added to which it was heavy. At 54,600lb or 24,818kg (some F-4 Phantom IIs would weigh almost 62,000lb or 28,182kg) the F4H rewrote the rule book and ushered in a totally new era for fleet defence fighters: the age of missile-carrying, electronic interceptors with a Mach 2+ speedometer and a combat radius of almost 1,000 miles (1,600km). Such performance was not cheap and it was paid for in size and weight. In turn, this had its price too. With a major increase in the gross weight, the wing loading went up to the extent that it compromised

The world's first nuclear carrier, the Enterprise became the first ship to put to sea with Tomcats on board when VF-1 and VF-2 sailed aboard this super flat-top in September 1974. Eight pressurized water-cooled reactors power the ship through four geared steam turbines.

The 1950s saw remarkable developments in US naval aviation reflected through evolving technologies, new and bigger carriers and an emphasis on nuclear weapons. One of Grumman's finest models, the F9F-6 Cougar incorporated the excellence of the company's first jet fighter – the Panther – with a new swept wing. Rushed into service during 1952 to give the Navy a jet fighter equal to the Soviet MiG-15 in the Korean War, nearly 2,000 were built.

flexibility, bringing high landing speeds and reduced low-speed control. The conventional design philosophy was hard pressed to accommodate all the factors but still the demand for higher performance and greater capability increased.

By the late 1950s when the F4H was getting into its flight test programme, serious concerns were expressed about the perceived threat and the ability of the new generation of Navy fighters to meet it. Intelligence reports were fragmentary but gave a grim forecast. Hard on the heels of Soviet atomic bomb tests came an expanding family of air-to-surface missiles capable of hitting stationary or slow-moving targets from great distances. Deployed in 1956, the AS-1 Kennel was carried by the Tu-16 Badger C and could deliver a nuclear warhead to a target 90 miles (144km) from a high-altitude drop point. The AS-2 Kipper had a slightly greater range and was supersonic through

a programmed autopilot with active radar for terminal homing. The AS-3 Kangaroo stand-off weapon was designed to hit area targets such as ports and harbours with a 800-kiloton warhead. It was carried by a Tu-95 Bear and had a maximum range of 400 miles (640km) , a speed of Mach 1.8 with autopilot control and no guidance.

Of the greatest concern was the AS-4 Kitchen. With a single rocket motor producing a maximum speed of Mach 4.6, the AS-4 had a range of up to 285 miles (456km) , terminal homing and a 350-kiloton warhead for attacks against battle groups and carriers. Carried by a Tu-95 Bear and later by the Tu-22K Blinder supersonic bomber, it represented the unique way Soviet design teams were decentralizing the threat by creating an air-launched challenge to US delivery systems – which is what the carrier was quickly becoming for conventional and nuclear weapons. Added to submarine-launched

cruise missiles of more questionable performance, the new class of Soviet weaponry posed a serious challenge and it was its appearance at the end of the 1950s that forged a new requirement. While the F4H showed great promise from the day of its first flight in May 1958, it was limited by the technology of its time.

Events were overwhelming the ability of aircraft designers to keep pace with expanding challenges and the emergence of new threats. What the Navy needed was a fighter that could engage the cruise-missile carriers before they released their weapons, or at least engage the weapons after their release. In the second half of the 1950s, however, only short-range missiles had been developed and were generally seen as supplements to the traditional cannon armament. This required the defending fighters to engage their targets at relatively close range – just a few miles at most – but with threats spread out across the sky there would be insufficient aircraft to tackle each target and many would get through. The Air Force chose to resolve the problem of destroying large formations of approaching bombers with the equivalent of a sledgehammer, backing the Douglas MB-1 Genie which had a special 1.5 kiloton nuclear warhead and a range of 6 miles (9.6km). Fired into a formation of approaching bombers, Genie would destroy by blast or shock wave. A live test was conducted in July 1957 when a Northrop F-89A Scorpion fired a Genie across the Yucca Flat, Nevada, test range 15,000ft (4,545.5m) over the heads of watching USAF personnel! The lethal radius was over 1,000ft (303.03m). The Navy's solution was less dramatic because the maritime-based threats it faced were of a different kind. Approaching bombers with cruise or stand-off weapons targeting carrier battle groups would not fly in the massed formations feared by the Air Force. To combat the sneak attack or the simultaneous attack from different directions

many miles apart, aircraft designers made the fighters faster and more capable. But it was a solution bound to run out of plausible applications and the technology of the late 1950s gave little succour to concerned Admirals.

These were early days for air-to-air missiles. The first examples of the now famous Sidewinder family, designated N-7 by the Navy for its version of the missile, broke new ground. Produced by a brilliant team of engineers at the Naval Ordnance Test Center, China Lake, California, the precursor XAAM-N-7 was the first to tackle the problem of passive infra-red guidance direct. These were also early days in the then extraordinarily exotic field of electronics, when hot vacuum tubes and crystals were familiar components and field-effect transistors and solid state devices had yet to be invented. The first Sidewinders were tested in 1953 and went into operational use during 1956. Two years later the Chinese Nationalist F-86 fighters used Sidewinders to shoot

down fourteen MiG-15s from the People's Republic, the first time they were used in anger. However, McDonnell and the Navy selected another missile for the F4H. The yet-to-be-named Phantom II would carry six AIM-N-6A (from 1962 known as AIM-7C) Sparrow III missiles, introduced into Navy service by the F3H Demon.

A serious limitation with the Sidewinder was its relatively short range and constrained targeting arc. Anything other than a tail-end attack was unlikely to result in a hit and early versions had a maximum range of little more than 2 miles (3.2km) until the improved AIM-9C available in the early 1960s extended that to 11 miles (17.6km). Yet this was still far below the Navy's requirements. At 380lb (173kg) the Raytheon Sparrow III was twice the weight of the Sidewinder but it had semi-active, continuous wave, radar homing and a range of 25 miles (40km). This was better, but still not close enough to the requirement for an effective, long-range

One of the all-time carrier heavyweights, North American Aviation's A-5 Vigilante expressed the strategic mood of the Navy when this 80,000lb (36,360kg) atom bomber joined the Fleet in 1961. It emphatically stamped a message of intent – that the US Navy was going to continue as a world force.

With more than 5,000 produced for countries around the world, it would be hard to classify the F-4 Phantom II as a failure but it does typify the end of the line for metal aeroplanes and iron bombs and even in Vietnam it was hard pressed by the MiG-21.

interception of multiple targets. It was not a new quest. Beginning in 1955 the Sparrow II had been developed by Douglas with just that problem in mind, adopting fully active radar homing and designed for integration with the proposed Douglas F5D-1 Skylancer. This was the first serious attempt to integrate weapon system and launch platform, but the supersonic airframe evolved from the subsonic F4D-1 Skyray and was seriously compromised by adaptability and a burgeoning array of black boxes. The Navy axed both aircraft and missile.

Yet even as the Navy accepted the logic of Sparrow III armament for the F4H it still brooded over the expanding threat

envelope to its vital, expensive carrier assets. Using the failed marriage of the Sparrow II and the F5D-1 as a precedent for renewed efforts at producing a cruise-killer, the Navy put together a specification based around the requirement for a Fleet Air Defense Fighter or FADF. This time a new weapon system built to operational needs would drive the specification for a new launch platform. The Navy reasoned that it was better to put the control of the intercept in the missile rather than in the airframe and build into the missile range and flexibility to seek and destroy. Then whatever was needed in the way of black boxes and launch requirement could drive the speci-

fication for a new aircraft. This was not yet the integrated weapon-system approach that would dominate procurement several decades hence, but it was a start along the right road.

In 1957 the Navy requested proposals for this new fleet defence system and this time, instead of responding to the marketing from a specific contractor, the Navy decided what it wanted and how the system had to perform. That was simply stated: a defence concept that could seek, attack and destroy attacking weapons before the defending aircraft or the carrier battle group came within their range. It was decided that each carrier-launched missile platform would have to deal with up to eight separate targets at the same time in an integrated system which reflected the belief of the day – that missiles would take over many of the functions previously carried out by the aircraft itself. This was not a uniquely American view. In Britain, the infamous (as some would say) Defence White Paper of 1957 decreed that there would be no new manned fighters and that piloted aircraft would be replaced by missiles, thus legitimizing the lack of government support for the aircraft industry. In turn, this would result in the English Electric Lightning being the last manned fighter of wholly British design.

For the US Navy's Fleet Defense Fighter requirement a purpose-built aircraft would have to carry eight missiles to an altitude of 35,000ft (10,606m) and take up station 150 miles (240km) from the carrier that launched it. There the FADF would use its own radar to locate targets, but active homing radar on each missile would guide

it to the assigned threat. Early in 1960 contracts were awarded for the missile and its carrier. Bendix beat off the competition from fifteen other contenders and got the job of developing the missile, known as the XAAM-10 Eagle, and Douglas was authorized to develop the aircraft – an unlikely looking missile truck given the company model number D-766 which the Navy designated the F6D-1 Missileer. In one sense the requirement was in the right direction. It put a look-down Doppler radar system out where it mattered, in the threat environment closer to the aggressor and, because the scan and track system could cover all threats down to the surface of the sea, it encompassed all known classes of air-to-surface weapon. However, because of the earth's curvature and surface-skimming threats, the defending carrier could not see many of the weapons that could be thrown against it.

The F6D-1 Missileer had a bulbous fuselage, two crew members seated side by side,

an unswept, shoulder-mounted wing and twin engines attached to the fuselage with chin intakes. The bulbous nose was dictated by the size of the large, pulse-Doppler, track-while-scan radar, the first such developed for a fighter. The Pratt & Whitney TF30-P-2 turbofans were specially selected for the Missileer because of their fuel efficiency. With a speed of Mach 0.8, the Missileer had to loiter on station for up to six hours and map the multiple threat environment before simultaneously launching selected Eagle missiles at individual targets. The XAAM-10 Eagle was by any standards a big missile, with a length of 16ft 1.5in (4.89m), a maximum diameter of 1ft 2in (0.35m) and a launch weight of 1,285lb (584kg). It comprised two stages, including a solid propellant booster and a long-burn, solid sustainer carrying the missile a distance of 126 miles (202km) at a maximum speed of Mach 4. The Eagle's active seeker was derived from the Bomarc surface-to-air missile.

Tangling with aircraft such as the extremely capable MiG-21 shown here gave Navy pilots a taste of what was to come unless designers took a quantum leap forward in warplane technology. In the late 1960s the Soviets were clearly catching up the West and threatening to add technical superiority to a numerical advantage.

A product of the early 1950s, the Douglas A-4 Skyhawk allowed the Navy to conduct close support operations and light interdiction, adding new roles and capabilities. The A-4 would open new opportunities for Navy and Marine aviation that would stiffen the need for fleet defence and combat air patrols far from the home carrier.

Grumman was responsible for the missile's airframe.

The Missileer was not expected to defend itself, which was a reasonable enough assumption for the job it was designed to do. Soviet maritime aircraft were long-range bombers and cruise-weapon platforms were unlikely to be protected by fighters. The Fleet Air Defense Fighter was not expected to tangle with MiGs nor to fly against manoeuvrable attack aircraft. It would rely for its survival entirely on the premise that it would destroy an incoming aggressor at a greater range than the latter could reach its

adversary. Although the Missileer and its revolutionary Eagle missile would not survive long in the turmoil of Washington politics, that concept would prevail through another still-born venture until compromise and advanced technology merged it with a true dogfight capability. But, at $3.4 billion, the Missileer/Eagle combination was a costly programme and one that would come under close scrutiny from the new Defense Secretary Thomas S. Gates.

Most of the programme's development had taken place under the tenure of Defense Secretary Neil H. McElroy, who in

1957 had been president of the soap company Proctor & Gamble when summoned to office by President Eisenhower. McElroy replaced Charles Wilson, who for almost five years had been unable to control the Pentagon in its ambitions to acquire the world's biggest arsenal and seed global intelligence operations. But McElroy went the way of Wilson and failed to shackle the runaway plans that threatened to blow the lid off the national budget at a time when deficits were a sign of national failure rather than a topic for Congressional debate. So it was that Gates arrived at the Pentagon in 1959 with firm expectations from Eisenhower that the Department of Defense would play its part to get a balanced budget in Fiscal Year 1960.

Enter TFX

President Eisenhower had, by law, to leave office at the end of his second term, a departure marked by the inauguration of a new President in January 1961. Like all outgoing administrations, government matters are tidied up in the preceding election year, leaving options open for the incoming administration. It was in the nature of the man for Eisenhower to leave the very cleanest slate when he departed. In the late autumn of 1960 Gates ordered the Navy to cancel the Missileer/Eagle programme but allow continued research (not development) testing on the Eagle missile, which was considered to be a potential winner. The real nail in the coffin had been the highly specialized nature of the Missileer, which was useless for any other role and thus had an expensive, single-point, application. The FADF requirement was to be left open, preserving choices for the incoming administration. In a seemingly unrelated move, but one which would prove highly significant in satisfying the fleet defence requirement, Gates ordered the Air Force to refrain from

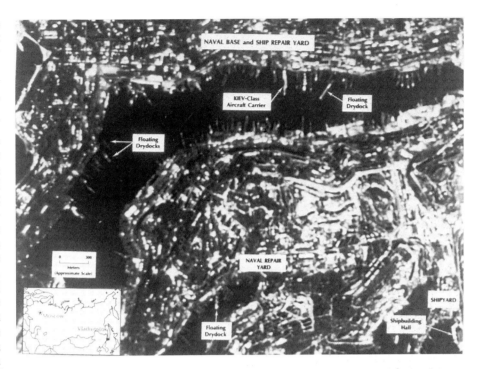

Reconnaissance photographs were a vital component in the intelligence war surrounding naval operations and Soviet expansion through the policies of Admiral Gorshkov was evident. Here naval facilities at Vladivostok clearly show the substantial build-up in facilities and support infrastructure for the impending Soviet carrier programme.

issuing requests for proposals on its TFX (Tactical Fighter Experimental) programme until the new Secretary of Defense had taken office.

The TFX had been drawn up to meet Specific Operational Requirement 183, which defined the fighter-bomber replacement for the Republic F-105 Thunderchief. SOR-183 had itself evolved from new research into variable-geometry wings. As a weapons delivery platform the F-105 was good, but the roles of tactical bomber and dogfighter were sufficiently far apart to give aerodynamicists and engineers a serious headache over optimized wing/fuselage shapes. It seemed an ideal candidate for variable-geometry wing platforms which, by virtually redesigning the wing in flight, could give the aircraft excellent low-speed lift and control stability without detracting from its supersonic performance. Nevertheless, despite several research projects proving that, in practice, wings could be pivoted in flight – forward for low speed, back for high speed – serious mechanical and engineering problems would delay the application of the concept.

Then, in 1958, engineers at the Langley Aeronautical Laboratory, a field site belonging to the National Advisory Committee for Aeronautics (NACA) found a solution. By adopting an idea from Britain's aircraft industry they discovered that these particular problems would go away if the single-hinge mechanism were divided into separate pivots for each wing,

Escorted away by two F-4 fleet defence fighters, a Soviet Bear maritime reconnaissance bomber flies close by the Kitty Hawk during its passage through international waters. Frequent and increasing encounters highlighted the sustained interest taken by the USSR in a global presence.

with each located outboard of the fuselage centreline. In this way the blended inner wing and fuselage juncture would provide a deep structural unit where the pivot box could be located. Langley's director John Stack, who would leave at the end of the year when the NACA metamorphosed into NASA, brought this idea to the Air Force. The former test pilot, now acting commanding general of USAF Tactical Air Command, Brig-Gen Frank K. Everest took this idea and organized a closed conference with senior TAC officers and representatives from industry to sell the use of variable-geometry for the F-105 replacement. It was just what was needed, he said, to optimize performance for low and slow missions as well as fast fights at altitude. On 14 June 1960 this was formalized into SOR-183 and TFX was conceived.

The birth of the Air Force TFX programme waited for the inauguration of the Kennedy administration in January 1961 and the attentions of the newly appointed Defense Secretary Robert S. McNamara. It called for a Mach 1.2 ground-hugging penetration capability as well as Mach 2.5 dash at altitude, a transatlantic, unrefuelled ferry range and operability from short, unprepared, 3,000ft (909m) strips. Coming from the Ford Motor Company with a reputation for

hard-nosed decision-making, McNamara wanted to save money wherever he could; in time, and somewhat unjustly, this would lead to his being called 'Mack the Knife'. At the Pentagon he quickly reviewed all defence programmes for possible cuts. The administration was already pledged, in its election campaign, to a major expansion of strategic and nuclear forces and wanted to whittle away at the not-so-visible secondary defence projects to help to claw back some of that outlay. McNamara coined a new phrase that would reverberate through Congressional halls thereafter whenever government agencies wanted funds for a new technology venture: commonality. By merging seemingly disparate requirements, said McNamara, great savings can be made by having a single programme that served the needs of several users.

Taking advantage of the open-policy legacy from the Eisenhower administration, McNamara wanted to merge the Air Force TFX and the Navy FADF programme into a single effort. He met senior officers from the services and consulted with Dr Harold Brown, head of Defense Research and Enginering. On 16 February, to the consternation of the Air Force and the Navy, he ordered all four services to explore the possibility of a common aircraft for their separate require-

ments. The new Defense Secretary envisaged a single aircraft that could satisfy not only TFX and FADF requirements but also serve as a close support aircraft for the Army and the Marine Corps. In June the Army and the Marine Corps said they could not adapt the same aircraft for their purposes and flatly refused to be dragged into the programme. Bitter acrimony flowed between the service chiefs and these 'bow-tie bastards' as the new army of civilian money-savers were dubbed. With unprecedented authoritarianism, the new guard in the Kennedy White House swept aside convention and told the service chiefs what they would have to do to squeeze their requirements into the 'commonality' funnel.

The problems were awesome. The Navy set an upper weight limit of 50,000lb (22,727kg) on their FADF and allowed it a maximum length of 66ft (20m), set by the size of carrier deck lifts. They wanted a 4ft (1.21m) tracking radar providing the 200-miles (320km) range sought for early intercepts and that dictated a large diameter nose, and for optimum co-operation between pilot and weapons officer they wantd side-by-side seating. The Air Force optimized a design which came out at an aeroplane with a 75,000lb (34,091kg) gross weight, terrain-following radar and a high-Mach dash capability dictating a slender nose and tandem seating. But it was the separate performance specifications that compromised design considerations, and all along the Navy insisted that the two could not be reconciled.

Concerned at the cancellation of the Eagle missile, the Navy did successfully campaign to fund low-level work on the concept. That activity arose from Fighter Study 1 set up to examine the case for pursuing the AWG-9 radar project from the now cancelled Missileer/Eagle programme. It showed an indisputable need for a new missile to fill the air defence requirement out to at least 100 miles (160km) from the launch aircraft. The new missile developed from the Eagle was, appropriately, called the Phoenix, with the weapon designation AAM-N-11, later known as the AIM-54A. The combination of radar and missile was the most ambitious air-to-air weapon yet attempted and the AWG-9 was derived direct from the advanced ASG-18 pulse-Doppler, lookdown, fire-control system designed for the YF-12A Mach 3 interceptor. The ASG-18 had itself evolved from the ASG-1B

While protection of the carrier battle group grew along with the capabilities of carrier attack planes in the 1960s, Soviet aircraft nosing around the sea lanes gave US Navy intelligence important information about the expanding threat and many aircraft were interrogated electronically while being escorted away.

designed by Hughes for the cancelled North American F-108 Rapier, a Mach 3 interceptor with a design gross weight of 102,000lb (46,364kg)! But none of this would work if the airframe requirements between the two services could not be matched in a flyable aeroplane.

The one area where both services did agree, however, was in the application of variable geometry. Each could see the benfit for its own applications: the Air Force for diverse mission roles; the Navy because it significantly cut deck landing speeds, improved the dogfight potential and yet allowed high dash speeds. For different reasons the two services wanted optimized performance at both high and low energy levels. Variable-geometry wings would provide that in a way other, high-lift devices could not. Only by redesigning the wing in flight, adapting it for different flight regimes and performance requirements, could each service satisfy both ends of its specification. The Air Force liked to call it the 'mission-adaptive' wing and it promised just that: to change the mission of the aircraft according to set geometries. The NASA work proved that the engineering problems with swing-wings could be solved and it was perfect for the TFX and the FADF. But still it left the general configuration unresolved.

The Bogy of Commonality

After both the Air Force and the Navy told the Secretary of Defense that they could not reconcile their very different requirements into a common airframe and engine combination their judgement was overriden and they were ordered to get on with it anyway. In August 1961 McNamara told the Navy that it had to accept a modified specification – and that was that. They would get a 3ft (0.91m) diameter radar antenna with less performance than stipulated, accept a 55,000lb (25,000kg) all-up weight limit, 10 per cent higher than the maximum desired, and be given their side-by-side seating configuration, as requested. The final insult came when McNamara told the Navy that it would not be in overall charge of its Fleet Air Defense Fighter, because the specification was to possess 'commonality' with the TFX programme and that would be managed by the Air Force. Many Navy fighters are successful as land-based combat aircraft, but there is not a happy history of land-

Long-range cruise missiles launched by ship or aircraft posed a real threat to the carrier and its complement of attack squadrons. Almost 50ft (15m) long, this AS-3 Kangaroo entered service in 1961 and could be launched by the long-range Tu-95 Bear. With a range of about 400 miles (640km) it carried a nuclear warhead and would usually have been targeted against harbours, ports or coastal cities.

based fighters with sea legs.

On 29 September 1961 the Department of Defense issued its RFP for the integrated TFX; the Pentagon tried to subsume the Navy's Fleet Air Defense requirement into Air Force nomenclature and all reference to the FADF was quietly erased. Instead, because it was to be an Air Force project, it would get a USAF designation and be known as the F-111. Respondents included Boeing, General Dynamics, Lockheed, McDonnell Douglas, North American and Republic. Acknowledging its lack of naval expertise, General Dynamics teamed with Grumman in a joint proposal submitted, along with other bids, during December; General Dynamics would play prime contractor and Grumman would build the aft section, tail unit and landing gear for the Air Force version, assemble the entire Navy version and integrate electronic equipment into the latter. Boeing was ranked first with the General Dynamics/Grumman bid second, but none of the submissions was acceptable. Boeing was weak in having proposed an untried engine, the General Electric MF295, while all were low on crew escape, on-station loiter times and performance at both high and low altitudes.

After a second round of submissions requested in April 1962 and delivered a month later, the first two ranking designs remained the same and, while declaring Boeing and General Dynamics/Grumman to be near the required design targets, they were still far from producing acceptable concepts. Again they went back to the drawings boards and in a third set of refinements submitted during June the two top contenders came out strongly, with Boeing in the lead but its prime competitor closing the gap. The Pentagon sent them back once again to hone the blueprints. At the fourth submission in September Boeing were the clear winners, getting the vote from the Air Force Council, the Air Force Logistics Command, the Bureau of Naval Weapons and the Chief of Naval Operations Adm George W. Anderson. As a member of the Joint Chiefs of Staff, Adm Anderson worked with Gen Curtis LeMay for the Air Force, Gen David Shoup for the Marine Corps and Gen George Decker for the Army, all under the chairmanship of Gen Lyman Lemnitzer.

During the period of the TFX design refinement, which went on unabated for the first nine months of 1962, Adm Anderson was increasingly alarmed at the way the Navy's priorities in the specification were slipping and that Grumman was unable to get General Dynamics to agree to critical design changes vital for the retaining of the Navy's part of the specification. To achieve commonality said

McNamara, the Air Force and the Navy would have to accept a certain amount of compromise and 'relax' (abandon) certain criteria originally considered sacrosanct. But what upset the CNO was that, not only would the primary structure have to be the same for the two services, but as far as possible the assemblies, systems and subsystems – even components – had to be the same. Since adopting standardization with the British during World War II, the Navy had prided itself on developing a set of equipment which maximized the efficient use of hardware and minimized cost and procurement. Now it was having to reinvent 'standardization', turn it around and call it 'commonality' which, to many of the men on Anderson's staff, sounded like 'conversion' – to the Air Force way.

The real problem lay at the interface between the Office of the Chief of Naval Operations, staffed by career officers with an impeccable service record and working single-mindedly for the future of the service, and the Office of the Secretary of Defense, staffed by civilian bureaucrats living their lives in the revolving-door between think-tanks delving in theory at industry R&D establishments and the upper echelons of the Pentagon. It was from the bureaucrats that McNamara drew strength to sustain the doomed TFX

concept but it was to them that the Navy had to appeal for rationality in approving elements in the specification and the ensuing contract. At the fourth presentation Boeing was selected by Adm Anderson, for the Navy, and Gen LeMay, for the Air Force, as prime contractor. This recommendation was passed to Navy Secretary Fred Korth and Air Force Secretary Eugene Zuckert and the two services then prepared to work with the Boeing concept in wrestling down the burgeoning weight, which even at that stage threatened to ground the programme.

It was not to be. When the two Secretaries passed the recommendation to McNamara and his assistant, Undersecretary Roswell Gilpatrick, the decision was reversed and word came back down the line that the General Dynamics/ Grumman team were to be awarded a contract for eighteen F-111A development aircraft for the Air Force and five F-111Bs for the Navy. When Boeing heard about this it contested the reversal claiming, correctly, that its competitor had a more expensive proposal. But Boeing's bid had only 60.7 per cent commonality compared with 83.7 per cent for the General Dynamics/Grumman proposal, and commonality was the golden key.

Moreover, General Dynamics was a Texas company, the home of Vice-President Johnson and Undersecretary Korth. But there was another reason: McNamara had wanted to keep reins on the Air Force and when he was appointed CNO in August 1961 Adm Anderson had been told that, with the Joint Chiefs of Staff, he was expected to support the Secretary in keeping LeMay in check. Although Anderson made it clear that he would have no part in such a conspiracy, both General Dynamics and Boeing were primarily Air Force contractors and McNamara found it comforting to know that, by selecting General Dynamics, Grumman would be there to maintain the Navy's interests.

Boeing managed to get high-level attention for the matter and Sen John L. McClellan formed an investigating committee, asking McNamara to defer the awarding of the contract until judgement had been made. Interpreting it as an affront to his authority, McNamara went ahead and awarded the $439 million contract on 24 November 1962. Although Adm Anderson rated Grumman highly and had high regard for their design record, he was furious over the clandestine way the final decision had been made, overturning the Joint Evaluation Board and the decisions of the Air Force and the Navy chiefs. McNamara's staff became paranoid and sent messages to the chiefs of the Air Force and the Navy instructing them on what to say when they appeared before the McClellan committee, which was still scheduled to take place during spring 1963. Terse response only increased the fear that the civilian leadership could face a revolt. McNamara's staff then bugged the offices of the Air Force and Navy chiefs in an attempt to uncover misdeeds which could be used against them if they argued for Boeing.

In the end all it did was to stiffen resolve, but it was the beginning of a decade of uneasy peace between the military and the Democratic civilian leadership which reached its peak during the Vietnam War as the White House tried to micro-manage operations from desk-top maps and the bean-counters tried to take control of the contracts. Only with the Reagan/Bush leadership of the 1980s and the early 1990s was White House meddling eased; but that is a different story.

Back in 1962 the hearings droned on for several weeks, one side fighting it out with the other and all to no avail. The

With inertial guidance and a single-stage rocket motor, the AS-4 was developed for use against naval targets and shore installations. With a range of 300 miles (480km) and a top speed of Mach 4.6 it would have been difficult to knock down.

legislators on Capitol Hill decided that McNamara was perfectly within his rights to award the contract to the General Dynamics/Grumman team and that no miscarriage of justice had taken place, despite protestations from Boeing. As for Adm Anderson, the long drawn out hearings brought nothing but plain truth from the CNO, including the Navy's disquiet over the entire TFX issue. Before the year was out he received a visit from Korth and Gilpatrick to say that the President was not going to extend his tenure as Chief of Naval Operations and that he could take up a position as ambassador to Portugal if he wished. As it was, when McNamara asked George Anderson to meet him the former CNO gave the Secretary of Defense such a drubbing on integrity and the principles of ethics that he literally reduced the man to tears. As for McNamara, he went too far and tried to influence Robert Kennedy who saw to it that the President knew the full story.

Kennedy wanted to award Anderson the Distinguished Service Medal but McNamara made sure that he himself would be out of the country when that prestigious event took place in the Rose Garden at the White House; so the President advanced the date so that the Defense Secretary would have to attend. Before leaving for Portugal, Anderson spent an hour with the President, who assured the former naval chief that he fully understood what had been going on and that he was not prepared to accept intervention by 'little Czars'. Shortly thereafter Kennedy was dead and McNamara was replaced by Clark Clifford. There was, Anderson thought, justice after all in American democracy.

At a projected $5.4 billion, the 'commonality' programme represented the largest production contract ever made for a single aircraft type. Two versions of the TFX would be produced: the F-111A for the Air Force and the F-111B for the Navy, with only minor differences (visually the shorter nose on the F-111B was the most prominent) to shoe-horn the 'commonality' aircraft into each service niche. As related earlier, the Navy was none too happy with the lead role being assigned to the Air Force, but it had extracted a price for that: the Navy would pay no money for the development of the F-111B until the first production aircraft was delivered. The Air Force would be prime funding agency and as such would

The Soviet SS-N-2 Styx anti-ship missile, in service during the early 1980s, was a serious weapon keenly respected if only because it had been sold around the world. Packing a lethal punch, it has a range of up to 50 miles (80km) and a high subsonic speed.

Feline Propwash

Grumman will be for ever linked to a range of fighters associated with members of the cat family, the first of which, the F4F, took to the air in 1937 but spent three years in protracted gestation before it entered service in 1940. Named Wildcat in October 1941, just six weeks before America went to war, the US Navy had about 130 operational F4Fs when Japan attacked Pearl Harbor in December 1941. Like so many companies swept into the uncompromising demands of war, Grumman had to expand on a massive scale and total production increased from 158 aircraft of all types in 1940 to 2,247 two years later. The aircraft was selected by the British and served initially as the Martlet; F4Fs saw service from the Arctic Ocean to the deserts of North Africa.

By 1942 the Wildcat was in the vanguard of US Navy operations against the Japanese and propelled the company into the forefront of American aeroplane builders. In all, 7,825 Wildcats were built of which 1,123 went to the Royal Navy, but it was in the Pacific that the F4F made its name. It was while flying Wildcats with Marine squadron VMF-121 in January 1943 that Capt Joseph J. Foss became the first air ace of the Second World War to equal the twenty-six kills of the highest scoring American ace of the First War, Eddie Rickenbacker. By this time the ratio of kills to losses was almost 6:1. At the war's end, Wildcat pilots were credited with 1,327 kills, a figure greatly overtaken by Grumman's second shipboard monoplane fighter, the Hellcat.

The Grumman F6F Hellcat grew out of initial design work, from studies that began almost four years before America went to war, to find a successor to the Wildcat using the 1,700 hp Wright R-2600 fourteen-cylinder, radial engine. Incorporating improvements that accrued from experience with the Wildcat design and operations, the F6F first flew in June 1942 and Hellcats were fighting the Japanese by August 1943. Production aircraft had the 2,000hp Pratt & Whitney R-2800 engine. The aircraft rapidly became the mainstay of Navy and Marine Corp units on fighting flat-tops and all the leading aces in the Pacific war flew Hellcats. When production stopped in August 1945 Grumman had built 12,275 Hellcats and only 270 had been lost in combat against 5,156 kills, a loss ratio of less than 1:19.

Too late to see service against the Japanese, the F8F Bearcat was a further improvement upon the Hellcat, incorporating similar safety features but with added speed and manoeuvrability. Albeit unsolicited, the Grumman proposal got the Navy's attention and the first aircraft took to the skies in August 1944. However, orders for almost 6,000 F8Fs were cut when the war ended, even as the first Bearcats were sailing to war aboard the carrier the USS *Langley*. Arguably the best propeller-driven fighter to see service in the US Navy, the Bearcat was too late for World War II. When the Korean War began it had been superseded by the new generation of Navy jets, also from the Grumman stable. The Bearcat's lasting claim to fame came on 16 August 1969 when Darryl Greenamyer took his privately-owned Bearcat through calibrated traps to secure the world speed record for piston-engined aircraft at 483.041 mph (777.7kph).

Developments in the Soviet Navy during the 1960s saw a major commitment to produce fixed-wing models, traditionally an area ignored by the Soviets. These Yak Forger VSTOL aircraft are seen on the deck of the Minsk, a Kiev class carrier built in the early 1970s. When the US Navy was planning a successor to the F-4 it was intelligence about the construction of ships such as this that forced the pace to find a new and more potent replacement for the Phantom.

have to deliver a workable product compatible with the Navy's TFX requirement. It was not for this reason alone that the entire TFX programme failed as a multi-service aircraft, but the fact that the Air Force had to pay for the Navy's changes was enough to ensure that the flat-top flyers drew the short straw when it came to budget allocations within the programme.

From the beginning it was recognized that the Navy TFX would take longer to develop. It was more advanced in that it incorporated a superior suite of electronics to satisfy the Navy's long-shot intercept needs and the AWG-9 radar system had to be integrated with the AIM-54A missile. The potential for weight growth was enormous and Grumman realized that it was an insoluble issue until major development had produced a working aeroplane. Only then, reasoned the contractor and the customer, would they worry about weight. The first three of five F-111B development aircraft (eventually seven would be built)

would be produced regardless of weight but the fourth prototype would begin a weight reduction programme which would lead to acceptable levels for the production aircraft. At least that was the idea. In 1964, when Grumman had about 6,000 engineers working on the project, optimism ran high that the F-111B would open a new outer perimeter fleet-defence capability only dreamed of hitherto – or that was what the public relations machine said. In that other world of fantasy and make-believe, politicians endorsed orders totalling 705 aircraft for the Navy version alone.

Despite the physical similarity between the two versions of the F-111, the F-111B for the Navy had a shorter length, 66ft 9in versus 73ft 6in (20.23m vs. 22.27m), so that they could be accommodated by the deck elevators. Performance requirements stipulated by the Navy included a longer loiter duration than that required by the Air Force, so the F-111B had its wing span increased from 63ft to 70ft (19.1 to 21.2m)

and a corresponding increase in wing area from 525sq ft to 550sq ft (48.21 to 50.51sq m). The Navy version would not carry the Texas Instrument AN/APQ-110 terrain-following radar and the General Electric AN/APQ-113 attack radar would be replaced by the Hughes AN/AWG-9 search radar. Grumman would adapt the Air Force design to carry six AIM-54 missiles, two of which would be carried in the internal weapons bay and four on swivelling pylons attached to the outer, movable, wing sections.

Weight, of course, was to be the main problem for the F-111B, or at least it was the aspect of the aircraft that the Navy fastened on to as it fought desperately to shake loose from the TFX agreement forced upon it against all service advice. When the General Dynamics/Grumman team got the TFX contract it gave the Navy assurances that the fleet version would have an empty weight of 39,000lb and a gross weight of 63,500lb (17,727 and 28,864kg), now 8,500lb (3,864kg) over the

Two views of the Soviet carrier Novorossisk, third in the class of four Kiev carriers built as the pinnacle of Admiral Gorshkov's plan for a blue-water navy operating from warm water ports. It was the emergence of a powerful Soviet navy from what had been a predominantly coastal defence force that added complexity to the balance of forces involving the US carrier battle groups. Note the angled flight deck and forward missile housings for cruise and anti-ship weapons.

weight it had been told it would have to accept and 13,500lb (6,136kg) higher than its preferred empty weight. By mid-1963 the empty weight had risen to more than 40,000lb (18,182kg). When the F-111B was rolled out from Grumman's Bethpage, New York facility on 11 May 1965 the empty weight was 46,300lb (21,045kg) but, calculated on the basis of the first prototype, the gross weight had soared to a phenomenal 77,700lb (35,318kg)! The effect of the weight increase took its toll on performance. The single-engine climb capability sank from a projected 595ft/min (180.3m/min) in late 1962 to 270ft/min (81.82m/min) in 1964 and less than 190ft/min (57.6m/min) at rollout. The landing approach speed for the F-111B went up too, from 113 kts in 1962 to 125 kts in 1965.

On 18 May 1965, five months after the first flight of the Air Force F-111A, the first

F-111B took to the air from Calverton, New York at the start of a relatively trouble-free test period. Nevertheless, underlying problems boded ill for the 'Texas swinger'. It was simply not a Navy fighter. With a high angle of attack in the approach pattern and glide slope phase, and a highly sloped forward canopy, the pilot had difficulty in seeing the carrier deck. At 66ft 9in (20.22m) the F-111B was 6ft 9in (2.05m) shorter than the Air Force version with a sweep capability of 16 to 72.5 degrees; the F-111A would use the 26 degree forward sweep position for landing while the Navy would use the 16 degree sweep for both take-off and landing. On carriers, normal parking spots would put the aircraft diagonally in a box 55ft x 55ft (16.67 x 16.67m), irrespective of wing sweep.

But none of the differences between service variants mitigated the underlying

problems, which may be divided into three groups: weight, aerodynamics and engine. The weight problem spoke for itself and Grumman implemented a Super-Weight-Improvement Program (SWIP) from the fourth prototype in a determined effort to get it down to acceptable operating levels. Yet the fundamental problem was built into the design when the Air Force rigidly adhered to its requirement for Mach 1.2 at sea level. This enhanced the structure, which added weight, which needed more fuel, which added still more weight. When it rolled out in May 1965 the F-111B's projected range was 44 per cent below specification. At the first Navy Preliminary Evaluation, or NPE, in October 1965 the F-111B was given an emphatic thumbs-down. The design team met criticism by suggesting a set of high-lift devices in the form of slats and flaps, more fuel to get the range back up to requirement and a

Throughout the decade of the 1960s the US Navy would wrestle with the problem of getting an effective fleet defence fighter capable of matching the threat while killing the intruder in large numbers at great distance. That search began with a F3D Skyknight lookalike, the F6D-1 Missileer. With a bulbous fuselage and side-by-side seating for pilot and weapons officer, a superb long-distance radar and six long-range missiles, the aircraft framed the basis for the F-14/AIM-54 Phoenix combination to emerge a decade later.

Paradoxically, the next step in the Navy's search for a fleet fighter was triggered by a US Air Force require-ment for a successor to the F-105 Thunderchief, the first supersonic tactical fighter bomber to enter service. Operational throughout the 1960s, the F-105 was stretched to the point of compromise and what the Air Force wanted was a fighter bomber with supersonic dash at low level, Mach 2 at altitude and rough field operation.

major reworking of the structure to shave off precious pounds. It was a game of reciprocal challenges: because the aircraft was low on range the internal fuel capacity was increased from 16,000 to 26,000lb (7,273 to 11,818kg) which offset SWIP work to cut weight.

An examination of the many problems faced by the F-111 is outside the scope of this book, but some relate to the emergence of the VFX specification and the eventual development of the F-14. The general shape of the aircraft had been subject to considerable work with 6,000 General Dynamics engineers assigned to the project. NASA had performed more than 20,000 hours of wind-tunnel testing from which it was learned that the aircraft was not as aerodynamically clean as was expected or forecast in the proposals. Drag was a big problem characterized by poor transonic performance, directional stability and manoeuvrability. Before its first flight, the F-111 had accumulated 25

million man-hours of development which, along with the wind-tunnel time, was the highest ever committed to an aircraft of its size. Indications of serious drag problems were evident in these tests, but in the extensive flight trials of the F-111A they were defined to a higher fidelity. Most serious was tail drag, contributing as much as 30 per cent to total drag figures versus a theoretical, optimized 5 per cent. This was impossible to change without a complete redesign of the empennage and that, of course, was impossible.

One problem that would consistently plague the F-111 and carry forward to its Navy successor was the engine. Begun as a private venture at Pratt & Whitney, the JTF10A was the first turbofan with an afterburner. It was designed as a 20,000lb ((88.97kN) thrust class two-shaft, axial-flow engine and bore the military designation TF30, by which it would be known in its long and not altogether uneventful life. The design of the engine

originated in 1958 when Pratt & Whitney conceived a subsonic engine for a commer-cial airliner proposed by Douglas but never built. When the TFX came along the company dusted off the design, attached a large afterburner and stressed it for Mach 1.2 at sea level, the first time an engine had been so designed. The three-stage titanium fan section was integrally mounted with the six-stage, low-pressure compressor section to form a nine-stage spool. The seven-stage high-pressure compressor was primarily fabricated in nickel alloys and the eight annular combustion cans burned JP-4 or JP-5 fuel delivered by hydraulic pump at up to 4,000lb/hr (1,818kg/hr) and by centrifugal afterburner pump at greater flow rates.

The 'blow-in door ejector nozzle' (BIDE) exhaust shroud concept was not well suited to afterburning turbofan designs, producing a 30 per cent loss of ideal net thrust at the nozzle in subsonic speed, or 5 per cent at supersonic speed

When the Navy wrote its fleet defence requirement between 1960 and 1962 it anticipated as a successor to the F-4 Phantom an aircraft with great range to fly CAP on deep strike at great distance. Within a year of being told by the Pentagon to combine its requirement with the Air Force's in a common fighter the Navy would issue a request for a replacement to the diminutive A-4 Skyhawk. The A-7 Corsair II, seen here, would emerge for service at the end of the decade giving added responsibility to escort fighters.

with afterburner. Although the afterburning turbofan brings advantages in high thrust augmentation and low cruise SFC (specific fuel consumption), it challenges the designer with the need to compensate for a large boattail in the non-afterburner mode and facing high back-end drag and thrust loss. In flight tests with the first prototype the engines suffered compressor stalls close to the aircraft's maximum performance and above Mach 2. At that speed the engine would stall if the aircraft were put through high-g manoeuvres, but at Mach 2.35 it would happen spontaneously and without warning in straight and level flight. Careful study of the flight trials led to the inevitable conclusion that a lack of practical testing had given the engine inlet design engineers too few data from which to produce optimized inlet/airframe/engine geometries.

Never built before, afterburning turbofans were notorious in theory for demanding very carefully designed inlets,

and wind-tunnel tests of candidate configurations were totally inadequate in obtaining the data and detailed fluid dynamics information essential in arriving at the right inlet. This would be a basic and time-consuming flaw throughout the aircraft's life, but for the Navy F-111B it was a disaster. The problem arose from channelled ducting bringing supersonic air through a quarter-round inlet, thus creating pressure anomalies at the compressor face. Although the problem would eventually be resolved, it played no part in the F-111B since it came long after the demise of the Navy aircraft. However, lessons that began to be learned from 1965 would, paradoxically, provide the tests essential in getting it right on the aircraft's successor, which would use a derivative version of the same engine.

By mid-1966 the cost overruns, weight increase and performance deficit added concern to confusion in Congress where the legislators puzzled over the pro-

gramme. A moratorium on the TFX issue imposed by Sen McClellan when President Kennedy was assassinated in November 1963 ended in mid August 1966 when McClellan demanded answers and reconvened the Senate Permanent Investigations Subcommittee. This time the Navy would be ready. In the first round of hearings held between 26 February to 20 November 1963, when Sen McClellan examined the legality of McNamara's contractor selection, the Subcommittee was broadly divided in two on favouring the General Dynamics/Grumman team over Boeing. This time the Subcommittee wanted to know why the unit flyaway cost of the F-111B had jumped from $2.9 million in 1963 to $8 million less than three years later. New members sided with McClellan and older members had the poor technical record to ponder, factors which would give McClellan greater leverage in the hearings and on the floor of the Senate.

Within days of Sen McClellan announcing the end of his 'moratorium' Defense Secretary McNamara took the unprecedented step of attempting to run the F-111 programme from his own office in the Pentagon. On 25 August 1966 he held the first in a regular series of weekly meetings to solve problems with the aircraft and the programme in general. McNamara shunned involvement with the uniformed military and the Pentagon's project officer was not invited to the meetings. But it cut little ice with Sen. McClellan and the Navy made it known that it was out to get its F-111B version

cancelled. In fact, for some time Grumman had been edging away from the joint endeavour with General Dynamics and quietly started the process of looking at alternatives. Unhappy with some technical choices forced on the programme by the prime contractor General Dynamics, Grumman were working up their own solution which could be applied to a new, all-Navy, aircraft to replace the F-111B. One area where Grumman differed from General Dynamics was in the design of the wing box and in the materials selected for it. Even as they accompanied their senior partner in defence of the maligned F-111B,

Grumman had their own, very different ideas about a substitute.

But the industry too had been looking at alternatives, particularly competitors. Leaking stories about its intentions, McDonnell made it known that it was working on a swing-wing version of the F-4 Phantom II and early in 1967 it defined such a project. Known as the F-4J(FV)S, it had a completely redesigned wing with shoulder-mounted pivot boxes in a fixed inner wing section, variable-geometry outer wings with a sweep of from 19 to 70 degrees. The wings incorporated hinged leading-edge flaps and trailing-edge, full-

From 1962 to 1969 the US Navy would fail in its attempt to get a fleet replacement for the F-4 Phantom because of the policy of commonality. What Defense Secretary McNamara did was to give the Navy time to come up with a product appropriate for the next generation instead of the F-111. Weight problems, structural fatigue, poor engine inlet and exhaust design and excessive drag penalties revealed a flawed design.

The picture for which the Navy eternally gives thanks that it can see only in an artist's impression: two Navy F-111B fleet defence fighters streak across a rocky shoreline. Departing from the Air Force version only in the shorter nose, the F-111B was overweight and had a performance considerably below that of the F-4, the aircraft the Navy wanted it to replace.

span ailerons and spoilers, the undercarriage was redesigned and fixed to the fuselage and the tail area was increased and anhedral eliminated. Later in the year McDonnell would offer Britain's Royal Air Force a version of the swing-wing Phantom designated F-4M(FV)S in efforts to attract it away from an Anglo-French proposal which would eventually emerge as the Jaguar. Despite these initiatives, and although it favoured the cancelling of the F-111B, the Navy was still firmly under a directive to make the Texas 'swinger' work.

During March and April 1967 a new Navy Preliminary Evaluation was held on the fourth and the fifth F-111B prototype,

now the subject of the SWIP which made major internal changes to cut out unnecessary weight. Materializing from this and other recommendations was the Colossal Weight Improvement Program, or CWIP, which sought to remodel the exterior. The CWIP resulted in a reduction of the empty weight to 46,112lb (20,960kg) but the gross weight went up from 77,692 to 79,002lb (35,315 to 35,910 kg)! The nose area was changed, the forward canopy was reshaped to aid visual approach, the position of the landing gear was moved back to avoid tail-dip on bucking carriers, and the AWG-9 electronics boxes were moved from a position behind the cockpit

to the new extended nose. Other changes included the raising of the pilot's seat and providing increased flap deflection. In the original configuration, four AIM-54 missiles were carried on underwing pylons. In the CWIP version two missiles were moved to engine-mounted pylons.

Despite appalling problems built in with the original, inadequate design, the SWIP and the CWIP action did result in an aeroplane compatible with carrier operations, although its performance never came up to required standards. The first three models failed to gain the advantage of these slimming and remodelling activities but the two pre-production aircraft (numbers six and seven) did conduct carrier trials with their improved TF30-P-12 engines. Lighter than the earlier models, these engines produced 20,000lb thrust (88.97kN) with afterburner, an improvement of 1,500lb (6.67kN). Largely at the insistence of Congressional opponents rallied by Sen. McClellan, production of the F-111B had been stopped after the first two aircraft had been delivered; but they served a useful purpose in directing attention more precisely to test results which would aid in the definition of a replacement for the F-111B. It was only a matter of time before it would be totally abandoned.

In summary, as the Navy viewed the programme in mid-1967, it was clear that the idea of 'commonality' had sunk without trace but at great cost. Nevertheless, concluded the Navy, elements of the blue water TFX were salvageable: carried over from the aban-

doned Missileer, Eagle had been resurrected as the AIM-54 Phoenix, a weapon system giving good results despite weight increases and cost overruns; the variable-geometry wing (which General Dynamics insisted on calling the 'variable-area-sweep-camber-and-aspect-ratio' or VASCAAR wing) was a viable solution to adaptive mission requirements; and the TF30 promised good fuel efficiency for long range and loiter. It also made sense to employ invested capital; the government and industry had spent $1.25 billion (at 1960s prices) on Eagle/Phoenix and the engine alone.

Enter Grumman

During the spring and summer of 1967 the Navy held extensive, but informal, discussions with Grumman about a new specification for a replacement aircraft.

Under the terms of a Navy Anti-Air Warfare Study, ostensibly for the purpose of seeing what was needed to get the F-111B on track but in fact a think-tank for redefined mission needs, the Navy and Grumman agreed on a purpose-built aeroplane that would carry the Fleet Air Defense role into the next century.

In the period between the award of the TFX contract at the end of 1962 and the realization almost five years later that the entire Air Force/Navy 'commonality' concept had been a disaster, the spectrum of threats catalysed into a redirected threat. The Navy mission had not changed appreciably but the new generation of carrier-based aircraft joining the fleet had clarified operational goals. In addition, new Soviet long-range aircraft posed new and expanded threats that could not be addressed by anything then on the drawing board. In a classified document of the period the Navy reported that 'The oper-

A serious design flaw in the engine inlet interface brought numerous problems throughout the lengthy development of the F-111. The quarter-round inlet buried under the inboard wing section had numerous boundary layer flow challenges never fully met by the aircraft's design team.

ational and intelligence communities tell us that we have at best a parity situation in 1968 with regard to the Soviet Tactical Air Threat. Russian fighters have a disturbing edge in vehicle maneuverability.' Worst of all, concluded the Navy's analysts, 'The Russian philosophy of attaining a broad base of technological development through flyable hardware has created a recognized technological gap which will become a serious operational gap by 1967.'

What the intelligence community reported about impending Soviet air threats was glimpsed at the Domodedovo air show in July 1967 when Western guests saw the Mach 2.9 MiG-25 Foxbat for the first time. Although it was unlikely to emerge as a danger to US naval forces, it nevertheless represented the first in a new generation of Soviet fighters and long-range aircraft that would threaten the security of carrier battle groups. By this time too the Soviet cruise missile and

stand-off threat had expanded and the need to confront the enemy at the outer perimeter was more urgent than ever before. During the summer of 1967 Grumman suggested to the Navy a new fleet-defence fighter concept optimized around the avionics, weapon system, missiles and engine of the F-111B and which added depth to the Navy component of the now defunct TFX concept. It grew out of a study Grumman conducted for the Navy known as VAFX and another for the Air Force known as FX; although FX was conceived as defining a stablemate for the F-4 Phantom, due largely to the shock effect of the MiG-25, it emerged as successor to the F-4 in parallel development with the F-14.

For the Navy, VAFX clearly pointed to the need for dogfight roles within the combat air patrol function of the fleet air defence mission. That broadened the weapons suite to include a gun, with Sidewinder and Sparrow for close-in

combat as well as Phoenix for the distant punch. Experience in Vietnam had shown that the old-fashioned cannon had been rejected prematurely from the weapons suite of modern combat aircraft. A version of the F-4 Phantom had been produced with a 20mm M-61 Gatling gun specifically at the request of the Air Force. Clearly defined mission requirements in the fleet air defence and air superiority missions were not met by the F-111B and, as the classified Navy summary on VAFX reported, 'there is now a higher requirement for Air Superiority'. In several ways the F-111B was less capable in that role than the F-4 Phantom, which had a 50 per cent greater acceleration than the Texas 'swinger'. The changed nature of the threat had broadened the requirement even more than it had been at the inception of the TFX, but radical new ways to build combat aircraft would accommodate those needs.

Grumman had been out of the fighter business for almost ten years, since

In time and after the Navy had successfully mobilized opposition to its version, the F-111 was successful in the roles that it was used for by an Air Force that had to rewrite the mission around the aircraft it finally got. The only truly supersonic long-range deep penetration bomber operated by Strategic Air Command and an effective successor to the F-105 in Tactical Air Command, the F-111 failed the Navy but left a slot wide open for a far superior aircraft.

The search for a fleet defence fighter accelerated during 1967 when it was clear that the Navy would not get what it wanted in the F-111. Having worked closely with General Dynamics on the F-111B, Grumman was in good shape to see what it had done wrong. In Design 303-60, submitted to the Navy in January 1968, Grumman put the crew in tandem, permitting longerons to run the length of the fuselage which could be less bulky and avoid the heavier structure of the F-111. Gone too was the clumsy intake geometry, replaced by clean intake boxes leading to separate engine pods. But in other respects it was still too much like the F-111.

completing the production line on the F9F Cougar, but in the interim it had been deeply involved in revolutionizing naval airborne early-warning and tactical electronic warfare. The airborne Navy of the late 1960s was a generation beyond that of the late 1950s and Grumman knew well, through its development of the E-2 Hawkeye and the EA-6 Prowler, that a FAD fighter with long sea legs could be a defence force multiplier. It was in the fundamental rethinking that accompanied the demise of the F-111B that the airborne

command and control system evolved. Now, with quantum leaps in avionics and electronics, naval combat could be directed by an airborne battle director far beyond the horizon and out of the carrier's radar reach. This was the defence-in-depth sought in the Navy's original requirement but denied by limited technology and rigid adherence to the disastrous ideology of 'commonality', fine in principle but unsuited to the different needs of the Air Force and the Navy.

As steeped as it was in the latest tech-

nology for fleet defence, surveillance and attack co-ordination, Grumman badly needed another big fighter contract and the dollars that it would bring. For much of the 1950s Grumman had been building aircraft at the rate of 500 to 800 a year, but since 1960 the annual rate had been around 220. Intriguingly, the most prolific seller was the Ag-Cat, a biplane crop sprayer designed in the 1950s. While high production levels are not necessarily commensurate with high profits, a low level will never provide the capital base for investment. However, disproportionate to the low production quotas, Grumman enjoyed global fame. Built for NASA's Apollo programme, the company's Lunar Module was giving it a household reputation across the world.

This contract had not made a huge profit for Grumman, but over the crucial period during which the company would manoeuvre itself back into the fighter market the total success record of that programme would do nothing but good when bean-counters in Congress sought value for money. As the company's public relations men would write in 1969 when substantiating Grumman's claim to build the next Navy fighter: 'The taxpayer can be assured that he's getting the best for his defense dollar from the company whose spacecraft landed two men on the moon.'

The need to secure a major new defence contract was not lost on Llewellyn J. Evans, just forty-eight years old and both President and Director of the Grumman Corporation. He approved the assignment of Mike Pelehach, for twenty-five years an aircraft systems engineer and design analyst and latterly in charge of the VAFX and the FX study, to head the new design initiative that Grumman would put to the Navy as a replacement for the F-111B. That aircraft would evolve from the new operational roles defined by the changed threat environment and give the Navy guidance on what it should look to for its revitalized FADF. Evolution would be a key part of the new aircraft and in the last few months of 1967 Grumman concluded that the new requirements called for two aircraft, delivered sequentially. First, a repackaged F-111B would fit good elements of the General Dynamics/Grumman TFX work into a newly engineered fuselage and wing assembly using innovative design concepts and high-strength titanium alloys for reduced weight, while a second concept coming along later would incorporate advanced systems and an Advanced Technology Engine then being developed.

Grumman briefed the Navy on what it thought was a better fighter concept, more than a redesigned F-111B, and lobbied quietly for support in the Pentagon and on Capitol Hill. As luck would have it, just when the Navy wanted a strong advocate for its dedicated Fleet Air Defense and Air Superiority fighter, the dice of opportunism rolled in its favour. Relieving Adm David L. McDonald as Chief of Naval

Jet Cats

Production of the Hellcat and the decision to retain the piston engine for its intended replacement the Bearcat, all but excluded Grumman from competing for the first series of jet-powered, shipboard fighter contracts. Instead, in January 1945 McDonnell introduced its twin-engine FD-1 Phantom, and in October 1946 Vought flew the single-engine F6U Pirate. Neither these, nor the North American FJ-1 Fury which flew in November 1946, made the impression intended. Nevertheless, the failure of these three types to meet expectations kept open the door for second-generation Navy jet fighters from McDonnell and Grumman in the form, respectively, of the F2H Banshee and the F9F Panther. These two manufacturers would dominate the Navy's decks for the rest of the century.

Grumman's F9F Panther emerged from an unpromising four-engine concept known as the XF9F-1, rationalized to carrier requirements through a single-engine design. The F9F-2 adopted an Americanized version of the Rolls-Royce Nene engine and emerged as a Hawker Sea Hawk lookalike, except that the exhaust exited through a pipe under the rear fuselage rather than through the bifurcated side-fuselage outlets adopted for the Brtish design. The Panther was rugged, seaworthy and, with a detachable nose and rear fuselage/tail sections, easy to get to. Only 5ft (1.51m) longer than the Hellcat, its folding wings facilitated deck-spotting. The right aeroplane at the right time, it entered service in May 1949 well in time for the Korean War, when it became the first Navy jet to see combat.

Grumman built 1,385 Panthers and 1,988 of its derivative successor, the F9F Cougar. Too early to incorporate advanced aerodynamics from German research facilities overrun at the end of the European war, the Panther had a conventional wing but Grumman tested a swept wing on a variant of the F9F. This was to give the aircraft a comparable performance to that of the swept-wing MiG-15 encountered in Korea, and to keep up with the North American Fury and a swept-wing variant of the Douglas F3D Skyknight. With a 35 degree sweep, reduced span and 20 per cent more area than the straight wing Panther had, the F9F-6 Cougar was the precursor to the definitive model, the F9F-8 with a further 12 per cent wing area through its extended root chord.

Panthers saw front-line service until 1956 and Cougars for a further four years by which time they were seriously obsolete. Overwhelmed too by extraordinary advances in technology, the last single-engine Grumman cat, the F11F Tiger, saw front-line service for only four years from its 1957 introduction. The first Navy fighter to get an area-rule fuselage for reduced transonic drag, it was the first supersonic shipboard aircraft and the first to do Mach 2 in level flight. The Tiger was built just twenty years after Grumman's first design entered service, but fell prey to the tides of change and only 201 were built. Instead of perimeter defence, the carrier task force now had to reach out far beyond the battle group and attack enemy aircraft before they could release cruise and stand-off weapons. A new kind of fighter was needed and for a while McDonnell's F-4 Phantom II filled that gap until it too became redundant and stood aside for the last feline fighter: the Tomcat.

Operations from 1 August 1967 was Adm Thomas H. Moorer, an able exponent of an all-Navy aircraft. Replacing Paul H. Nitze as Secretary of the Navy was Paul R. Ignatius. Both men were concerned at the appalling situation regarding the F-111B and nobody wanted to take the responsibility for it. Adm McDonald had presided over the whole affair since he replaced Anderson in 1963 and spoke wisely to Adm Moorer about new brooms and clean decks. As for Secretary Ignatius, all he wanted to do was to keep an even keel and not rock the boat until Defense Secretary McNamara left office, which it was rumoured he would be doing in 1968.

There was, however, one man close to both the Navy Secretary and the new CNO who could convey the internal relationship which had deepened between the Navy and Grumman over the preceding year: Vice-Adm Thomas F. Connolly, deputy to Adm McDonald since November 1966 and now deputy to Adm Moorer. It was Connolly who would brief his new chief on the closely guarded secrets of Navy manipulation to jettison the F-111B once and for all and make way for a new aircraft. The time was just right. Congressional hearings on the Fiscal Year1969 budget would be held in the spring of 1968 and the new CNO and his civilian head would be the subject of much questioning in the House of Representatives and the Senate. There were a crucial few months in which position policies could evolve for a determined attack on McNamara and his bureaucrats; time in which to get ready for a new assault on the troublesome child of TFX. But more than that, the Navy was stymied on funds for the production of F-111Bs (which it did not want anyway) until the budget subcommittee received answers to hitherto insoluble problems.

To date it had spent relatively little on the F-111B programme and was only due to allocate funds for production aircraft. If the new CNO and the new Navy Secretary could demonstrate to Congress that more money would be saved by switching to a completely new, dedicated Navy aircraft they would carry the day. It was a tight time for the Federal budget, with Vietnam claiming much of defence spending and belt tightening all around the Capitol. To prepare the way, Vice-Adm Connolly arranged to brief Adm Moorer on the new fighter proposal arising from the VAFX study and received a warm reception. At Adm Moorer's behest he took the idea to Secretary Ignatius in an attempt to garner support, but his reception there was hostile to say the least. Ignatius listened tight lipped as Connolly explained about the new proposal and how everyone from the President down would be tainted by the infamous TFX and its sorry legacy unless something were done quickly to undo the damage. This might not have been the most diplomatic way for the deputy CNO to behave and all it did was to forewarn the Navy Secretary on plans afoot. Loyal to McNamara, he would try to stop the mutiny, but it was too late.

Grumman's plan was simplicity itself and that was what made it attractive: to blend the existing TF30 engines into a completely redesigned airframe, spread them on either side of the fuselage, integrate the avionics and the weapon system and put the two crew members in tandem above, rather than in, the forward fuselage, affording good visibility for take off and landing as well as in air-to-air combat. In briefing the CNO and his deputy, Grumman provided charts which all knew would persuade Congress. One showed the cost projections inherent with the current F-111B option. Because the Navy would pay for the F-111B as an annual procurement on the basis of aircraft accepted, the curve maintained a steady upward trend. The other showed budget projections for the new proposal. For three years funding for the new aeroplane would rise steeply and exceed the steady procurement figure for the F-111B; but after three years the costs for the new aircraft would level off while procurement on the F-111B would

continue to rise. The message was clear. It would cost less for the Navy to scrap plans for F-111B purchase, fund development of a completely new aeroplane and buy it in from a single-source contractor.

In September 1967 the Navy defined the new fighter through what it called the VFX requirement. The basic fighter proposed by Grumman as an outgrowth of the F-111B would be VFX-1 for the Fleet Air Defense role while the advanced version, using the same airframe but different engines, would be known as VFX-2, for both FAD and the Air Superiority requirement – quaintly referred to as the Other Fighter Role. During the closing months of 1967 the Navy defined the content of Fighter Study II which sought to re-evaluate missions, roles and requirements, an evaluation which included the F-111B (in its CWIP-modified configuration, now referred to as Navy II F-111B) and the VFX proposals from Grumman. It was impressed that Grumman had sought to maximize work already under way and not to begin with an altogether clean sheet.

The idea was that Grumman would produce the VFX-1 to give the Navy experience with the new fighter before switching to the ultimate version, defined as VFX-2. The engine Grumman proposed for the definitive VFX-2 was a new turbofan incorporating advanced materials such as high-nickel alloys, titanium and ceramic composites in place of the conventional steels used in the then current generation of turbofans. Defined in the Advanced Technology Engine programme, jointly funded by the Navy and the Air Force, it was to bring its own problems to the VFX.

Encouraged by the potential customer, Grumman completed its initial VFX configuration and presented it to the Navy in January 1968. This initial design, known as the 303-60, was the definitive F-111B reworking and the first iteration in a sequence of evolving configuration changes to meet the VFX specification. But first there were the Congressional hearings and crucial decisions about the flagging F-111 programme. Where once it had fallen to Sen John McClellan to probe source contracting on the TFX programme during hearings in 1963 it was now up to Sen John Stennis, acting chairman of the Senate Armed Services Committee, to judge the merits of the F-111B. On one matter Congress was united: if there were to be another programme to carry out the mission first mooted for the TFX it would

be hard fought over in competitive bids and not left to a single contractor.

Anticipating that, in November 1967 Adm Moorer, Chief of Naval Operations, began Navy Fighter Study II which would be conducted with industry in general as well as Grumman in particular. During the course of this study the Navy would evaluate proposals from McDonnell Douglas, North American Rockwell and Ling-Temco-Vought and reach conclusions in a final report to be issued on 1 April. There was little chance that Grumman would lose to competing bidders; none could match the familiarity with Navy requirements or compensate for the working experience of Grumman's F-111B team.

In some ways it was a bad time to make final judgements on the F-111B. The fifth prototype, the first aircraft to carry all the changes brought about through weight savings and reconfigured systems, represented an intermediate step to yet another proposal from industry for a better Navy version. A hypothetical F-111B seriously re-engined to meet Navy requirements and incorporating 40 per cent titanium, 30 per cent aluminium and steel, 5 per cent boron and 25 per cent other materials would cut the airframe weight to 24,000lb (10,909kg). Unit flyaway cost was predicted by the Navy to remain within $9 million, or $10.45 million including R&D, for a production purchase of 232 aircraft. In a proposal submitted by Navy Air Systems Command during February 1968 the 'new' Navy II F-IIIB went some way to setting targets which Grumman's initial contender for VFX – the 303-60 – would have to match.

At the March 1968 hearings specially convened by the Senate Armed Services Committee to discuss the F-111B, Navy Secretary Ignatius supported the F-111B/Phoenix programme and urged approval from the legislators for early production. He drew upon the sinking of the Israeli destroyer *Eilat* by Soviet-built Styx missiles deployed by the Egyptian Navy on 21 October 1967 as an example of the danger faced from a new generation of Soviet anti-ship missiles which left US naval forces vulnerable to a similar fate. When asked for their opinion, Adm Moorer and Vice-Adm Connolly gave a less politicized response and clearly showed the advantage of a VFX aircraft over the F-111B. Split cleanly during intense questioning, the two factions stood their ground but the argument that swung the day was that 'Other Fighter Role' which called for close-in dogfights to fulfil the air superiority mission. It was no contest: the F-111B was a good supersonic strike aircraft and, potentially, penetrating, low-level bomber, but it could not survive against a Phantom let alone the next generation of Soviet combat aircraft.

Between December 1967 and May 1968 Fighter Study II, and the VFX submissions from industry summarized in the Navy's report of 1 April 1968, the Navy produced analytical results from a theoretical fly-off between the F-111B and the VFX-1 designs. At 40,000ft (12,121m) the new concept had ten times the climb rate of the F-111B and the time taken for it to accelerate from Mach 0.8 to Mach 1.8 was 2 minutes versus more than 6 minutes for the F-111B and 3 minutes for the F-4 Phantom. Turn rates for the VFX-1 were spectacular and these figures said it all. Despite the rearguard action by Secretary Ignatius, in its Fiscal Year 1969 budget the Navy cut from thirty to eight the number of F-111Bs put up for funding request. Already $350 million had been earmarked

for production funds and the Navy knew that if it went ahead with the order for the F-111B now it might never get rid of it whereas that money – which Congress did not contest – could be put to good use in getting the Navy an aircraft it really wanted, albeit one at present on paper only.

It was proving a bad time for the entire programme. On 29 February 1968 the British government cancelled an order for fifty F-111K attack aircraft, reneging on its original decision of 22 February 1966 to buy ten and of 15 March to buy a further forty. On 17 March 1968 the US Air Force put the first F-111As into Takhli Air Base, north of Bangkok, at the start of an operational evaluation phase. Eleven days later, on 28 March, one of those aircraft failed to return from a bombing mission over Vietnam. That same day on the other side of the world, the Senate Armed Services Committee cancelled funds for further work on the F-111B. In May, when the matter was brought before Congress, legislators refused to sign any more cheques for F-111B development or procurement and

the Navy TFX was dead. Less than two months later the Navy would go out to industry for bids to build the VFX-1.

By this time Clark M. Clifford had taken over as Secretary of Defense from McNamara who left in February 1968, three months after President Johnson sacked him from the Pentagon he had presided over for almost five years. In December 1970 the Senate Permanent Subcommittee on Investigations delivered a damning report on TFX, claiming that 'vital financial resources were squandered in the attempt to make the TFX program produce satisfactory results.' It also went on to say that McNamara's insistence that the F-111 prime contract should be awarded to General Dynamics 'can at best be described as capricious, lacking in depth and without factual substantiation.' As for the Air Force version of the F-111, that went on to become an effective strike aircraft and low-level penetrating bomber but its reputation will always be unfairly linked to the unrealistic dreams of a car builder from Detroit who went to the Pentagon with a big idea.

complex as it was, presented the optimum package for performing the Navy's VFX mission. Although refinements had added capabilities and cut weight, the Phoenix was big to hang on the airframe and expensive to buy. If the drag-inducing Phoenix could be dropped in favour of the Sparrow and Sidewinder missiles the aircraft might be lighter and more manoeuvrable in the fighter role. So the 303G was designed around that possibility in an effort to see how far the Phoenix was driving the aircraft's capabilities and performance. It incorporated the same AWG-10 radar and missile configuration as the F-4 Phantom, which Grumman knew was a potentially serious competitor to the F-14, and came out slightly smaller than the other 303 design choices. Nevertheless, the 303G came out at only 1,600lb (727kg) lighter than the all-Phoenix version and proved a disappointment.

In the weeks following the adoption of the 303E for further design iteration, the configuration was refined from the 303B into more or less the aeroplane that Grumman built as the F-14. By mid June 1968 the shape was defined but much debate ensued about the positioning of the wing pivot, both fore and aft and in and out from the fuselage centreline. Furthermore, at this stage, design 303E incorporated a single fin, although some design engineers were from the outset pressing for a twin-fin configuration. Moreover, while opting for separate engines with their own independent auxiliary systems in pods, the engineers knew that they were building in a serious flight-control problem should one engine fail on reheat. With twin thrust lines 9ft (2.73m) apart, the aircraft has both a drag penalty and, with one engine out, a potentially disastrous yaw slicing moment. But, to counter these unwelcome side-effects, the obvious advantages were clear and decisive.

So it was that by the time the Navy released its RFP to industry on 21 June 1968 Grumman was far along with its definitive design and on 1 October, when the five development proposals were submitted for evaluation, except for a single fin, the aircraft had all the characteristics of its final design shape. One feature undecided at the time of submission was the wing, which some believed should employ supercritical section as defined and investigated by Dr Richard Whitcomb of NASA's Langley Research Center. It was Whitcomb who devised the

In yet further design options, Grumman examined a fixed-wing alternative seen here in the form of the 303F concept. Similar in most respects to the definitive F-14, the greater wing area needed for low-speed handling made it much heavier and cut mission performance.

wasp-waist, area-rule, transonic fuselage for the supersonic fighters of the 1950s and who was frequently to be heard saying 'We've done all the easy things, let's do the hard ones!' The area rule concept had already won him the Collier Trophy and had been incorporated into the General Dynamics F-102.

Whitcomb had an uncanny ability to conceptualize a radical design innovation and to demonstrate its viability through slide rule and wind tunnel. His supercritical wing was a way to raise the drag-divergence Mach number close to Mach 1 by giving a wing a flattened upper surface and a downward curve at the trailing edge undersurface. Lift would be lost by the shape of the top surface but compensated for by the design of the undersurface. The shape of the upper surface was intended to make the airflow over that area supersonic but to reduce shock waves, which translates into reduced drag. The supercritical wing evolved over a four-year period of research at Langley and raised considerable interest in the military and industry. It promised greater range through improved aerodynamic performance close to Mach 1, offering a reduced fuel consumption. These were attractive attributes in a long-

range interceptor for the air superiority and fleet-defence role where fuel weight was a critical factor.

Langley's supercritical wing programme was moving into full swing when Grumman worked over the Design 303 configurations during the autumn of 1968. Responding to good results from small-scale models in wind tunnels, NASA decided to try out a full-size supercritical wing by substituting one for the conventional wing on a Vought F-8 Crusader, chosen because the variable incidence wing on that fighter was easy to remove and replace and the aircraft type had a genuine supersonic capability of measured value against which the new wing could be tested. Additionally, the high mounted wing did not have to support landing gear and could be measured 'clean' of any peripheral equipment or appendages. But there were several unknowns about Whitcomb's supercritical wing and Grumman had reservations about moving too swiftly to adopt an untried concept.

However, Grumman demonstrated advantages in adopting a supercritical wing for the F-14, wind tunnel tests, showing clear improvements in maximum lift over drag values and better buffet lift coefficients in the transonic area as measured by root strain gauges. But wing trailing edge pressure values were not as good so that there was a mixed message. Grumman management opted to retain a conventional wing design but to maintain a close eye on the F-8 tests. Although approved as early as mid-1968, these tests did not start until April 1971 and by that time the F-14 design was decided upon. Carrying arguably the most aesthetic wing of all time, the F-8 Crusader with the SCW made its first flight on 9 March 1971 piloted by Thomas C. McMurtry. As early as 29 February 1972 NASA held a symposium at Edwards Air Force Base, California, to announce the findings of the test programme, which demonstrated a 15 per cent increase in efficiency at the transonic region. Whitcomb received a $25,000 prize from NASA and industry incorporated the results, but mostly on passenger aircraft and military transport designs. It came too late for the F-14.

As submitted in October 1968, Grumman's VFX contender set a standard by which other aircraft in the US and elsewhere would be built for the next several decades. Most notable would be the Sukhoi Su-27, preceded by the T-10 on which design work began during 1969 with the podded-engine concept, and the MiG-29, albeit with fixed wings. There had been a precedent for the Grumman F-14 design in the North American A-5 Vigilante which, like the VFX contender, had two engines set wide apart with space between the inlet boxes for a forward fuselage to grow out of a broad, flat, aft section supporting the tail surfaces. The main section bridging the two intake boxes and housing the wing pivot assemblies would be affectionately known as the 'pancake', linking the large aerofoil-shaped aft surface between the two engines to the forward fuselage, which had a round cross-section. This centrebody area would generate more than half the lift of the entire aircraft.

Another feature of the F-14 that took note of recent research base was the relative location of the horizontal tail surfaces. Work at NASA showed benefits from having the tail surface below the wing level and Grumman positioned it at the lowest practicable location. This is particularly important for variable-geometry wings and was to serve the F-14 well for the Navy's requirements. As submitted in October 1968, the 303E design had an unswept span of 62ft 10in (19.04m) with a 20 degree sweep at the leading edge. At a maximum sweep of 68 degrees the wings had a span of 37ft 7in (11.34m), but as originally conceived the aircraft had an oversweep to 72 degrees whereby the trailing edge overlapped the horizontal tail surface. The original submission incorpo-

The Convair F-102 and F-106 (the latter is shown here) incorporated advanced area-rule that typified the transformation in aeronautical design during the 1960s. First put forward by NASA's Dr Richard Whitcomb, it was to prove a winning solution to aerodynamic performance problems in the transonic region. Whitcomb went on to design the 'supercritical' wing which Grumman examined for the F-14 but rejected as untried.

rated folding tail tips which, with the over-sweep, presented a maximum span of 27ft 1in (8.21m). The earlier F-111B had no oversweep because the vertical level of the tail was contiguous with the wing trailing edge and this limited the deck span to 33ft 11in (10.28m).

Another aspect unique to the October 1968 submission was the single vertical fin with ventral strake folded for landing. Because Navy fighters must be as short as possible, there was an operating need to prevent trailing edge sweep and fin tip overhang which would extend the aircraft's overall length. Moreover, the height above deck must be no more than 17ft (5.15m) for all functions, including engine change-out. Because the span of an aerodynamic surface increases its effectiveness for a fin/rudder assembly, this translates into height. The surface area was obtained by broadening the base length of the tail while keeping the overall height to 16ft (4.85m). The vertical trailing edge of the tail kept the overall aircraft length to 63ft (19.1m). For all its compromises to meet the Navy's operating requirements, Grumman chose the single fin design for its better performance at high angles of attack and its lighter weight. The strake was added to provide directional stability in the event of an engine shut-down at high speed.

The design of the wing was given much attention and the need for combat agility through low wing loading remained paramount in selecting the optimum configuration. In the initial design submission a wing area of 541sq ft (49.68sq m) was selected, incorporating a manoeuvring flap system. This more than compensated for the weight inherent in the large surface area and produced a net weight gain over alternative configurations. Throughout, priority in wing design was given to the combat manoeuvre with low take-off gross weight a close second, followed by transonic combat agility and, lastly, the deck spotting factor. A key aspect of the variable-geometry wing was to have a longitudinally destabilizing device forward of the centre of gravity in supersonic flight. This can be provided by free-floating canards locked for supersonic flight – but they could jam – or extendible doors – but they have a fixed configuration. Both are difficult to incorporate without extending base drag. Early in the maturation of the Design 303 series, Grumman opted for an extendible glove vane and

A precedent for the F-14 geometry had been set by several aircraft designs, first and most prominent of which had been the fixed-wing North American Vigilante, with boxed inlets and high lift devices.

Clean Sweep

The variable-geometry wing incorporated by General Dynamics in the TFX design during 1961 had its theoretical origins almost thirty years earlier. It was after the writings and calculations of Adolph Buseman in Germany and Robert Jones in the USA were published that the advantages of a wing designed to be geometrically variable in flight were seriously put forward for development. These two theoretical engineers showed the advantages in swept-wing angles for supersonic flight by calculating the reduced wave drag. It was only a matter of time before the obvious advantages of a fixed, straight wing for subsonic flight and a fixed, swept wing for supersonic flight were combined into a variable design allowing the pilot to re-engineer the wing in flight according to the speed.

Known as 'polymorphous' wing geometry, the restructured shape of an aeroplane's lifting surface may take many forms. In the broadest definition, auxiliary lift devices such as slats, flaps and variable tip droop restructure the wing so that it is adapted to varying conditions of flight, matching the requirements placed upon it by the flight envelope. In reality, 'polymorphism' refers to wings that can change their planform, typically the aspect ratio, while lift attenuators are variable camber devices. It is the balance between all these that materially affects the aerodynamic efficiency of the aeroplane at various stages in flight. For example, wing tip deflection in supercruise (sustained supersonic flight without reheat) reduces the nose control moment, increases the fin area effectiveness and enhances the compression lift which in turn optimizes the potential efficiency of the airframe/engine combination. A third, but less frequent, means of remodelling is the variable-incidence wing which may be useful in certain circumstances for altering the AoA without disturbing the attitude of the fuse-lage to the flight path.

The two possible in-flight planform changes are variable aspect ratio and variable sweep angle. By engineering the wing so that the outer sections are telescoped into the inner, a change in aspect ratio is made possible through in-flight extension. But it is variable sweep that provides the opportunity to optimize cruise lift/drag values for widely differing flight envelopes and it was this that caught the imagination of aircraft design and engineering teams. Most coveted of all was the possibility of moving the sweep angle in flight, thus opening up the aircraft's optimized flight envelope without landing. But it was no advantage bought without cost and penalties had to be accommodated.

Typically around 30 per cent of the all-up weight of a modern combat aircraft, the structural weight would grow by 10 per cent and the hydraulic equipment and services (usually around 7.5 per cent for a fixed-wing aircraft) could increase to 8 per cent for variable-sweep aircraft. Benefits to offset these penalties included reduced engine weight, perhaps from 14 per cent to little more than 12, reduced fuel, from 38 per cent to little more than 28, and a better payload for a given all-up mass – 16 versus 9 per cent. Conversely, with a common payload requirement, the all-up weight could fall from 84,000lb (38,182kg) for a fixed wing aeroplane to 45,000lb (20,455kg) for a swing-wing equivalent. It was the high all-up weight of the variable geometry F-111B that made it almost impossible to get the weight down as required; with the swing wing bonus built in, the only way out was to employ increasingly exotic materials.

spent most of the year refining it through the several wing shapes.

As originally conceived, the extendible vane was to be located where the leading edge of the fixed part of the wing joined the engine intake boxes, pivoted so that it would normally be retracted within the mould line of the aircraft. It was there primarily to provide the longitudinally destabilizing surface forward during supersonic flight, reducing trim drag and enhancing manoeuvrability. In addition, by extending it deflected down 60 degrees at the leading edge, it was to have given greater lift during take-off and landing. When Grumman designed into the wing a hinged, slotted flap, wind tunnel tests showed that this would reduce leading edge upwash and that the glove vane would not be needed during take-off and landing. So the glove vane would be extended only from Mach 1 and used exclusively to counteract the decrease in stability at supersonic speeds. This is covered in more detail later.

Grumman Triumphant

Between 1 October and mid December the five competing engineering development proposals from the Contract Definition Phase were scrutinized and evaluated by Naval Air Systems Command (NAVAIR). From this McDonnell Douglas and Grumman emerged as the front runners and although Grumman's submission was not the cheapest it was the best overall. For nearly three months the five competing companies had been exposed to rigorous examination and one of the most exacting contract standards devised for military procurement. Still smarting from the failures of the Kennedy administration to get the dual-role TFX organized into a satisfactory aircraft for both the Air Force and the Navy, Congress was in no mood for a walkover involving additional billions of taxpayers' dollars. Even so, the basis on which the F-14 contract would be negotiated assumed that the stable economic policy that had kept inflation low and monetary policy tight for much of the 1960s would continue at least for

The definitive F-14 shape owed much to the requirement for a rugged airframe and Grumman chose to place the wing pivot points outboard of the fuselage on a broad and flat 'pancake' structure to which the forward nacelle, tail and landing gear would be attached. Note how the horizontal tail is below the level of the wings. Twin tails were incorporated after a contract award based on a single fin concept.

the following three or four years. This was not to be so and the changing patterns of economic fortune in the USA would soon cast a shadow on the Navy's newest fighter.

None of this was known on 17 December 1968 when the Navy began a detailed analysis of the contract proposals from the two finalists. On 14 January 1969, just six days before Richard Nixon was inaugurated as the thirty-seventh President, Grumman was informed that it had won the F-14 contract. After Congress had been notified, the contract for six development aircraft was signed on 3 February. All along, the five contenders had been required to submit detailed technical, schedule and quality criteria for not only the research and development (R&D) phase but also for the duration of the initial production contract, which was expected to run from 1971 to 1977. Industry had been concerned about the start-stop trends from governments that changed political face and there had also been concern about the threat to the financial stability of aircraft companies trapped in the uncertainties of economic changes. Adm Elmo R. Zumwalt, Chief of Naval Operations from 1 July 1970, defined the nature of the Grumman contract in a report to the Navy Secretary John H. Chafee in 1972:

> The detailed definition of the total procurement package concept was implemented in an attempt to reduce the uncertainties of program requirements. Moreover, other new contracting methods were introduced to influence the procurement and administrative functions of the total procurement package concept. These techniques include a Variable Lot clause to permit the Navy the option of ordering varying quantities of aircraft based on a pre-established nominal quantity (i.e., plus or minus 50 per cent) at a pre-agreed formula for deriving ceiling prices in each fiscal year. The development contract included a ceiling price that was 125 per cent of target cost as well as provisions to discourage configuration changes and minimize cost growth. Two basic indicators were utilized to structure the cost of the program – national economic growth and corporate business base.

Although Grumman was not to know it at the time, this was the peak of their post-war corporate performance. Just eight days after the Navy had informed Grumman that they had won the contract for the F-14 the first of the company's Lunar Module

spacecraft* was tested for the first time in earth orbit before its ultimate role of landing two men on the moon, which it would achieve on 20 July 1969. But the company was about to embark on a contract the dollar value of which exceeded anything it had been called upon to deliver since World War II. It was make or break because Grumman had lost all hope of F-111 production when the F-111B had been cancelled in May 1968 and the LM contract would expire in mid-1971 when the last of twelve lunar landers had been delivered to NASA.

Under the terms of the contract Grumman agreed to build six R&D aircraft plus 463 production F-14As and F-14Bs. Congress had given approval in the FY 1969 budget for three prototypes and would give approval for the last three when it reviewed the FY 1970 budget requests in the spring of 1969. The end objective of the Defense Department requirement was for a procurement buy of a total 716 production F-14s to replace the F-4s with

---

* NASA contracted for fifteen Lunar Modules and ten were launched into space of which six landed on the lunar surface. Cancelled moon landing missions deleted the last three and their subsystems were assigned as spares. The last LM landed on the moon on 11 December 1972. Although not relevant, it is interesting to note that the loaded Lunar Module had about the same gross weight as an empty F-14.

the Navy and the Marine Corps. At fixed 1970 rates, the initial R&D phase, including the six pre-production prototypes, would cost $705 million for the F-14A and $228 million for the F-14B. Procurement of 463 production aircraft was projected to carry a unit flyaway cost of $7.5 million, or $10.4 million if total support and spares costs were included and $12.4 million per unit for full programme costs including amortization of the R&D.

During the first half of 1969 the Navy revised its estimates of operational flying requirements and the impact on spares, training and support to reduce the all-in production unit cost from $10.4 million to $9.7 million. If amortized costs on R&D (including the six prototypes) were factored in, the total F-14 programme would show a cost of $11.7 million per aircraft. The Navy was quick to demonstrate to Congress the efficiencies in rolling on with extended procurement, showing a reduction in total programme costs to $9.6 million per aircraft for a production run of 722 (including prototypes) and $8.1 million for a buy of 1,200. In all of these calculations, the flyaway cost – the actual build price of the aeroplane as it stands on the runway – is broken down into 46 per cent for the airframe, 27 per cent for the avionics, 23 per cent for the engine with the remaining 4 per cent making up ancillary and miscellaneous items. In terms

The flat underbody directly below the fuselage pancake presented a slab-bottomed wedge between the two engine pods, yielding the cleanest inlet/engine/exhaust geometry possible and putting stores points and pylons in clean air for good separation characteristics.

of the total programme, the Navy estimated that the total invested programme cost broke down into 73 per cent for the flyaway hardware (the aircraft on the runway), 19 per cent for spares and 8 per cent for support equipment and people. Spares include engines and avionics, and since these represent a significant fraction of the programme cost any problems here may seriously affect the total budget.

The R&D Contract

The R&D contract Grumman signed on 3 February 1969 was on a Fixed Price Incentive (FPI) basis with a target price of $388 million, including a target profit of $35.5 million and a ceiling price of $44.9 million (125 per cent of the target cost). It included the procurement of the six prototypes (Lot 1) and options on seven production lots, each of which could vary between 50 per cent and 150 per cent of the estimated quota. For instance, Lot 2 was for six aircraft, Lot 3 for thirty and Lots 4 to 7 for ninety-six aircraft each with Lot

8 quoting a buy of forty-three. But under the terms of the contract Lot 2 could vary between three and nine (50–150 per cent) while Lot 3 could vary between fifteen and forty-five, and so on. The ceiling price was the maximum the government was prepared to pay and any additional costs incurred would be borne by Grumman. Penalties and awards were to be made for guaranteed performance values in the categories of empty weight, minimum approach speed, acceleration time at altitude, specific range, maintainability and cost. In the best of all outcomes this allowed Grumman to lower costs yet increase profits or, conversely, to suffer reduced profits for escalated prices. There was even a penalty clause for late delivery of five test aircraft to the Board of Inspection and Survey Trials.

The development schedule defined by the contract specification called for a first flight of the F-14A on or before 1 January 1971, the first flight of the electronics and avionics aircraft (prototype #4) in May 1971, carrier suitability trials to begin (aircraft #10) during October 1971,

completion of the aerodynamic evaluation in February 1972 (prototype #8) and air-to-air weapons systems demonstration beginning in May 1972 (aircraft #11). The original Grumman Design 303 submission with the single vertical tail had an empty weight of 35,294lb (16,043kg) and a design gross take-off weight of 52,740lb (23,973kg). The aircraft was designed to carry two Pratt & Whitney TF30-P-12 turbofan engines rated at a normal thrust of 10,750lb (47.82kN), a military thrust of 12,290lb (54.67kN) and a maximum afterburner thrust of 20,250lb (90.1kN) limited to 45 minutes. It had ten integral tanks for JP-4 or JP-5 fuel, with two in the wings (3,480 gall, 15,660 litres), two in the wing box (3,148lb, 1,431kg) and six in the fuselage (7,712lb, 3,505kg) for a total capacity of 14,340lb (6,518kg) or 2,109 gall (9,491 litres).

Armament included one M61A1 Vulcan cannon mounted in the port side of the lower forward fuselage with a 950-round feed drum and mountings for six AIM-54A Phoenix, AIM-7E or AIM-7F Sparrow or the AIM-9D Sidewinder. It is

Little more than half the lift derives from the moveable wing panels, the balance being provided by the flat underside. The outer sections of the mid-fuselage on the underside of the pancake provide ample space for six large missiles such as the AIM-54 Phoenix, putting stores relatively close to the aircraft centreline.

Unlike the complicated design of the F-111 wing/body interface, where pivoting outer stores pylons had to compensate for varying degrees of sweep, no stores are carried on the moveable wings of the F-14. When cleaned up for supersonic dash the aircraft has no drag-inducing appendages thus ensuring greater aerodynamic efficiency and better performance from a given energy band.

true to say of this aircraft that it literally was designed around the armament it was primarily intended to carry, for the width of the aft centrebody and the separation of the engine pods was dictated by the space needed to accommodate four Phoenix missiles, two pairs of two in tandem, in that part of the aircraft. A wide variety of conventional bombs and rockets could be carried on standard launchers and multiple adapter racks and Grumman wrote into its proposal provision for two external fuel tanks holding 6,120lb (2,782kg; 900 gall, 4,050 litres).

In the period between the formulation of the original TFX mission objectives and the definitive VFX proposals of 1968, the expanded role of global naval responsibilities translated into a reshuffling of mission priorities. Now the primary mission was one of fighter escort with combat air patrol as a subfunction for the air-superiority role, secondary objectives including deck launch intercept (DLI) and interdiction. The dogfight function was even more clearly defined and a new generation of Soviet air threats matured quickly through

the 1960s to bring traditional air combat back into the fighter pilot's agenda; continuing experiences reported from Vietnam showed how wrong it had been to think that the days of the fighter were numbered and that air defences were invulnerable. A new generation of electronic aids grew up through the Vietnam years to return the manned combat aircraft to centre stage once more. It was profoundly clear by now that the F-111B would have been pitifully inadequate for the roles the F-14 would be increasingly called upon to fill.

The projected F-14 performance with the RFP design was rated in each of four mission sortie categories: escort (with four Sparrows), long-range escort (with four Sparrow and two 450 gall [2,025 litre] drop tanks), fleet air defence (combat air patrol role with six Phoenix and two 450 gall tanks), and interdiction (with fifteen Mk 82 Snakeye bombs and two 300 gall [1,350 litre] drop tanks). For each mission category Grumman quoted separate performance figures with stores dropped and stores retained. For the fleet

air defence role the proposed (single fin) F-14 had a loiter time of two hours at a radius of 150 nautical miles (nm) (277.5km) or a combat radius of 547nm (1,012km) for a total sortie duration of 2.75 hrs. The warload varied with mission, 2,000lb (909kg) being assigned to both escort and long-range escort roles. For the fleet air defence role the aircraft carried 6,000lb (2,727kg) of stores and for the interdiction role a load of 8,475lb (3,852kg). The F-14 had the highest performance capability in the escort role, with a maximum take-off weight of 52,740lb (23,973kg), a sea level climb rate of 9,600 ft/min (2,909m/min), a ceiling of 41,000ft (12,424m) and a combat range of 1,623nm (3,003km). At the other end of the spectrum, for the interdiction role the aircraft had a maximum take-off weight of 66,843lb (30,383kg), a climb rate of 6,280ft/min (1,903m/min) and a range of 1,585nm (2,932km).

In examining the initial proposal from Grumman, the Naval Air Systems Command concurred with the primary engineering judgements about the aerodynamics and the structure but disliked the single fin and rudder assembly. At the last minute Grumman switched to a twin-fin design with a single, fixed, under-strake at the rear of each engine nacelle, dispensing with the complex folding action of the previous type. With twin fins the aircraft's silhouette is reduced and the two strakes help to maintain directional stability under high-g loads during combat manoeuvres when the fuselage and the wing can mask clean air to the tail surfaces. Although the twin fins together weigh more than the single fin, Grumman found that it was easier to engineer them into the upper surfaces of the rear engine nacelle and fuselage assembly

than to attach the single tail to the wedge-shaped afterbody. Overall, the twin fin assembly had a smaller weight impact than the single tail.

So confident had Grumman been of getting the F-14 contract that in late 1968 the company had ordered long-lead procurement items to ensure that scheduled events and development gates were met on time. With the contract signed, the company had just twenty-two months to complete the detailed design, build the the first prototype and fly it. By March 1969, three months after go-ahead, the design was frozen. Detailed design would be assisted by a unique process known, almost affectionately, as EMMA –

Engineering Mockup Manufacturing Aid – and would be used for fit-checks on hydraulic lines, electrical wiring, control systems and black boxes. Whereas most mock ups are made from wood and plastic without an internal structure to mirror the definitive product, EMMA was identical in every respect to the prototypes and looked like a real aeroplane, but without the expensive metals and materials from which flight-worthy aircraft would be built. EMMA was fabricated from sand-cast aluminium and low-cost steels to copy all the elements of the real aircraft's internal structure and would even be used to hang up a real engine for fit and alignment checks with systems location spotting.

The optimized marriage of engine inlet, landing gear housings and weapons stores points in a blended airframe/engine design is seen here where short-, medium- and long- range weapons are mixed and attached to the fixed parts of the structure. Inlet geometry posed fewer problems for air-flow management and eliminated the need for complicated boundary layer control.

New Materials

The real F-14 would use more exotic materials and Grumman broke ground in the extensive use of titanium, this metal making up almost 25 per cent of the empty weight compared with 9 per cent on the F-4. Titanium grew to importance in the aerospace industry during the 1960s, from limited use in high-temperature regions in the late 1950s to universal application a decade later. However, high strength-to-weight ratio, corrosion resistance and good high-temperature characteristics were offset by forming problems due to its low modulus of elasticity. Hot-forming techniques developed at the beginning of the 1960s provided the breakthrough needed for the widescale use of titanium throughout the industry. By 1969 Grumman had perfected an improved hot-forming process that allowed the production of 2,000 titanium components a month without a cold-preforming process that had previously been necessary. These

new materials-forming technologies played a key role in producing the F-14 as an enduring combat aircraft retained in the inventory for decades.

Another new area was in the effective application of pure and alloyed titanium made possible through chemical milling and the introduction of electron beam welding in the critical wing carry-through box which, in that element alone, saved more than 1,100lb (500kg) in weight over more conventional construction. Electron beam welding was also applied to other airframe elements and, to ensure a real quality improvement in purity, vacuum chamber welding maintained high energy levels and resulted in a seam with greater strength and durability in stress. To fabricate them, components would be placed in the vacuum chamber which would then be sealed. The welder would use a telescope to observe and control the precise alignment of the components. With the intense energy of the beam focused to a spot with a width of no more than an eighth of an inch (0.32cm), the weld penetrated deeper

into the join and produced a stronger bond with less distortion, obviating the need for extensive milling which usually followed conventional welding operations.

By using techniques such as these, Grumman could design large structures into the airframe too big for traditional forges or presses, saving weight by eliminating the need for mechanical fasteners. Moreover, with the use of mechanically controlled welding operations the seams and joins were made more precise, while vacuum welding significantly reduced weld vent porosity through oxidation. To perform this work Grumman invested in two huge electron beam welding machines each with the capacity to weld wing planks 26ft (7.88m) long. One machine would weld wing pivot and wing spar assemblies while the other would be used to weld the huge titanium wing carry-through structure. With the capacity to fabricate up to 160 aluminium and titanium skins per day in sizes up to 20ft by 12ft (6.06m x 3.64m), Grumman had invested in a new, high-capacity production facility built to

The search for an optimized engine inlet was stimulated by NASA and US Air Force laboratory research programmes during the mid and late 1960s. In addition to Grumman, North American Rockwell was given a contract to study optional shapes and work with government research teams to advance the state of the art. North American had set the trend not only with the Vigilante but through engine inlet design for the XB-70 Valkyrie, shown here. This laid the basis on which company- and government-funded studies evolved to produce the new generation of design concepts.

Work on the Air Force/NASA inlet geometry studies in which Grumman and Rockwell participated led direct to the B-1 design shown here, optimized again for a broad performance band. Between the F-111 and the F-14 a completely new way of thinking about performance matching had arisen to influence, then dominate, combat aircraft design. It is interesting to note that, in fact, the two-dimensional box inlet with variable camber ramps had first been applied early in the 1960s in the Concorde airliner.

integrate all operations from the taking in of raw materials through cleaning, heat treating, stretching, milling and trimming. Alongside the facility housing these huge machines, other buildings provided chemical milling and finishing equipment.

Significant amounts of composite materials were designed into the F-14 from the outset. By using boron-skinned, aluminium honeycomb core stabilizers to save weight, Grumman helped to pioneer the wide application of next-generation materials which would become commonplace a decade later. The company introduced boron into wing fences on the A-6 Intruder during 1965 and spurred a major development programme at the Materials Laboratory, Wright-Patterson Air Force Base, Dayton, Ohio, where two R&D programmes emerged. One involved

the production of boron wing tip box beams and the other researched the production of a complete wing box structure out of boron. From this work Grumman developed a third boron research programme, applying the accumulated knowledge to the development of advanced wing designs for future aircraft. It would not be available for the F-14 but it typified the new concept of continuous development where small-scale applications in one project underpin basic research for others.

It is this approach, forged through programmes such as the F-14 and the Air Force F-15, that typifies the revolution brought about by the new generation of combat aircraft that would enter service in the mid-1970s. In several important respects the F-111 epitomized the ultimate

design and fabrication technologies of conventional 1960s aerospace practice, but the F-14 and its generation-mate the F-15 ushered in completely new design and manufacturing techniques that would stand the test of time. Between the F-111 and the F-14, reflected largely in the materials and manufacturing methods employed, the industry took a significant step into the future and set trends that would succeed and be consolidated through to the end of the century.

Systems Engineering and Aerodynamics

No greater demonstration of new, even innovative, design trends can be found than in the overall approach to systems engineering and aerodynamic integration. In the age of propeller-driven combat aircraft, a powerplant was selected for an airframe according to specific criteria and bolted on to the appropriate end of the aircraft. With the first generation jets, engine and airframe were brought together from separate development paths and matched according to the available space and volume. When supersonic flight bcame routine, engine and airframe design took on new rationales. Engines designed to move at supersonic speed were required to ingest air and slow it to subsonic speed, use it to burn a fuel and eject exhausted gases through an optimized nozzle. Performance trade-off resulted from a poor design fit between the engine and the airframe through inlets and nozzles. When straight-line speed became less important than engine performance and efficiency throughout the entire length of its power band, the match of airframe to inlet and exhaust was a crucial factor in engine/airframe integration.

Optimized, fighter aircraft require an inlet geometry capable of supplying high quality air to the engine compressor surface at a uniform pressure, with the least amount of drag in a design offering the lowest weight. The definition of 'high quality air' is associated with measurements of pressure recovery, distortion and turbulence, all of which must be kept under control. Pressure recovery, which is the amount of air flow for the engine to handle, is the average of all the total pressures across the flow area. The total pressure equals the value of the static pressure plus the dynamic pressure. So long as these are kept in balance there will be no losses. Distortion is the profile shape of the pressure recovery pattern and identifies localized peaks or troughs in the uniform flow, essentially describing the magnitude of 'lumpiness' in the air flow. Turbulence is defined as the speed at which these local distortions take place and is expressed as the frequency with which the distortions occur. Airflow through the engine, thrust and SFC will be affected by distortion and turbulence, but the most serious effect will be to induce engine stall, surge or a sudden increase in temperature.

Standard fighter inlet design lagged somewhat and Grumman did a survey of all existing types to select the one optimized for the VFX specification. An alternative D-shaped design had been favoured by several manufacturers, including Dassault with the Mirage F.1 fighter shown. While giving a clean, undisturbed flow of air it failed to provide optimum air delivery for all the performance requirements of the aircraft.

While optimizing straight-through air flow, an alternative inlet to the two-dimensional box, rejected because of its complexity, was the round inlet adopted for the SR-71. Necessitating a moveable cone spike to accommodate different flow volumes and auxiliary flow devices to boost air volume at take-off, the design was too complicated for the F-14.

Taken to excess, distortion or turbulence on their own can stall an engine. Devoid of measured distortion, if the dynamic inlet flow is pulsing rapidly with high enough amplitude it will have the same effect as massive distortion with no turbulence. Insidiously, moderate effects of distortion and turbulence together can, when coupled, have an even greater impact. Engine designs optimized for one or the other are prone to upset the balance between distortion and turbulence and this amplifies the effect of each. The Grumman engineers faced with exacting requirements for engine performance over a broad area of the flight requirements envelope chose to design a simple, technically robust product that could be extended in complexity where necessary, but only to the minimum required for success.

To an unusual degree, the VFX specification called for a broad range of flight capabilities, any one of which would have been a specification for a unique mission or role calling for a distinct aircraft design. Just as the mission-adaptive wing produced a clear need for variable-geometry wings, so would the engine inlet geometry have to adapt for different environments. Only in this way would Grumman get the F-14 to excel in every task for which it was designed. The F-14 became a watershed in

American Swing

After the aerodynamicists Buseman and Jones had shown how optimized swept wings would be for high-speed flight, it was only a matter of time before tests got under way. In 1945 the Langley Aeronautical Laboratory began work on skewed wing angles, and under the guidance of John Campbell tests were conducted on models in wind tunnels. Various angles were tried and, although skew angles up to 60 degrees were evaluated, a sweep of 40 degrees was found to be optimum for this model. Directed by Charles Donlan, later to become a luminary in NASA's manned spaceflight programme, a research effort began in 1947 to determine the effects of variable sweep for low-speed handling with aircraft primarily designed for high speed.

Using the 7ft x 10ft (2.12m x 3m) wind tunnel at Langley, engineers tested the variable-sweep wing on models of the X-1 and found improvements in longitudinal stability. It was during these tests that in-flight variations in wing-sweep angle were found to be preferable to fixed changes made before take-off. Progressive sweep movement during flight would bring the greatest benefits from this technology and it was as a direct result of the Langley tests that Bell Aircraft proposed the development of a full-scale test aircraft based on a German design. Known as the Messerschmitt P.1101, the experimental, vari-able-sweep aircraft had been brought to the USA after the war, delivered to Wright Field and handed to Bell in August 1948. The P.1101's wing could be swept between 35 and 45 degrees in any one of three fixed positions. What Bell wanted to do was to use the basic airframe design and demonstrate how in-flight wing sweep would benefit performance and handling.

The Bell test aircraft, known as the X-5, was in fact a completely new structure based on the design of the P.1101. Powered by a single Allison J35-A-17A turbojet of 4,900lb thrust (21.8kN) the first of two X-5s took to the air on 20 June 1951 with Jean 'Skip' Zeigler at the controls. A major problem with sweeping the wings arose with the change in the centre of pressure and the centre of gravity. To compensate, the high mounted wings were made to slide forward and back along the fuselage according to the sweep angle, 20 degrees in the fully aft position and 60 at the fully forward position. In sweeping from fully swept to fully unswept the wing assembly moved on rails on either side of the fuselage centreline a distance backwards or forwards of 2ft 3in (0.68m). The X-5 was a vicious little brute to handle and the second aircraft crashed killing its pilot Maj Raymond Popson; but the fault lay in the aircraft's design and not the concept of the variable-geometry wing.

the exacting science of optimized engine inlet geometries and came at a time when government funds were being reinvested in basic R&D programmes lacking for most of the 1960s.

Sucked away by space projects and moon landing goals, NASA funds had left aeronautics research with little support. Toward the end of the decade, the Lewis Research Center returned again to fundamental studies in aeronautics essential for progress in these areas. Lewis had been one of the early research establishments under the National Advisory Committee for Aeronautics, replaced from 1 October 1958 by the nascent National Aeronautics & Space Administration which had its mind on other matters. Through

additional work at the Air Force's research laboratories at Wright Field and work in support of the Air Force Advanced Manned Strategic Aircraft (AMSA)* programme, inlet research study contracts were awarded to North American Rockwell, Republic Aviation and Grumman. It was through this latter work that the company performed tests that resulted in the refined blending of the F-14 inlet/outlet geometries with the body parts.

* Begun in 1965, AMSA sought to define the configuration of a successor to the B-52 and laid the groundwork for a wide-spaced nacelle design that would influence US and Russian fighter concepts. It led eventually to the configuration on the B-1 bomber.

The problems inherent in inlet/engine geometries were too big for analysis and required extensive wind tunnel testing. In the days before computer aided design and computational fluid dynamics equations were wrestled by images on video screens, wind tunnels were the only way to resolve seemingly insoluble problems. In the run up to the contract award on the VFX proposal, NAVAIR supported the critical examination of alternative geometries to balance several critical factors. Inevitably, some loss of engine thrust and increase in SFC are unavoidable with any configuration but the end game is achieved when these are minimized as far as possible. To achieve minimal excesses on these power and consumption deficits, Grumman examined a wide range of alternative inlet geometries for trade-off tests leading to the optimized shape. In all cases it was essential to uncouple the air flowing into the engine inlet from the disturbed boundary layer air coming off the fuselage.

From a menu of optional inlet configurations, tried and tested in the preceding two decades of jet aircraft design, there were several candidate types. Circular inlets applied to aircraft such as the A-12/SR-71 family possess an efficient structural shape and low duct weight but they require a moveable cone-shaped spike capable of being withdrawn and extending to accommodate different flow volumes according to speed – greater at slow speeds, less in the supersonic region. Moreover, complex auxiliary air flow devices are needed to provide the extra volume of air for take-off and landing and these compromise the basic simplicity of the circular intake. Half-round shapes, such as those used on the Mirage IIIG, are theoretically efficient but these feed a single engine with a symmetrical flow along an extended duct with little change of vector, similar to that obtained from a circular inlet with a straight-through duct. Their main drawback is that they provide optimized flow volume at the upper end of the aircraft's performance envelope and are inflexible at subsonic and transonic speeds.

Quarter-round inlets situated in the armpit of the wing–fuselage junction have low weight and short duct length. This location does afford some precompression from the junction, facilitating a smaller inlet area, but the complexity and diversity of accessories essential to make the quarter-inlet work are too many to make it a desirable choice. In the example of the

Whether or not the Soviets copied the emerging trend for two-dimensional box inlets, Soviet designers adopted this design for the 1970s generation of MiG-29 and Sukhoi Su-27 series. Work on the MiG-29 and the Su-27 began during the early 1970s to a specification based on the need to counter the coming generation of Western fighters such as the F-14 and F-15. Here the MiG-29 shows off its F-14 lookalike inlet geometry.

F-111, a basic susceptibility of the TF30 engine to compressor stalls did nothing to help to solve problems with the inlet/duct geometry; in fact, it masked major problems inherent in the quarter-round inlet design. Under the Triple Plow modification programme an improved splitter plate was added together with a notched side plate, redesigned intake lip, increased cross-sectional inlet area and relocation of the entire inlet structure 4in (10cm) further out from the fuselage side. Yet still it failed to cure the problem completely. As a consequence of tinkering with the F-111 inlet and engine, the fuselage had to be modified and that brought problems of its own. Moreover, the basic design produced relatively high distortion and turbulence and the inlet was vulnerable to high angle of attack where the boundary layer built up between the fuselage and the wing glove. Grumman had been closely involved with the whole sorry story and were determined not to repeat it with the F-14.

Another option was the D-shaped inlet used by Grumman on the F11F Tiger, an aircraft capable of exceeding Mach 2 when fitted with the General Electric J79. Like the half-round inlet, the D inlet has no auxiliary devices and no moving parts. That it was capable of delivering smooth air to the J79 at such a speed was due to the recontouring of the forward fuselage such that a small bump precompressed the air ahead of the inlet and washed the boundary layer around the lip. But even this was a straight-line speed capability without the full and flexible range sought for the F-14. Just how delicate is the match between inlet, duct and engine was experienced by the British when they installed afterburning Rolls-Royce Spey engines in their F-4K Phantoms. Stalls and blowouts frequently experienced with this engine were probably caused by high airflow levels and reduced tolerance to distortion and turbulence through the inlet/duct geometry.

In all of these shapes and inlet configurations only one set of flight conditions could satisfy the particular geometry adopted for a specific performance requirement. Put simply, subsonic combat aircraft such as those which had evolved through the late 1940s could be amply accommodated by a fixed geometry inlet which, at most, needed supplementary auxiliary inlets to increase the ingested air volume in the lower speed range. Transonic flight requirements, such as those that emerged in the early 1950s, would also be met by fixed inlet geometries but with bypass systems available for matching the air taken in to the air required by the engine across a wider performance corridor. By the early 1960s supersonic fighters evolved with straight-line speed requirements that could be met by fixed inlets clear of boundary bleed or wing/fuselage turbulence, but the new generation of fighters such as the F-14 had to fly and fight at peak performance from low to high speed.

Selected for the Anglo-French Concorde supersonic transport aircraft, by the Soviets for their equivalent Tu 144 and by North American for the RA-5C Vigilante, the two-dimensional box inlet with variable camber ramps was also chosen by Grumman for the F-14. The two-dimensional wedge shape provided an external compression inlet with three horizontal ramps like flat doors, one behind the other along the flat, upper surface of the forward inlet box, a design that gave high

A fine study of the F-14 powering into a gentle right turn and showing variable camber doors on the upper section of the boxed inlet. Note the ventral strakes which assist with control at high angles of attack when the fin is in the body wash.

Considerable drag may result from poor boattail design and, again, the F-111 demonstrates how not to model the aft end of a combat aircraft. In this design the tail contributes 30 per cent of total drag with a commensurate reduction in theoretical performance.

Set on each side of the thin, tapered, aft fuselage wedge the two exhaust nozzles selected for the F-14 were of the convergent–divergent iris type (CD-iris), seen here in low thrust (left nozzle) and high thrust (right nozzle) configuration. One-piece leaves made to translate fore and aft as needed remodel the shape of the interior.

pressure recovery, low distortion and low turbulence. External compression allowed four times the airflow range than mixed (external plus internal) compression. The shape of the inlet gave natural airflow regulation across a wide range of aircraft speeds and flow adjustment by the simple action of opening and closing the compression ramps. Best of all, the design was insensitive to the angle of attack, which put good air to the compressor face under all types of manoeuvre. It was possible to build in over-collapse on the ramps for greater air ingestion under critical low-speed conditions. Furthermore, to obviate the need for a boundary layer bleed system, the intake

lip was situated 8in (20.3cm) away from the forward fuselage, thus ensuring the delivery of clean, uniform air to the box.

Supersonic air coming into the inlet produces three oblique shock strokes and a terminating normal shock. The first occurs at the fixed ramp leading edge along the top of the intake and the others are determined by the position of the moveable ramps. The two front ramps are connected to each other by hinges and to the structure, with the second ramp's centre of rotation positioned in the subsonic section of the inlet. The position of this second ramp determines the cross-sectional area of the throat and the geometry of the

subsonic diffuser. This also controls the slot height for excess air and the volume of the boundary layer bleed discharged through the variable exit flap on top of the wing glove, doubling as an auxiliary inlet. All three ramps doors and the auxiliary flap on top have servoactuators for precise and automatic positioning. A vital part of the design is that the system should operate according to sensory inputs which do not require actions by the pilot. In essence, the F-14's two-dimensional inlet with variable geometry ramps was simple and highly effective without the technical complexity of spikes, cones, cowls, suck-in doors and other devices essential for circular, half

Frames and longerons encapsulate the forward fuselage nacelle which provides generous room for the two crew members. Equipment bays are in easily accessible locations, maintainability being a key feature of the detailed design.

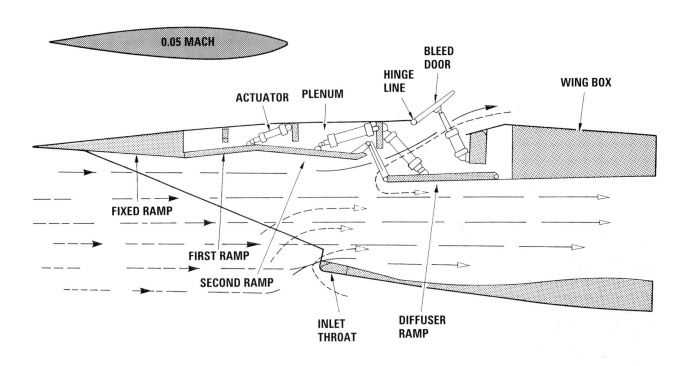

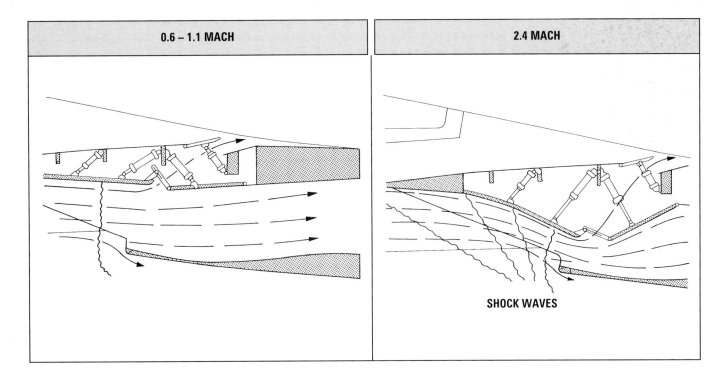

The F-14's engine air induction system.

The Variable Grumman

In November 1946, not long after research on variable-sweep wings began at Langley, Grumman started work on what would eventually emerge as the world's first variable-sweep fighter design. Conceived for the purpose of collecting design data for a swept-wing version of the F9F Panther, Design 83 was submitted in September 1947 with a clipped delta wing, high-mounted T-tail and conventional, aft fuselage exhaust, not at all like the Panther upon which it was supposedly modelled. Designated XF10F-1, two prototypes were ordered in April 1948 but successive changes mandated by the Navy resulted in the clipped delta being changed for a variable-sweep wing in support of a new fighter requirement to which the aircraft, now bearing little resemblance to Design 83, was built.

Grumman's Gordon Israel was chief of the design team that tackled the compromising requirement for transonic speed and good handling characteristics. A succession of Navy requirements loaded the design with radar equipment, extra fuel, bigger and heavier armament and the inevitable weight growth. Utilizing a single pivot point, the high-mounted wings could be hydraulically swept in flight from 13.5 to 42.5 degrees and would incorporate Fowler flaps, full span slats and ailerons supplemented with spoilers. The main landing gear retracted into the bulbous fuselage beneath the single Westinghouse J40 turbojet. It was the engine that proved the aircraft's Achilles' heel and eventually killed it off.

With the Korean War giving strong assurance that the XF10F-1 would be placed in production, Grumman engineers prepared the revolutionary aircraft for its first flight from Edwards Air Force Base in California. That took place on 19 May 1952, but the airframe and engine problems dogged the test programme until production contracts cancelled in April 1953 spelled doom for the venture and trials were stopped by an order to ground all aircraft powered by the troublesome J40 engine. Nevertheless, it was experience with variable geometry that resulted in Grumman's partnership with General Dynamics on the ill-fated F-111, without which the F-14 would probably have looked very different.

Load analyses on wing structure and lift devices showed the advantage in keeping a clean moveable section, providing the engineers with the opportunity to build one of the strongest combat aircraft in the inventory.

circular, quarter circular and D shapes.

Simplicity was an important aspect of the engineering considerations on inlet ramp control. Grumman wanted the automatic system to operate with as few sensor variables as possible and sought to strap the servos to indicators on Mach number, angle of attack and airflow requirement for the engine at a specific time. But the quantity of control engineering needed to react to the three sensory inputs was large and the greater number of ramps and positions was found to bring little clear advantage to the performance band. Tested in the wind tunnel and confirmed later in flight tests, the ramp adjustments were to be carried out by measuring the Mach number and on that alone commands were delivered to the servoactuators. However, signals on the angle of attack, total temperature and the rpm of the low pressure compressor were measured. Grumman placed sensors at strategic locations for each: a conventional pito-static probe showed both the static pressure and the total pressure to determine the Mach number, pressure differences measured at alpha sensors in two holes perpendicular to each other revealed the angle of attack, and a platinum resistance probe measured the temperature for the determination of mass flow.

Safety was a key aspect of the design with tolerances high on ramp angles, the varying limits being +/- 0.3 degrees in supersonic flight and +/- 0.6 degrees at subsonic speed. The control unit consisted of a computer programmed to operate according to specific functions with output to the ramps and the single bleed door. The measured values come in analogue signals and are converted to digital form for controlling the hydraulic pressure in the servoactuators. Each ramp door and the single bleed door in each inlet box is given up to a hundred commands each second by the high-speed control system. In normal operations the ramps remain fully open until Mach 0.5, when they move to the 50 per cent closed position. Safety was uppermost when both inlet systems were designed to operate independently of each other. In the event of a control system computer failure, the servos drive the ramps to the optimum subsonic positions for landing. If a failure occurs below Mach 1.2 the ramps will float to the fully open position, and at a speed greater than Mach 1.2 they lock into position. In all cases the inlet is capable of providing smooth, clean air up to the Mach 2.5 requirement of the VFX specification.

When the specification was written, range and acceleration were an integral part of the requirements for fleet defence at the perimeter and in one-on-one dogfights in tight combat. The

The structural backbone of the aircraft is the wing carry-through box which supports two pivots and accepts bending and torsional moments. Seen here clearly is the reflexed pancake structure giving the upper fuselage its characteristic shape.

Parallel production lines for F-14 Tomcats and EA-6B Prowlers at the Calverton facility emphasize the dominant position as Navy supplier held by Grumman throughout the late 1970s and the 1980s.

airframe/engine combination had to work with maximum efficiency and smoothness to achieve that, but the threats from high boattail drag and reduced engine performance from the variable throat exhaust nozzles were great. All aircraft exhibit drag because of the exhaust, in some cases up to 30 per cent of the engine thrust, and some have excesses that live with them throughout their operational lives; it is, after all, difficult to reconfigure the tail end of an aircraft completely when the relative position of the aft fuselage, the engine exhausts and the tail assembly are all integrated as a functioning part of the original design. Again the F-111 stood as a warning to Grumman's VFX design team. With the tail drag fully 30 per cent of the aircraft's total drag (compared with an optimized value of around 5 per cent), the F-111 had a much reduced supersonic dash range and reduced ferry range, only a few minimal improvements making marginal differences to operational aircraft.

The performance spectrum written up for the F-14 called for a special type of exhaust nozzle. The engineers at

Grumman were faced with several alternative design options which, by the late 1960s, had changed along with the pace of jet combat aircraft evolution. When jet aircraft had low accelerations and operated in the subsonic region, a simple exit pipe sufficed, sometimes with a shroud to pump cooling air along the engine and over the nozzle. This had the advantage of increasing the convergent-nozzle thrust and was known as the ejector nozzle, but when afterburners became the fashion a wide range of convergent orifice dimensions were necessary. The nozzle exit area had to be smaller at subsonic speeds and greater at supersonic speeds. To achieve optimum exit volume for changing thrust levels, designers devised four types of convergent-divergent nozzle, the most common of which in the 1960s was the variable-flap ejector or VFE.

Applied to aircraft such as the F-104 Starfighter, the F-4 and the XB-70, VFE flaps were longer with internal contours to shape the exhaust gas flow and 4 per cent of the engine flow tapped for cooling. But the weight of the varable flap rams and actuators amounted to 20 to 40 per cent of the weight of the engine and the design was judged to be too heavy for the F-14. Lighter in weight but sensitive to engine/inlet matching, blow-in door ejector (BIDE) nozzles were adopted for the SR-71 and the F-111 as an improvement on the VFE. The BIDE nozzle concept allowed the petals, or ejector flaps, to float on the optimum balance between the pressure of the air flowing across the nozzle from the atmosphere and the pressure of the exhausted gases from the engine. Furthermore, blow-in doors float to achieve a balance between the ambient air and the internal pressure, taking augmenting air in to maintain the nozzle pressure when the afterburners are not operating.

The third type of convergent-divergent nozzle was the variable plug (VP) design in which a conical plug moved in and out, or a sleeve extended or retracted, to change the exit area. This design showed great promise and Grumman examined the advantages of a refined VP incorporating a fixed plug in the centre of the exit pipe, capable of collapsing or expanding like flower petals alternately increasing or decreasing the exit volume, for supersonic and subsonic flight, respectively. Engineers disliked the large external flaps necessary for the 'divergent' section and several test

With outer wing panels mated to the pivot points on the carry-through box the aircraft begins to take shape, exterior skins following the reflexed shape of the upper pancake. Each wing carries two pivots, one of which can fail while leaving the wing still supported.

runs were made with discouraging results. Flap sections would separate or disintegrate and, when they did work, add generally to the area turbulence, creating a large boattail effect on the airframe. It was seen as more appropriate for very large engines and by the end of the 1960s too little development work had been done to generate faith in its ultimate potential.

The fourth candidate nozzle design was the Grumman convergent-divergent (CD) iris which in tests in wind tunnels proved that it could outperform all the others. It had a low installed weight, less impact on theoretical aircraft performance and was simpler in design. It was the one selected for the F-14 and combined convergent and divergent sections into one-piece leaves which translate fore and aft according to the flight requirement. At subsonic speeds the leaves extended rearward and, from the outside, appeared to close up like an iris, providing a convergent internal shape

and a smooth external boattail. In full afterburner the leaves are retracted forward, providing an internal convergent-divergent nozzle configuration. Self-cooling fan air is drawn from between the afterburner shell and the liner without the necessity for doors and flaps. This unique Grumman design was ideally suited to the F-14 and set a trend that would be followed by successive developments.

A key feature of the design would be the integration of the engines into the airframe and the correct spacing of the exhaust nozzles. Afterbody effects in single-engine aircraft are bad enough. With twin-engine aircraft the problems are so complex that they do not lend themselves to simple mathematical procedures. Grumman enlisted assistance from NASA's Langley Research Center under a NAVAIR contract and performed wind tunnel tests on five aft fuselage configurations, from closely-spaced F-111 type exhaust outlets to widely-spaced interbody structures keeping the nozzles far apart. By using a unique double-force measuring and balancing system NASA carefully measured the nozzle/fuselage interference drag in each design. Several nozzle attachments were tried out with each of the five backend shapes and confirmed the preference for a CD-iris system widely spaced – which suited the airframe design team since they had first projected a wide spacing for optimum missile carriage in quiet air beneath the fuselage and between the engine housings.

For widely spaced exhaust nozzles, VFE designs imposed a 13 per cent loss of thrust in subsonic operation compared with 10 per cent for BIDE and less than 5 per cent for the CD-iris design. At supersonic speed in afterburner, the CD-iris imposed a 7 per cent loss compared with 8 per cent for the BIDE design. Overall, Grumman projected and later measured a 15 per cent reduction in the specific fuel consumption in cruise compared with the next best inlet/nozzle configuration. Changes during development would eliminate the variable position, bleed air door on top of the inlet, opting for a fixed inlet which would allow a constant flow of air through a 100sq in (645sq cm) aperture. During much of 1969 Grumman tested both the inlet and the exhaust end of the propulsion box and configured the shape and ramp positions to accept air flow of up to 270lb/sec (123kg/sec) to the inlet. During February 1970 Grumman delivered a test inlet to Pratt & Whitney for evaluation with the F401 engine planned for the F-14B and compatibility tests were then conducted with the TF30-P-412 (the redesignated TF30-P-12 assigned to the F-14A), clearing the design for flight trials.

Wing Design

Power and fuel efficiency were vital elements in accomplishing the aircraft's mission but new ground was to be broken in giving it manoeuvrability and a flexible

In an advanced stage of assembly, the wings now have flaps and systems are being installed. Several key assemblies were put together at Bethpage then taken up Long Island to Calverton where they were mated with the main assembly.

operating envelope. The design of the wing and control surfaces, the selection of materials and the geometry of the pivot mechanism were unique to the F-14. There had been only one operational variable-geometry combat aircraft to date – the F-111 – and some had suffered wing box failure with the resulting loss of the aircraft. During 1968 static fatigue tests on the F-111 wing carry-through box – the section designed to transfer wing loads to the fuselage and contain the pivot structure – failed when cracks appeared at 50 per cent of the design life. Designed in the early 1960s, the F-111 wing carry-through box was made from sections of D6AC steel bolted together. Grumman had experience

of that programme and knew how to improve on the concept. Instead of using the tried and tested method, bringing weight and cost penalties, the company opted for the electron-beam welded titanium wing box described earlier, a revolution at the time but the first effective, lightweight, structure of its kind in a variable- geometry fighter.

Lightness too was to be a feature of the wing itself, made stronger for less weight than might have been expected for a fighter of its size by giving the F-14 a thickness/chord value of 10.2 per cent at the pivot and 5 per cent at the tip. Because of this the F-14 can have thinner skins than might otherwise have been necessary and

the extra weight is avoided. By comparison, the F-4 has a wing root thickness/chord value of 6.4 per cent, the Mirage has 4.5 per cent, the MiG-21 has 4.3 per cent and the F-104 has 3.4 per cent. Fitted with numerous high lift devices, the F-14's slender, variable-sweep wing has an aspect ratio of 7.16 with wings swept forward and of 2.07 with wings swept back. This compares with 2.82 for the F-4 and 2.88 for the F-15, both fixed-wing aircraft. The taper ratio, measured as a ratio of the outer and the inner wing chord, represents the load distribution and is typically around 0.25 (meaning that the tip chord is 25 per cent of the root chord). A wing of constant chord will have a ratio of 1.0

The geometry of the boattail is seen clearly here along with the speed brake, tail fillet and systems trunking along the mid-fuselage spine. Note the wing fold screw jacks serving the variable-geometry outer wing panels with their high lift devices. Three-section flaps and four-section spoilers are visible on the trailing edge of the wings.

The substantial speed brake and CD-iris exhaust nozzles evolved through a complicated series of design iterations for minimum drag. Screw jacks for the moveable wings are visible too.

while delta aircraft would have a taper ratio of zero if the tip recedes to a point. The F-14 wing is designed to distribute loads along the span so the variable section has a high taper ratio of 0.31.

The very design of the wing and the moveable control surfaces was a balance between many factors and the choice between several alternative options. The weight of the aeroplane was driven up by the performance/range/armament mix in the VFX specification. The rejection of a fixed wing for the optimized Design 303 configurations was based on the fact that a swing-wing offered greater flexibility in carrier operations (lower landing speeds and better wind-over-deck requirements),

and saved a great amount of weight; a fixed wing would have had an area of 745sq ft (68.4sq m) and increased the F-14's empty weight by 14 per cent (4,920lb; 2,236kg).

The selection of a variable-geometry wing, however, brought with it unique requirements and a novel approach to flight control, involving attitude and manoeuvre functions shared between the wing surfaces and the horizontal tail. In the original VFX submission of October 1968 the all-flying horizontal tail was skinned with a boron-epoxy composite sheet and had a span of 33ft 2.5in (10.1m) but in the detailed design that took up the first three months of 1969 the span was adjusted to 32ft 8.5in (9.9m) and the tail was given a

total surface area of 140sq ft (12.86sq m) with a leading edge sweep back of 51 degrees. It was through differential movement of the tail, acting as tailerons, that primary roll control was established with coupled motion of the tail controlling pitch.

The F-14 was designed to carry leading edge slats and trailing edge flaps with spoilers but no ailerons. The full-span, two-segment slats had constant profile and were mechanically linked for a 7-degrees deflection in combat manoeuvres and 17 degrees for landing. The three-segment, full span, single-slotted flaps on each wing double for roll control and direct lift control. The two outer flaps are supplemented by the inboard auxiliary flap section at the 20-degrees (fully forward) sweep angle, but these are prevented from operating at progressive sweep positions because that part of the wing is shrouded as it slides into the aft fuselage slot.

The two outer flaps on each wing operate at a 35-degrees deflection for landing and 10 degrees for manoeuvring at wing-sweep angles of up to 55 degrees. Three mechanized, four-section spoilers (flaperons) are attached to each wing upper surface. In the absence of ailerons they augment the differential tailerons for roll control at all sweep angles up to 57 degrees (a limit originally set at 63 degrees). Beyond 57 degrees the asym-

metric deflection of the horizontal tail surfaces is ample for full roll control. This is due to the ineffectiveness of the wing-mounted roll devices at the high hinge sweep where roll inertia and damping are relatively low.

Initially, Grumman wanted the spoilers to operate as direct lift controls enabling the F-14 to hold a constant 10.8 degrees angle of attack in the approach so that, with a 15.5-degrees downward view across the nose, pilots would have a full view of a carrier's stern down to the water line. The four-section spoilers were designed to travel 5 degrees up to kill lift and alter the glide path without changing the pitch of the aircraft. This was later changed to 7

degrees, the pilot selecting 'spoilers up' by a single switch and controlling the rate of descent direct through a thumbwheel which modulates the angle of the flaperons. If switched to a post-landing deceleration mode, a touchdown sensor in the main landing gear deflects the flaperons to 55 degrees and they serve as a brake to spoil wing lift and reduce the rollout distance by 765ft (232m). They were the first load-bearing structures on an aircraft made from composite materials.

As mentioned earlier, in the early Design 303E configuration Grumman put in triangular glove vanes at the wing leading edge/intake box juncture (the wing glove) to provide additional lift during

The extreme outer section of the wing carry-through box may be seen in this side view, together with the stout landing gear assembly.

The upper port wing pivot can be seen clearly as the F-14 prototype nears completion. The relatively spacious crew compartment is fronted by a windscreen typical of 1970s design with a thick frame.

take-off and landing. They were considered unnecessary for that job but retained for their primary function – to compensate for the rearward movement of the centre of lift as the speed increased. Although it was possible for the pilot to deploy the glove vanes manually between Mach 1 and 1.4, at the upper value the glove vanes automatically pivoted out to the 15-degrees position to push the nose up and unload the tailerons. The glove vanes were limited, however, to deployment at wing-sweep angles in excess of 35 degrees to prevent pitch instability at subsonic speed. If the pilot selects a ground-attack mission mode the vanes will lock at the open position down to Mach 0.35. Later in the programme the vanes were found to be

superfluous to requirements and F-14A aircraft had theirs locked in position while the vanes on subsequent models were eliminated.

The reflexed design of the fuselage pancake aids the supersonic trim and cuts the pitch moment, contributing to the stability of the aircraft across the entire flight regime. When the original single fin and folding ventral strake were replaced by twin fins and dual strakes of reduced depth beneath the engines, Grumman applied a 5-degrees outward cant to the vertical tailplanes to reduce the effect of turbulent vortices from the wings and glove area at high angles of attack and in violent manoeuvres. The outward, canted, lower strakes have a significant effect on yaw

control and help to counteract twisting effects on the rear fuselage induced by the large vertical areas above. Finally, single-speed brake doors are fitted above and below the rear fuselage aft of the pancake, the lower door split by the slot for the tail hook. These doors can open to a maximum 60 degrees in flight with the lower door restrained to 18 degrees on landing and were designed to give the aircraft combat agility as well as stability in an optional ground-attack mode.

No aircraft builder closes off options for mission roles unless they compromise the design for the aircraft's primary function and flexibility and diversity of operation is a cornerstone of long-lived combat aircraft programmes. But, although it did not appear in the VFX specification, a ground-attack capability was built into the F-14 from the outset and that was reflected in the control system functions that integrated all moving surfaces on the wings and tailplane. Four primary wing-sweep programmes were provided: automatic, manual, emergency and ground attack; the first three covered fleet defence (combat air patrol and deck-launch intercept) and the last gave the F-14 an interdiction role that became enshrined in the aircraft's missions suite.

Key to giving the pilot ultimate freedom to concentrate on his adversary and get the best agility and manoeuvrability from his aircraft, the F-14 carries a Mach Sweep Program (MSP) system to optimize perfor-

mance/buffet advantages and match wing-sweep angles to speed. Optimum settings for the moveable wing and its lift and dump devices change rapidly with the Mach number and aircraft attitude. In his ability to control the battle, the pilot must put all his concentration on the targets, selecting when to engage, when to disengage, how to position his own aircraft with respect to the changing pattern of threats and how to keep his aircraft from harm's way. To focus on those battle management decisions the MSP frees the pilot from critical judgements about the flight condition of his aircraft. It provides improved combat agility in the turn, co-ordinates flap actuation with wing sweep and speed, decides when to augment roll authority through

the flaperons and protects the crew from putting the aircraft outside its safety envelope.

The MSP takes its primary information from a Mach sensor, maintaining the wing at the fully forward sweep angle of 20 degrees during take-off and progressively adjusts it to 22 degrees up to Mach 0.4. It remains at this position through Mach 0.75 when it resumes a progressive sweep motion until the fully swept angle of 68 degrees is reached at Mach 1.2. During this period the flaperons are inhibited (at 57 degrees) and roll authority is transferred exclusively to the tailerons. If the wings should inadvertently lock in the fully swept position it is still possible to get the aircraft down with up to 4,000lb (1,818kg) of

A superb shot of the tail area and speed brake actuator. Note the deeply recessed upper fuselage section above the pancake and the fuel dump line outlet at the trailing edge of the aft fuselage wedge.

With paint applied, the prototype F-14 looks every bit the futuristic fighter it was regarded as in 1970. With air data probe portending a vigorous flight test programme the aircraft was heavily instrumented using a telemetry system from NASA programmes familiar to Grumman.

fuel on board. As speeds vary dramatically and quickly during combat, the MSP controls the wing at an activation rate of 7.5 degrees/sec and the pivot mechanism is fully stressed to accept the limit load of 7.5 g, at which point the wing movement is reduced to 4 degrees/sec.

If selected, the manual mode allows the pilot to operate wing-sweep angles within the MSP limits, but he cannot position the wing to over-stress the aircraft. The emergency mode does, however, permit the pilot to completely override the MSP and put the wings into any position. The ground-attack mode locks the wings at 55 degrees of sweep to optimize aircraft stability during the run-in for a rocket or

bomb strike. Totally automatic, the engine compression inlet ramps have their own independent air data computer and hydraulic systems and operate according to the Mach number to shape the flow of clean air to the engines, leaving the pilot to fly with his hands on the controls without his having to shape the configuration of the intake geometry. Known as the air induction control system, it is independent also of cockpit controls, save for two circuit breakers and a pre-flight ground test system for cycling the inlet surfaces through the full range of travel. The test conducted after engine start takes about 20sec and is simultaneously performed on both inlets. This procedure also ensures

that hydraulic leaks are detected on deck.

In several respects the F-14 was proving to be a revolutionary aircraft, bringing new design and technology trends that would serve as precedents for new generations of high performance combat aircraft. Across the spectrum it was forging new ways of building aeroplanes. In materials by percentage weight the F-14 carried 24.4 of titanium, 36 of aluminium alloy, 18 of steel and 1 of boron, remarkable values for the 1960s, making it one of the strongest aeroplanes ever built. In structural design it was conventional but innovative in key places. Although the wing originally had a design surface area of 541sq ft (49.68sq m) (565sq ft, 51.88sq m, on aircraft built), the area

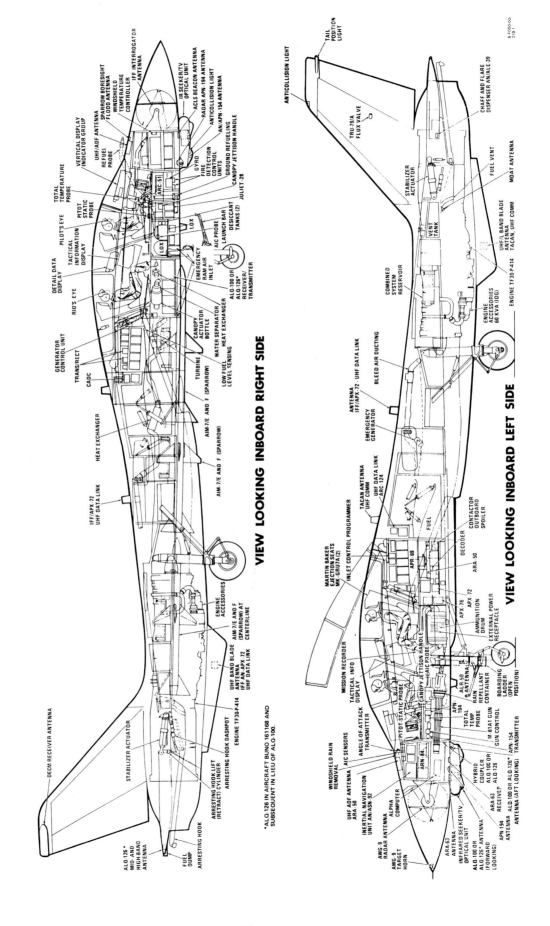

VIEW LOOKING INBOARD RIGHT SIDE

*ALQ-126 IN AIRCRAFT BUNO 161168 AND SUBSEQUENT IN LIEU OF ALQ-100.

VIEW LOOKING INBOARD LEFT SIDE

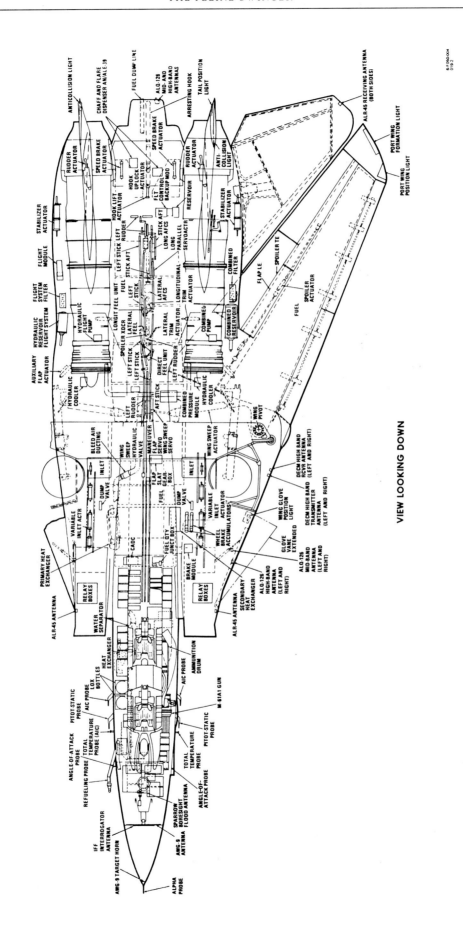

VIEW LOOKING DOWN

between and below the pancake, the glove area and the aerodynamic surfaces contribute a further 443sq ft (40.68sq m). If measured by itself, the moveable wing area renders a relatively high wing loading of 97lb/sq ft (4,644.4Pa), compared with 77.8lb/sq ft (3,725.1Pa) for the F-4 Phantom II. But the F-14 is designed to add lift through these other surface areas, giving an effective lifting area of 1,008sq ft (92.6sq m), 44 lb/sq ft (2,107Pa) with the wing at the forward sweep and 48lb/sq ft (2,298Pa) at full aft sweep. In this way, Grumman built the aircraft with a lifting fuselage which increases the lift coefficient up to 35 degrees angle of attack (AoA), while the wing actually loses lift above 10 degrees AoA.

The structural backbone of the F-14 is the centre section, or wing carry-through box, which supports the two wing pivots and accommodates variable bending and torsional moments as the wings are swept back and forth. Because it lies at the largest cross-sectional area of the fuselage pancake, the box must follow the aerodynamic profile of the reflexed shape of the upper fuselage section. Gull-shaped, it is 22ft (10m) in length and comprises a single-cell box beam in 6A1/4V titanium alloy which transmits the outer wing loads from the pivot to the fuselage nacelles and centrebody. It consists of four weld assemblies built up from thirty-three detailed machined parts. As described earlier in this chapter, electron beam welding replaced weighty rivets as the means of joining the sections. This was done successfully in an attempt to eliminate fatigue points and prevent cracks and fractures in the highly stressed box. Each box requires seventy welds, fifty-seven of which are square butt joints and thirteen scarff joints. The thickness of the weld varies from 0.5 to 2in (1.3 to 5.1cm) over lengths of up to 5ft 5in (1.64m) and the entire structure doubles as a wet fuel cell. At 2,065lb (939kg) the box beam came out 19lb (8.6kg) lighter than its target weight and the second least expensive element to fabricate, as measured in $/lb.

The wing pivots posed one of the more difficult design and engineering challenges. The F-111 pivot was designed to incorporate a large cylinder installed through heavy steel rings, but the F-14 had upper and lower titanium annular rings containing hemispherical bearings accepting lugs on each outer wing section. Instead of being parallel to each other, the

Displaying the strong forward landing gear about to get a larger-than-life test of its rigidity from a suspended drop test to simulate heavy carrier landings, this view shows the cavernous air intakes sloped to ingest the maximum air quantity at high angles of attack, with the flow volume controlled by the variable ramps.

angle of the two lugs at each pivot converges so that their axial loads intersect at the average wing centre of pressure. Because the centre of pressure moves forward and aft as the wing sweeps, the lugs are also inclined aft so that their axes converge at the average sweep position. Unlike the F-111, there is no carry-through pin and the space between the lugs is used for running lines and pipes into the moveable wing sections. Wing actuation is accomplished through a ball-screw located aft of the carry-through box and a slot accepts the trailing edge of the wing as the

sweep angle increases. A seal is maintained by a series of flexible plates with flaps and slats that telescope around the retracting wing surface.

Grumman used titanium for the upper and the lower wing panels and, because the moveable wings are wet, they must be fuel-tight to prevent leaks since there is no sealer to compensate for poor fixtures. At each rivet location where a hole is to be machine-drilled the titanium is chilled with Freon to prevent its heating up to its brittle point during drilling, which would take strength from the alloy. Slightly over-

A compact and integrated design, the aircraft displays clearly the layout of the main landing gear. As the gear retracts the wheels fold through 90 degrees to lie flat under the forward glove section outboard of the engines, providing a wide track and low slope between the centre of gravity and the wheel, affording stability while landing on a rolling deck; compare this with the narrow track of the F-111.

size, each rivet is driven home with great force to fuse it with the metal thus creating the fuel-tight joint. The main fuselage comprises a titanium alloy structure with conventional forgings and frames overlaid by a flush-riveted alloy skin. It is divided into several discrete modules for assembly and is of semi-monocoque construction with bulkheads, frames, longerons and skin panels of both honeycomb and sheet stringer construction. The horizontal tail is made up from honeycomb with steel root ribs, titanium beams and boron composite covers while the vertical tails are fabricated from bonded aluminium honeycomb. Structural strength is built into the specifi-

cation, calling for a fatigue life of 6,000 flight hours, 7,800 landings, 1,500 catapult launchings imposed by the Navy's C-7 catapult system (the F-14 loaded with fuel and maximum external stores) and 1,500 arrestor engagements.

To accommodate these accelerations (which are capable of launching the aircraft off the deck to flying speed with engines off and brakes on) the forward retracting undercarriage system incorporates shock-absorber legs fabricated from high-tensile steel. Operated hydraulically and with a single-use, air-storage bottle system as back up for emergency lowering and locking, the gear will fall by gravity if

all else fails. The main gear is attached to the wing glove outboard of the engine inlet boxes and inboard of the wing pivot point. Legs rotate forward to retract into a bay within the wing glove, the wheel moving through 90 degrees to lie flat over the leg. Originally the wheels carried beryllium disc brakes but these would be replaced with carbon discs, hydraulically powered and mechanically actuated by individual rudder toe brakes. The twin-wheel nose unit incorporates a shimmy damper with the steering electrically controlled and hydraulically actuated to within 70 degrees left or right of forward. The launch bar is lowered by turning the nosewheel about 10

The forward landing gear 'kneels' through strut compression during cat-launch to prevent the aircraft from pitching up prematurely and taking to the air before it has reached flying speed.

degrees to either side, with the strut compressed by about 14in (35.6cm) to reduce bending strain. By giving the aircraft a pitch-down AoA at launch, lift is inhibited until the F-14 rotates for flight.

As designed at the contract award stage, the F-14 was a superb step forward in performance, mission capability, design and manufacturing. The fuselage, wings and engine inlets were designed for minimal frontal area, offering 43sq ft (3.95sq m) versus 56sq ft (5.14sq m) for the F-111B and good aerodynamic efficiency. It was the first effective combat aircraft equipped with mission-adaptive engine inlet and wing geometry built in to give it near-optimum performance from less than 200kts to speeds in excess of Mach 2. As the Navy's next fighter it had everything going for it, but there were insidious combinations of unexpected events and unforeseen circumstances that would seriously threaten not only the design of the aircraft but the survival of the entire programme, none of which was properly foreseen in January 1969.

CHAPTER THREE

Tomcat Rising

Financial Problems Begin to Appear

During the first three months of 1969 the engineering design on the F-14 was finalized and in March the system and subsystem drawings were frozen. In all, Grumman expended 14,000 hours on aerodynamic and propulsion testing, in addition to the development of production and inspection methods for the revolutionary use of electron-beam welding and composites. The Navy drew up plans for flight testing and declared its intention to deploy the F-14 initially on *Forrestal* class carriers and subsequent vessels, replacing the F-4 Phantom. Later it would replace both the F-4 and the F-8 Crusader types on the *Midway* class carriers. Three versions of the F-14 were to be produced under the contract plan: F-14A as the standard aircraft with two Pratt & Whitney TF30-P-412 turbofan engines; the F-14B designed to the VFX-2 specification with the Pratt & Whitney F401-PW-P400 derivative of the JTF-22 advanced technology engine, providing a potential 40 per cent thrust increase along with a 25 per cent weight reduction and promising a 40 per cent better turn radius, 21 per cent better sustained g-operability and 80 per cent increased combat radius; and the F-14C with the advanced engine of the F-14B and new avionics and weapons for a greatly expanded mission envelope.

The Navy intended to replace the F-14A with the F-14B after sixty-seven aircraft, including prototypes, had been delivered. The potential order book for the American requirements ran to more than 700 aircraft, including some for four Marine Corps squadrons, and it was with these expectations that Grumman had set what it thought was a realistic price within a severely competitive marketplace. Within the restrictions of a fixed-price

contract there was little margin for error on costs and schedules. If predictions on labour rates and the national economic index were wrong, Grumman would suffer; in the fullness of time it would do worse than this and nearly die as a consequence.

According to conventional wisdom, new airframes and new engines must never come together in the same aircraft, but that was what Grumman set up in proposing the two-step programme involving three versions of the F-14. Paradoxically, although the programme was to change many times, this vulnerability was not the one that brought the programme close to disaster. Nevertheless, uncertainties on the true installed costs of the new technology embraced by the contract were exposed by spring 1969.

The first mock-up had been prepared for the contractor-selection phase and the second was made ready for inspection and acceptance on 23 May 1969. Where the first mock-up had a single tail fin the second had the twin fins which were canted outward by 5 degrees. At the mock-up inspection Grumman proposed, and the Navy approved, weight and development cost restructuring in efforts to save money. Although money had not yet become the problem that it eventually would, the Navy and the Department of Defense were concerned about restrictions pending on the whole defence budget and the new Nixon administration was proving firm on government expenditure. Not for nothing was the new budget secretary Casper Weinberger known as 'Cap the Knife'. The Navy also asked NASA to perform an engineering analysis and to evaluate the performance and weight estimates for the F-14A and the F-14B. These proved valid in what amounted to the first such exercise conducted by that agency.

The drawing release for EMMA (engineering manufacturing mock-up aid), the full-size lookalike for fit checks and

subsystem design integration, took place in May 1969 followed by detail parts fabrication in June and the beginning of assembly in November. Because the Department of Defense was concerned to watch all new programmes for their potential for overruns, the Navy chaired a DoD team mandated to examine F-14 programme costs and schedules. In September 1969 it declared that, under Instruction 7000.2, it found that 'the contractor has an effective system of management control; that the contractor has integrated cost, schedule and technical performance for both in-house and subcontract work...' In fact, in making its bid during 1968, Grumman had presented a production and subcontract plan that virtually spanned the continent, giving aerospace subcontracts on the F-14 to 3,700 companies in forty-one states. At its peak the F-14 would employ 10,000 Grumman employees at fourteen facilities, but the argument for putting out so much work was driven by economics: it was easier to subcontract than to justify a major building programme for new factories and assembly plants.

In several ways Grumman was becoming trapped by circumstances. Having signed a contract that set a ceiling price at 125 per cent of target cost, the company began to feel the chill of an economic winter. In the first nine months of 1969 it negotiated tight fiscal contracts with subcontractors, with equally tight delivery schedules. It formulated its company plan on historic trends in economic growth, averaging 3–4 per cent annually during the 1960s and based its projections of a secure period ahead on anti-inflation measures put in by the Johnson administration and a tighter monetary policy at the US Federal Reserve Board. Grumman anticipated a sound foundation for its business base, but changes to the economic figures began sooner than the ink was dry on the contract. During those first nine months wages began to rise alarmingly, powerful unions secured wage increases throughout American industry two or even four times the previous average and government spending cuts began to bite. Defence money went down from $79.4 billions in the year ending 30 June 1969, to $76.8 billions in the following fiscal year.

By mid-1969 Grumman began to make formal statements to the Navy warning of impending problems with the strict fiscal controls on the contract. Declining trends in the economy, an erosion of the corporate base and rising prices posed serious threats. Moreover, to Grumman's frustra-

tion, McDonnell Douglas were the beneficiaries to a new way of awarding contracts, one more sensitive and responsive to the vagaries of the national finances. A new way of negotiating procurement packages was introduced with the F-15. Just as the F-14 was the Navy replacement for the carrier-based F-4, so too was this new land-based fighter the front-line Air Force replacement for that highly successful aircraft. For much of 1969 the Air Force wrestled with competing designs and in December selected McDonnell Douglas to build the F-15, rejecting competing bids from Fairchild and North American

Rockwell. Known as a cost-plus-incentive-fee contract, McDonnell was given a greater leeway on costs, and the development side of its contract had higher guaranteed ceilings which allowed growth values of 150 per cent of target cost. To say that Grumman was upset is an understatement.

Construction of the first prototype begins

For the time being these problems were put on the shelf unresolved, while the

Systems and subsystems design on the F-14 broke new ground in redundancy and mission safety. New approaches to back-up and contingency provisions followed the practice used by NASA in the space programme, the F-14 being the first combat aircraft to use engineering and design technologies developed for space projects.

technical completion of the detailed design phase gave way to the metal-cutting period as the first prototype, YF-14A # 1 (BuAer number 157980), came togther. There were to be twelve prototypes, each identified by large numbers on the tails and each would have a specific set of objectives in the flight-test programme. Yet, even as the first aircraft was being built, there were challenges from within the Department of Defense which wanted as much 'bang for the buck' as it could get and sought to reopen the issue of 'commonality' once more. The McNamara legacy would not go away and the issue would strengthen

during 1970 as the F-14 neared its first flight. Intensive testing of the engine inlet design began during 1969 and, with the impending selection of a contractor to build the advanced technology engine intended for the F-14B, engineers designed it to accommodate a flow rate of 270lb/sec (122.7kg/sec). When Pratt & Whitney was selected to produce this engine, designated the F401, an inlet was delivered to them for tests. Later in 1970 further tests qualified both this and the inlet design for the TF-30-P-412 which would power the F-14A.

The development of the fuel system design evolved in concert with another test

rig which modelled the real aircraft. Duplicating the layout of tanks, pumps, feed lines, valves and flexible joints, the rig demonstrated changes in the centre of gravity as the fuel was consumed, the impact of the variable-geometry wings on fuel flow and tank transfer, and the routine procedures for deck fuelling, defuelling, jettisoning and in-flight refuelling. Tanks were assigned to specific engines according to location. The port engine would get fuel from the port wing, the port wing box tank and the tanks aft of the wing box. The starboard engine would be fed from the starboard wing and wing box tanks and

New composites were essential to weight reduction on the drawing board and not, as had happened often before, after the aircraft had flown. The use of composites was not new but the high quantities employed by Grumman in F-14 manufacture were novel.

the forward fuselage tanks. The split fuel feed system routes fuel from left and right pumps and lines pass through an isolation valve before penetrating the engine nacelle firewall. Hydraulic shut-off handles manually isolate the appropriate nacelles in the event of an emergency and these may be reset to reopen the fuel and hydraulic isolation valves without any maintenance action. The internal fuel capacity in the original Design 303 was 14,340lb (6,518kg); but the remodelled protytpes had a capacity of 16,200lb (7,364kg) while drop tank capacity was limited to 3,600lb (1,636kg).

The electrical power distribution was designed and tested on breadboards* with wire harnesses offered up to the EMMA for validation on the three-dimensional mock-up. Power for the aircraft is provided by two 60kVA engine-driven, air-cooled, generators supplying AC current to transformer rectifiers where it is converted to DC. Distribution is through buses with circuits protected by circuit breakers accessible both to the pilot and his NFO** (Naval Flight Officer) in the back seat. Each generator is driven by a hydro-mechanical constant speed drive unit coupled to a single engine and either can provide the 115/200V (400Hz) power required by the aircraft's systems. Emergency power is provided by an hydraulically-driven 5kVA generator which automatically cuts in at the loss of main AC or DC power. AC ground power provides current for the aircraft with engines off and an external ground-check panel controls the external activation of circuits.

One of the more advanced areas of design and innovation was in the hydraulics and supporting subsystems. Considerable experience obtained from working with lightweight plumbing in the NASA Lunar Module was applied by Grumman to the design and fabrication of the hydraulics system, and lessons learned

* A breadboard is a two-dimensional layout where all system elements, including subsystems, module assemblies and components, are laid out for integrated tests but do not conform to the three-dimensional layout in the real aircraft.
** The back-seat crew member has been called by several names, not all of them official! The term NFO refers to all non-pilot flight crew. Second crew members on Phantoms proudly hold to the title Radar Intercept Officer (RIO) while Grumman tried to call its F-14 back-seat crew member the Missile Control Officer. For the sake of old salts the term NFO is retained throughout this book but, for those who object, NFO means RIO.

Tailplane actuators and linkages share a tight space with hydraulic lines and electrical wiring in configurations least likely to incur critical failures during battle. The aft fuselage contains integral fuel tanks masked by the engines on either side.

from a programme that had more exacting weight constraints than any aeroplane ever built paid dividends when applied to the F-14. Fabricated from titanium at a total weight saving of almost 300lb (136.4kg), the pipes were shrunk on after being immersed in liquid nitrogen at -300° F and then brazed. The contribution to weight saving and safety in critical aircraft systems made by the Lunar Module experience was profound. Grumman made a special effort to protect the hydraulics and set up a special test stand to duplicate failures and cause problems in an attempt to seek solutions before the release of the manufacturing drawing.

Two independent systems were built into the aircraft, each powered by a separate engine, supplemented by electro-hydraulic power modules, a bidirectional transfer unit and a hand pump in the cockpit. They were known as the flight system and the combined system and they

are prime independent sources each pressurized by a single pump, the former by the right engine and the latter by the left. Because each system is separated from the other the very design of the dual system reduces the possibility that combat damage will disable the aeroplane and the supplementary power modules assist ground handling with power carts. The flight system mainly occupies the right side of the aeroplane and does not carry through into the wings, whereas the combined system is more extensively distributed throughout the airframe although elements are mainly located down the left side. Both hydraulic systems are designed to operate in parallel for primary flight controls, except the spoilers and wing-sweep and stability augmentation devices.

If one of the two systems should fail the other can provide essential pressure for operation, albeit with a reduced power capability. If both should fail back-up

F-14A Block Designations

Under the terms of the initial development contract Grumman was to produce twelve YF-14A prototypes with the BuAer nos. 157980 to 157991 inclusive. In addition the company built two mock-ups, the first carrying the single fin and rudder of the original Design 303E proposal and the second with the twin fins characteristic of all prototype and production aircraft. The second mock-up, a fit-check vehicle in 1:1 scale called EMMA, aided engineers in placing hydraulic pipes, electrical lines and subsystems and assemblies. EMMA had no skin and was fabricated from cheap materials. It would never fly and its only role was to serve as a pre-production tool for layout and detailed engineering interfaces.

The twelve YF-14A prototypes were each given a separate block number attributed as follows, together with the Bureau of Aeronautics number (in brackets) and the date of the first flight (FF): No.1 (157980) Block 01, FF 21/12/70; No.2 (157981) Block 05,

FF 24/05/71; No.3 (157982) Block 10, FF 28/12/71; No.4 (157983) Block 15, FF 7/10/71; No.5 (157984) Block 20, FF 26/11/71; No.6 (157985) Block 25, FF 10/12/71; No.7 (157986) Block 30, FF 12/09/73; No.8 (157987) Block 35, FF 31/12/71; No.9 (157988) Block 40, FF 28/12/71; No. 10 (157989) Block 45, FF 29/10/42; No.11 (157990) Block 50, FF 6/03/72; No.12/1X (157991) Block 55, FF 31/08/71.

Production line F-14A Tomcats were delivered in eighteen separate procurement orders spread over eighteen Blocks between the fiscal years 1971 and 1985. Block numbers were assigned from 60 to 140 in sequences at five number intervals (60, 65, 70, 75, and so on). In this period a total 631 aircraft were built and delivered of which 541 went to the US Navy. The first of these, the thirteenth F-14A built (BuAer 158612), first flew on 2 May 1972. Included in the 631 were the eighty purchased by Iran within a US government procurement order for 130 aircraft under Block 90.

These were assigned the designation F-14A-GR and the first was delivered on 27 January 1976. One of the aircraft ordered by Iran was still in the US on trials when the Shah was deposed.

Three Blocks (145, 150 and 155) of the F-14A+ (later designated F-14B) totalling thirty-eight aircraft were ordered in FY86, FY87 and FY88. The last production Tomcats were Blocks 160, 165 and 170, comprising a total thirty-seven F-14D models delivered in FY88, FY89 and FY90. The first F-14D was completed in March 1990 and the last Tomcat was delivered on 20 July 1992 after the remaining ninety F-14Ds which the Navy had planned to buy had been cancelled. Out of more than 400 F-14As which the Navy planned to upgrade to F-14D standard it was permitted to rebuild only eighteen and these were given the designation F-14D(R). In all, Grumman built 718 Tomcats of which 639 were retained in the United States and seventy-nine delivered to Iran where some still remain.

power sources provide a 'get you home' capability. There are some components which have no back-up power provision and these are either fail-tolerant to the degraded mission (in that they are not needed for the return to the carrier) or they have unique back-up devices themselves. The combined hydraulic system employs isolation circuits to restrict the distribution of fluid to the essential flight components and shuts off pressure to the landing system components until that facility is required imminently. The outboard spoiler system, which is not linked to either the flight or the combined hydraulic system, has its own independent, electro-hydraulic power module which supplies pressure for normal operation and serves as back-up to the main flaps and slats.

The back-up flight control system is automatically activated on loss of pressure in primary flight or combined systems and consists of an hydraulic power module linked to the combined system and provides power to the horizontal tail and rudder actuators. If combined hydraulic power is lost the main landing and nose gear assemblies receive pressure from the auxiliary unit, an accumulator charged with fluid from the combined hydraulic system. When this pressure falls below normal an emergency manual brake handle provides braking energy. Separate dual pneumatic pressure sources operate the canopy and provide an emergency

The aft starboard avionics bay in the forward fuselage nacelle and deployable glove vane in the wing leading edge are seen clearly as aircraft No.223 nears roll-out. In later aircraft the glove vane was deemed unnecessary and production aircraft had this cavity blanked off in manufacture.

extension of the landing gear from high pressure bottles through a common filler in the nose wheel well.

Another system that called for extensive full-size rigs and mock-ups to provide engineering layout guides was that concerned with environmental control. For this the cockpit and avionics module mock-up was a vital part in the designing of the optimum configuration. For the crew, the system provides temperature control, pressurized air for the cockpits, defogging, anti-icing, rain removal and pressure suit support requirements. In addition, the system also provides wing glove and canopy seals, temperature control for the avionics and the external drop tanks and cooling air for the missile subsystem and the AIM-54A. Cooling turbine and twin-ram air heat exchangers provide refrigeration for the air conditioning with pressurization by conditioned air through diffusers. High-pressure, high-temperature air from engine bleed ports passes through a primary heat exchanger and then to a turbine compressor from where it is delivered to a secondary heat exchanger and chilled.

Pressure is automatically maintained by the cockpit regulator above 8,000ft (2,424m) and held at that equivalent pressure to an altitude of 23,000ft (6,970m), above which a differential of 5psi (34.5kN/sq m) to the ambient pressure is maintained. Some pressurized air is delivered to the canopy seal, which automatically inflates when the cockpit is closed. Pressurized air delivered to the avionics equipment for cooling is dried by a dual desiccant system to prevent arcing from moisture. Air is changed every 12 minutes as it passes through the desiccant selector valve and timer which controls the dry air supplied direct to the radar wave guide at 30psia and further reduced to 15.75psia for pressurization of the infra-red equipment. Some electronics equipment in the cockpit is cooled by the flow of ambient air and the electronics in the equipment bays by exhausted air. Other equipment is force-cooled from the air conditioning system.

The excess of heat from the AWG-9 radar is removed by coolant fluid passing along cold-plates and cold-rails at a rate of 8gall/min (36 l/min). AWG-9 electronics warm-up is achieved by routing bleed air until optimum temeperatures are reached. The AIM-54A missile system also requires cooling fluid which flows into the missiles at 70° F and out to the environmental control system heat exchanger where it is rejected. Conditioned air from the secondary heat exchanger is also used to ventilate the ammunition drum and to expel explosive gases from the breech of the M61A1 Vulcan cannon. When the gun fires, an electrically-controlled modulating valve opens to admit ram air to the compartment and out through an exhaust door at the bottom of the gun compartment, expelling unburned hydrogen and carbon monoxide.

Cockpit conditioning is a prime function of the environmental control system, and for normal operation cabin air is divided equally between the cockpit air diffusers and the canopy air diffusers. To remove condensed moisture the pilot can select air temperatures up to 250° F and when defogging is selected all the air flows through the canopy diffusers located around the seal line. Windshield defogging and deicing are controlled by electrical heating elements between the windshield panes. Rain clearance for take-off and landing is effected by blasts of compressed bleed air at 45psi

Grumman's spectacularly successful Lunar Module took twelve astronauts to the moon during 1969–72, the period between the F-14's detailed design and early flight trials. The techniques and engineering worked up for the LM were transferred to the F-14 and the lightweight hydraulics were common to both programmes. New ways of joining small, light piping paid dividends in weight and cost saving on the Tomcat.

(310.5kN/sq m) and a temperature of 390° F which evaporates the water and prevents its accumulation. A special dispenser can produce a metered flow of chemical spray which helps to improve visibility during periods of heavy rain. In normal operations 100 per cent breathing oxygen is provided from two 2.2gall (10 litres) liquid oxygen converters designed for use with a pressure-demand regulator and compatible with a full pressure suit. Liquid oxygen is stored in the converter and changes to a gas at 70–80psi (483–552kN/sq m) from where it is routed to a heat exchanger and its temperature raised to a level comfortable for breathing.

Grumman: Problems and Progress

By mid-1970 the economic situation in the United States had worsened and Grumman was in serious trouble. Increased development and prospective production costs brought deep concern to the management. Less than two years earlier the contract had been negotiated on the assumption, but not the implication, that Grumman would produce more than 800 aircraft in the first three years of manufacture. By June 1970 that forecast had dropped to 357 aircraft over the same period. Between 1968 and 1970, as moon landing missions were shed or put back, NASA severely cut its Lunar Module programme with Grumman. Dropped too was a plan to use the Module for extended lunar surface operations and as the core of a telescope for earth orbit. Instead of producing three Gulfstream II aircraft a month it was building one, production for 1970 would be only 181 aircraft compared with 283 for the previous year and net income dropped by 8 per cent to $20.2 millions. Moreover, national economic decline reduced the opportunities for new programmes as the defence budget fell even further. Responding, Grumman cut 5,600 from its work force and gave up 150,000sq ft (13,800sq m) of floor space.

Grumman's contract to produce the F-14 included a requirement to provide support for the operational flight simulator and here an engineer is checking wiring and controls.

Nevertheless, progress with the F-14 was rapid and it had to be. The Navy wanted the flight-test programme results presented before the Board of Inspection and Survey (BIS) just seventeen months after first flight – half the time usually allowed – which was arranged for 31 January 1971 at the latest. The heart of the entire test programme, the System Integration Test Stand (SITS), arrived at Point Mugu missile range, California, on 21 January 1970 and from there software and hardware components would be integrated. Subsystems would be tested together under dynamic flight conditions, flight test results would be replayed there for ground evaluation and analysis, and flight-test equipment would itself be integrated and tested in the specially developed facility. Other test work would proceed apace on the other side of the country at Long Island.

At Calverton, New York, the world's largest anechoic chamber would check the integrated weapons and avionics for electromagnetic interference in a building 87ft long by 87ft wide and 42ft high (26.4m x 26.4m x 12.7m) with its own air conditioning, hydraulics, coolants, compressed air, electrical power and full support suite for the flightworthy F-14s that would be tested inside it. Also at Calverton a mobile laser theodolite would track the F-14 and its weapons on tests to an accuracy of 1cu ft (0.028cu m) at five miles and an IFF (identification friend or foe) CRT display would identify the F-14 in flight and track and position other aircraft. In addition, the new Automated Telemetry Station (ATS), the most advanced in the country, would capture data from aircraft in flight, process them in computers (itself a novel feature in the early 1970s) and display the data in real time.

The ATS pioneered a new way of testing aeroplanes and revealed the F-14 programme as not only a radically new window on future design and configuration selection but as a pioneer in its support capabilities through computers, telemetry and solid-state electronics. ATS was the most advanced and by far the most powerful flight test data processing facility ever made with instrumentation built around a new pulse-code-modulation (PCM) system straight from the space programme. It would capture data from 600 telemetry points, compared with a maximum of a hundred hitherto, and send 300 to the ground simultaneously,

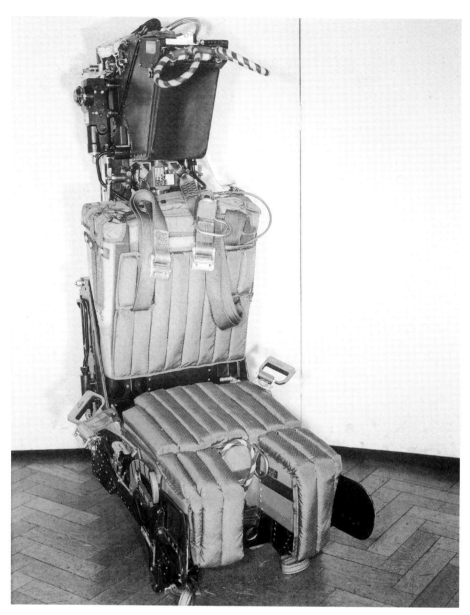

The Martin-Baker GRU7A ejection seat used in the F-14 was developed from an earlier model. It has a gas thrust generator and detonating cords with the seats timed to put the back seat out 0.4sec before the front seat.

compared with the current twelve at best. Special engine inlet and fuel system test stands would support the lengthy flight-test and development programme with prototype F-14s. In a novel application of an in-built capability, flight refuelling would significantly decrease the time required to conduct flight evaluation by increasing threefold the time spent in afterburner on each flight. By using the IFF tracker tankers could be positioned at the extreme ends of the flight runs

At Bethpage, Grumman set up the Structural Data Acquisition System to test

elements and check the integrity of the basic structural design. It also supported a Flight Control Hydraulic Systems test stand for hydraulics and autopilot tests. A key aspect of the Navy test requirement was for total compatibility with the Versatile Avionics Shop Test (VAST) system which it would introduce during 1971. This was an automated, avionic equipment suite, designated USM-247, for testing electronics removed from the aircraft and utilized a Univac 1240 computer. From the outset, Grumman set up special procedures to ensure that the programme met the stringent Navy requirements for VAST-qualified systems. But testing was not the exclusive preserve of Grumman and the Navy would take five of the twelve instrumented pre-production prototypes to the Naval Air Training Center at Patuxent River, Maryland, where it would conduct carrier suitability trials and structural, powerplant and performance-related demonstration flights.

Because the Navy wanted its BIS trials so soon after first flight, three more or less equally spaced programme inspections, known as Navy Preliminary Evaluations or NPEs, would be conducted. These were key gates in the combined vehicle and weapon system build-up programme, providing customer and contractor with useful reviews to pinpoint concerns, keep the pressure on the manufacturer and give the Navy a running diary on milestones. These NPEs would be performed by a team of Navy specialists drawn from the Point Mugu and the Patuxent River facilities. In the operations room at Calverton Grumman set up a Management Information System (MIS) to link to the Computerized Flight Test System (CFTS) and the F-14 Operations Center, the tracking and control hub for the entire flight-test system.

Set to last ninety days, Phase 1 of the first NPE was in detailed planning by mid-1970 and a 'squeeze team' of management personnel integrated the operating departments to keep all the human elements and the programme milestones on schedule. To keep the aircraft on track as well, a 'tiger team' of ten men was assigned to each of the twelve pre-production F-14s to identify problems or work faults appearing in the development, testing or engineering. To get those accomplished as quickly as possible, Grumman split the test phase into three components. The first would include hardware development testing to ensure that the many assemblies and sub-assemblies matched the specifications in the contract or the requirements set by Grumman. The second involved hardware and software testing to check on compatibility and interoperability after the sub-assemblies had been built up. The third provided a total evaluation of the entire system and a check on the performance of the integrated vehicle. As the components or assemblies were received from the subcontractors they were exam-

Tests with the ejection seat included a dummy fired from a redundant F-106 and live tests using the sled acceleration facility at the Naval Air Weapons Center, China Lake, where ejection took place at speeds of up to 600kt (1,100km/hr).

ined at Grumman and integrated into the SITS.

To a greater degree than was usual in a modern combat aircraft the F-14 included a large amount of equipment provided out-of-house, either by other contractors or by the government. Almost 25 per cent of the airframe by weight was procured from sub-contractors and that called for two levels of checking: qualification tests to confirm environmental and non-interference from electromagnetic sources and performance demonstration tests to prove the capabilities claimed by the subcontractors. After these the equipment was removed to the

VAST facility to prove that it would pass the Navy's requirements and the scrutineers who would examine it at the next NPE. From its experience on space programme contracts Grumman knew the value of putting its people into its major subcontractors, not only to keep watch on its products and troubleshoot when necessary, but also to give the vendor confidence in the team approach. As early as 1967 Grumman had built up a good relationship with the Rohr Corporation, working on advanced materials such as titanium and boron, and the goodwill it then built up gave it a strong start when it

The extensive flight test programme that began during early 1971 took advantage of high data transmission rate telemetry streams built into the test and data management systems. Aircraft were also kept longer in the air by the use of in-flight refuelling from tankers stationed at the end of each flight run, increasing air time and afterburner opportunities.

Test aircraft were given large numbers on the tail, this aircraft (No.10) being the one eventually used for carrier-suitability trials before it crashed on 30 June 1972 at Patuxent River.

used Rohr to help it to secure the contract.

Throughout 1970 progress was rapid. The wing pivot development tests which began in November 1969 went ahead throughout the first quarter of 1970 and boron horizontal stabilizer fabrication was completed on 20 March, with the static tests being completed on 8 May. On the ninth development test of a partial wing box test specimen on 2 June two lower lugs failed at only 1.5 times the design life, 9,000hrs versus the 12,000 called for in the specification. These were the most demanding tests ever conducted on an aircraft structural member and the loading tests measured in g force as a function of the wing sweep were unprecedented for a

fighter. Conservative estimates meant that operational loads calculated were higher than those that would be encountered, but the test specimen was examined and the faults isolated. Changes were made to a new test specimen and on 1 February 1971 a redesigned wing pivot demonstrated 7,000 test hours, equal to 15,120 flight hours.

Meanwhile, on 1 September 1970 fatigue tests on the boron tail successfully completed the equivalent of 12,000 flight hours, twice the design life. Moreover, it was tested to a temperature of 300° F and failed at 9 per cent over the maximum design load, a satisfying result for a composite that Grumman had been devel-

oping for more than three years. Engine inlet and associated tests were satisfactorily completed on 9 July 1970, two weeks before the final NAVAIR mock-up demonstration on EMMA was completed. The first aircraft began to come together during August as the forward fuselage was being stuffed with wiring, the engine inlet sections arrived from the Rohr Corporation and the aft section was delivered by Fairchild, another Long Island subcontractor. During September the first engines arrived ahead of schedule. On 25 October YF-14A # 1 emerged from Plant 1 at Grumman's Bethpage facility on the back of a flat-bed and slowly made its way approximately 50 miles (80km) north up

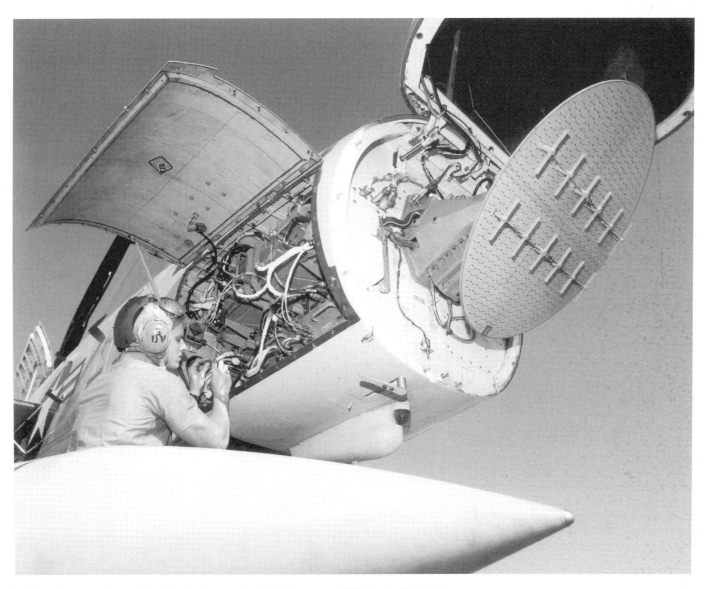

An electronics test engineer adjusts the avionics associated with the powerful AWG-9 radar. While the F-4B's radar operated only in pulse and the F-4J's in pulse and Doppler mode, the F-14 integrates six modes of pulse-Doppler operation through fifteen times the volume of sky.

As an integrated weapons platform the F-14 cockpit displays both front and rear areas dedicated to weapons systems management as much as they are to the control of the aircraft. The main display screen immediately above the control column is the Visual Display Indicator which provides the pilot with flight information, attack displays or terrain clearance data. Below that, obscured by the control column, the pilot receives navigation information, tactical situation and ECM data.

Long Island to Calverton where the final assembly took place, followed by systems checkout and ground vibration tests. By early December the first prototype was nearing its first flight in a month when the final tests were being conducted on the F-14's escape system.

The Martin-Baker GRU-7A rocket-powered ejection seat, developed from an earlier model, was subjected to twenty-two tests, including ejection from an F-106 based at the Naval Air Recovery Facility at El Centro, California. As the first YF-14A was being prepared for flight, a full cockpit mock-up was fired down the test track at the Naval Air Weapons Center, China Lake, at speeds of 100–600kt (185–1,112km/hr) for live tests with instrumented dummies to prove that the ground-level ejection sequence would work as designed; it did. In flight the

canopy is jettisoned and each crew member is ejected in a preset sequence with a lateral dispersion to prevent their collision; the NFO goes first up and to the left followed by the driver 0.4sec later, up and to the right. The canopy is jettisoned on manual command or as part of the normal ejection process by either crew member and utilizes a gas thrust generator and detonating cords.

Earlier in the year critical decisions had been made regarding the definitive F-14. On 27 February 1970 Pratt & Whitney had been selected to build the advanced technology engine (the P&W F401-PW-400) and on the same day Grumman submitted its proposal for the definitive F-14B. In addition to being the powerplant for the F-14B, the new engine had evolved from the JTF-22 as the progenitor of the F100 which would be used in the F-15 and the F-16.

The Navy version would adopt the same core section as the F100 but strap on a four-stage, versus a three-stage, fan and larger afterburner. With a diameter of 4ft 2.5in (1.28m) the F401 was 4in (10cm) bigger than the F100 and the dry weight went up from 3,020lb to 3,650lb (1,373 to 1,659kg) and the bypass ratio increased from 0.6:1 to 0.65:1. With a projected maximum dry thrust of 16,400lb (72.95kN) and 28,090lb (124.94kN) with afterburner, the F-14B would have had a 30 per cent increase in thrust-to-weight ratio, taking it from 0.75:1 to more than 1:1. With a lower weight and improved specific fuel consumption over the TF30, the F401 was better in these respects than the F100 and Grumman keenly viewed the adoption of the engine as a perfect match for the aerodynamic capabilities of the F-14.

First Prototypes Fly

From Plant 7 at the Calverton site the first prototype emerged ready for flight six weeks ahead of schedule. Taxi trials began on 14 December and went smoothly in the expectation of a flight before the end of the year. Already at least a month ahead of schedule, everyone wanted to get the F-14 airborne during 1970, although weather predictions were not good as Christmas approached. Grumman's chief test pilot Robert Smythe and the project pilot William Miller would put the aircraft to the air. On 20 December the aircraft performed well in high-speed runs over rough surfaces and the crew reported a satisfactory response when they lifted the nose wheel to test the control surfaces. Next day the decision was made to perform the first flight and shortly after 4:00 pm, with just nine minutes of daylight left, Smythe and Miller took the first F-14 into the air. Climbing to 3,000ft (909m) they took it around the airfield and back, did another pass at the same altitude and landed nine minutes later. Both men reported that it handled well.

After a brief respite over Christmas they resumed preparations for the flight test phase and on 30 December the YF-14A was back in the air, this time with Miller in the front seat. It was 10:18 am as the aircraft lifted off the runway at Calverton and made a broad sweeping turn toward the assigned test area some way to the south-east of the Grumman airfield. With chase planes accompanying it, the new crew performed stability checks and evaluated the flight controls, but just 25 min after taking off one of the chase pilots reported a thin stream of smoke trailing the aircraft. Then the combined hydraulic system failed and Miller turned toward Calverton at a steady 180kt (334km/hr), using the emergency nitrogen bottle to lower the undercarriage with just 4 miles (6.4km) to go. As they neared the field the second hydraulic system failed and the back-up emergency system was not responding. Then the aircraft began a gentle porpoising motion. There was nothing that could be done and with literally seconds to go the crew ejected as the aircraft crossed the trees at 25ft (8m) and 130kts (240km/hr). As the aircraft hit the ground and exploded in a ball of fire the two pilots were blown high into the air but landed safely within sight of the airfield

and the large crowd of workers and their families invited to see the test.

Grumman had built the hydraulics system to handle some of the heaviest loads ever designed into an aeroplane and had used proven technology that should not have failed across all three systems. What the engineers found after a determined scrutiny changed for ever the way hydraulics systems were installed. Vibration frequencies emitted from the engines at idle resonated at the fracture frequency of the hydraulics and their mountings. When Miller put one engine to idle in a simulation of single-engine performance it broke the lines and spilled the fluid. The solution was simple: use different fixtures for each system in the aircraft so that they resonated at different frequencies. The Navy instructed Grumman to remove the titanium lines, but kept the shrink fitting method and this

was used on later aircraft without problems.

Getting the flight-test programme back on track was not a simple matter of using the next aircraft. Each YF-14A prototype was instrumented during assembly for a specific set of test objectives. The first aircraft was to have conducted high-speed tests and generally explored the flight envelope; the second would conduct high AoA trials; while the third would define the structural limits, and so on. It was decided to move up the No.12 aircraft and re-instrument it to take over the job of the wrecked prototype, so the construction of airframe No.12 was accelerated and it was renumbered 1X. Meanwhile the wing pivot test finally came through, TF30-P-412 engine qualification tests were satisfactorily completed on 5 March 1971, and the No.2 aircraft took to the air on 24 May 1971. But the accident had an effect on the

Initial carrier trials confirmed the excellent deck handling and spotting capability. With wings swept the aircraft takes up less space than might be imagined from its size and with a measure of oversweep, where the wings overlap the underlying horizontal tail, the aircraft has good park and ride facility.

test schedule and changes made necessary by the accident investigation put back the development schedule by six months. This shifted the BIS trials first from June to December 1972 and then to February 1973.

For the first five months of 1971 Grumman pursued a vigorous design review of the affected components and systems, re-evaluated the already stringent safety and reliability requirements and re-examined the quality control and inspection procedures. With the second YF-14A the company began stall and spin trials, and for the latter the aircraft carried retractable canard strakes mounted on either side of the nose and immediately forward of the cockpit to inhibit spin tendencies. Tests with models thrown by hand into the spin tunnel at the NASA Langley Research Center indicated that the F-14 would be prone to flat spins with high rates of rotation but one-tenth, unpowered, radio-controlled models dropped from helicopters showed that there would be little susceptibility to spin unless the 'pilot' deliberately induced one through the controls and held them there. At the Langley Research Center model tests in a 30ft x 60ft (9m x 18m) wind tunnel revealed little tendency to spin, even with the Tomcat at an AoA of 32 degrees. Grumman replaced the strakes with the added precaution of a 22ft (6.7m) spin parachute capable of being deployed at 120–170kt (222–315km/hr). Spin tests were first conducted with the wings at the 20-degrees position and the intake inlets locked open.

Progress was rapid and initial tests with the No.2 aircraft averaged more than 2 hrs per flight in each of eighteen flights. Rapid flight testing was helped by three Grumman KA-6 tanker aircraft, each capable of dispensing 20,000lb (9,900kg) of fuel at up to 200gall/min (900 l/min) through buddy-pack in-flight refuelling equipment. An F-14 could be topped up in ten minutes. Flight trials and tests were limited only by the endurance of the pilots and, when the No.1X aircraft joined the programme in September 1971 to replace the first, lost, prototype, exploration of the high speed envelope began. Together these two aircraft logged seventy-one flights and 189 flight hours, an average of 2.7 hrs per flight, before the first Navy Preliminary Evaluation (NPE #1) began on 2 December 1971. In that time the proto-types demonstrated full wing-sweep

Aircraft deployed on carriers are usually lifted aboard by dockside crane but will usually depart from the carrier for their home stations by flying off as the flat-top nears port.

capability, a maximum flutter-free Mach number of 2.04 at 42,500ft (12,880m), a minimum 95kt (176km/hr) indicated air speed, a maximum 30 degrees true AoA, and perfect engine air inlet ramp control.

For NPE #1 Grumman cleared the aircraft for evaluation from Mach 0.9 at sea level to Mach 1.6 at 27,500ft (8,333m) and Mach 1.8 at 35,000ft (10,606m). The company had already proved that the aircraft was high on performance, demonstrating that it could accelerate from loiter to Mach 1.8 in 75sec and hold 6.5g at Mach 2.2 with flaps and slats. In tests with the best F-4 in the inventory, the F-14 would show a 40 per cent improvement in turn radius, a 27 per cent increase in manoeuvring climb capability, a 21 per cent increase in the rate of acceleration and sustained g force and a 20 per cent increase in the rate of climb. From these flights preliminary data confirmed that the performance projections made in the January 1969 NAVAIR forecast were either met or exceeded. These included acceleration, subsonic and transonic

buffet-free manoeuvrability, and carrier-approach-speed acceleration.

The swift completion of a wide range of performance tests was due in large part to the new ATS system installed by Grumman (which had, in fact, been developed for the A-6 Intruder programme and was not specifically set up for the F-14). Sitting at their consoles and watching read-outs from PCM-coded data coming in real-time via L-band (1.437–1.472GHz), engineers could process information through powerful (at that time) CDC-1700 processors and pass it through to the main CDC-6400 computer so that all information retrieval and processing had been done by the time the pilot returned. This, coupled with in-flight refuelling, was a radical transformation in flight-test procedures and was unprecedented in aircraft development. So much so that NASA purchased an ATS-based system for the Flight Test Center at Edwards Air Force Base; Rockwell's B-1 bomber was also evaluated through the equipment. Other aspects which Grumman held under

An early F-14A with VX-4 at Point Mugu, California. As the primary operational test and evaluation unit, it had a vital role to play in getting the Tomcat ready for operational service. Jeremy Flack/API

Variation on a theme as VF-33 displays changes to its motif and logo colours during the 1980s. Jeremy Flack/API

VF-84 abandoned its black tails and black-and-yellow nose banding around 1982, opting for a more subdued overall grey with yellow fin tips and black skull and bones. Jeremy Flack/API

Seen clearly here, the geometry of the intake box and internal ramp flaps to adjust air flow from subsonic to supersonic flight were crucial to the successful design of the F-14. Peter Davies

A Tomcat from VF-213 shows off its gun housing. The gun is a hark back to dogfight days that is rarely used in modern air combat, but the lessons of Vietnam were hard won, and not ignored when engineers put in the ultimate one-on-one weapon. Peter Davies

An F-14 with VF-84 visits the UK en route to a Mediterranean deployment aboard the USS Nimitz. Peter Davies

Just visible is the reflexed pancake of the aircraft's top decking on this Tomcat from VF-142, which first received the F-14A in early 1975. Peter Davies

Awaiting its moment of glory, a Tomcat from VF-14 takes time out from duty on the USS Independence and prepares for a display at RAF Greenham Common. Jeremy Flack/API

A Tomcat from VF-102 aboard the USS America shows off fine detail of stores pick-up points, and the integral boarding ladder and steps for the front and rear 'offices'. Jeremy Flack/API

Spotted on the aft deck area of the USS America, eight Tomcats from VF-33 and VF-102 crowd in with an S-3 Viking, an A-6 Intruder, an EA-6 Prowler and an SH-3. Jeremy Flack/API

With wings still in the overfold position, a Tomcat from VF-33 is manoeuvred to the launch position as each engine is run up differentially. Jeremy Flack/API

An evocative shot of a Tomcat with auxiliary fuel tanks awaiting the attention of launch crews on the USS America. Jeremy Flack/API

A Tomcat VF-102 being moved back into its deck slot. Note the stores trolley with Phoenix and Sidewinder missiles. Jeremy Flack/API

Operated by VF-143, an early F-14A with the original gun installation taxis from dispersal past Royal Navy Buccaneers. Later production aircraft had modified gun vent ports. Peter Davies

An F-14B from VF-143, line Tomcat squadron aboard the USS George Washington, and attendant spare fuel tanks below a leaden sky. Peter Davies

Showing signs of heavy use in foul weather, a Tomcat from VF-154 aboard USS Independence prepares for a mid-air top-up. Jeremy Flack/API

A visiting Tomcat from VF-11 based on the USS Forrestal puts in an appearance at the 1991 Paris Air Show. Note the nose probe added to later production F-14s. Jeremy Flack/API

Seen at RAF Mildenhall in August 1978, a Tomcat from VF-32 based on the USS John F. Kennedy. Aircraft from this unit shot down two Libyan MiG-23 Floggers in January 1989. Peter Davies

The pilot of a VF-14 Tomcat salutes with his refuelling probe as his aircraft completes its landing run. The acute angle of the tailplane helps increase friction between rubber and runway, slowing down the aircraft. Peter Davies

A USAF KC-135 tops up a Tomcat. With no mean range on internal and auxiliary fuel alone, the added bonus of mid-air refuelling improves the F-14's operational flexibility. Jeremy Flack/API

Mothballed Tomcats sit out their nine lives in the ghostly silence of Davis-Monthan air base. Jeremy Flack/API

An F-14A of VX-4, 'The Evaluators', moves around the deck during flight trials at sea. Wing folding necessitated by limited deck and hangar space is already a feature of the Tomcat.

control were weight growth (only one-quarter of the average of Navy aircraft projects), minimization of zero-lift drag growth to 5 per cent since the formal mock-up in May 1969, and improved thrust performance – as much as 12 per cent – from the TF30-P-412 engine.

The NPE #1 was successfully completed in just fifteen days after the two prototypes and six Navy test pilots had accumulated thirty-nine flights in 74 flying hours over a 9fi-day period, an unprecedented feat for US Navy aeroplane evaluation. Previous programmes held that two flying weeks were necessary for an average of eighteen flights accumulating 20.4 flight hours. When the test pilots pooled their experience with the two YF-14As they wrote a consensus review which highlighted as 'outstanding' specific aspects of the aeroplane's assets: its exceptional low approach speeds in power approach configurations; the visibility from both cockpits; the accel-eration in maximum afterburner; the take-off performance; its controllability at high angles of attack; its longitudinal control power; its transonic flying qualities; aeroplane handling during wave-off manoeuvres; the improved combat survival afforded by the non-pressurized fuel system; and the design of the pilot's cockpit.

Navy inspectors also applauded the maintainability features which they liked, including the daily and weekly engine-inspection access doors, the accessibility to nose compartments provided by the nose wheel kneel facility, and the improved maintainability due to the identical engine build-up configurations. In addition to notifying the Navy and Grumman of a few items which it wanted cleared for NPE #2, scheduled for June 1972, the evaluation noted several distinct improvements over the specified requirements: the weight had been held to 54,220lb versus the 54,420 (24,645 and 24,736kg) projected in January 1969, the escort radius had been shown to be 468nm (866km) with full weapons or 591nm (1,093km) with full internal fuel, versus a projected 460nm (851km), and acceleration from Mach 0.8 to 1.8 at 35,000ft (10,606m) in 2.02min versus a required 2.24min and a combat loiter time of 2.09hrs versus a specified 1.88.

Avionics and Missiles

By the end of the year the flight line had been joined by six more YF-14A pre-production prototypes. Aircraft No.4, the first instrumented for avionics and AWG-9/Phoenix testing, took to the air for the first time on 7 October 1971 before it was flown to Point Mugu to do its work. It was joined by the systems feasibility aircraft, No.5, first flown on 26 November, aircraft

Aircraft completed at Grumman's Calverton facility are flight tested at a special plant where systems and subsystems are checked and test pilots put the F-14 through its paces before its delivery to the Navy, which signs it on and then conducts its own checks.

Cost and Quality

Rising to the challenges set by the revolutionary approach to aircraft manufacturing, Grumman took significant steps to produce the F-14 at lower cost and to higher standards of quality than had been achieved in any earlier aircraft programme. On the basis of pioneering techniques from subcontract work on the F-111B, the company set up extensive subcontracting programmes of its own. With 30 per cent of the aircraft built by other companies in forty-one states, Grumman put an emphasis on work flow and integration. To avoid undesirable logjams on the production line Grumman co-ordinated the production and delivery of modular elements complete with systems, subsystems and assemblies, thus avoiding hold-ups due to temporary problems with particular units. This modular method was applied to the Integrated Design Analysis System (IDEAS), developed by the company as a tool for accurately determining internal structural loads.

IDEAS cut costs and reduced weight by eliminating excessive material and wastage from over-building structures where it was unnecessary. Although in 1969 money it cost $750,000 to develop, the analytical computer system for IDEAS integrated requirements from several groups providing aerodynamic, weight, loads and structures information. Grumman claimed that this technique 'ideally suits a manufacturing concept of building and controlling each module in its own colony for integration of discrete subassemblies going into the module'. These techniques were applied to the manufacturing of the F-111 aft fuselage structures and the learning curve was moved across to the F-14 production line. The company was able to make appreciable saving in areas where cost

overruns were traditional stablemates of high-tech combat aircraft assembly.

In looking to refine the manufacturing process and improve quality with cost savings, Grumman pioneered the use of lasers for better tool-measuring accuracy and manpower savings of up to 50 per cent. Used in tools fabrication, these devices could measure three-axis rotation with an accuracy of 2sec of arc at 60ft (18.2m) or measure the displacement in two axes with an accuracy of 0.00075in at 20ft (or 0.00000313 to 1). This mattered when Grumman had 45,000 production and tooling tools in use from the first production aeroplane. At the other end of the scale, cost savings were made by adopting uniform tools, connectors and terminals. For instance, instead of up to fifty wire crimping tools used on the production of electrical harnesses for other combat aeroplanes of the 1960s, Grumman used only two and that had an advantageous effect on the maintenance side as well.

There were in addition other, more humanly orientated, ways in which the company saved money. By running a programme of continuous monitoring on unit costs, savings were made in manufacturing and assembly until, within five years of the aircraft's getting into production, savings were being made which cut the cost of each aeroplane by $0.2 million. Some of these came from unusual sources. In a company-wide employee suggestions scheme, Grumman workers would personally profit from ideas that cut costs. In just one year the company paid $164,000 for such schemes and saved $13 millions a year. In full production each Tomcat took thirteen months and 80,000 man-hours to build.

A supersonic Tomcat squeezes water from moist air low down to lay a trail along normally invisible shock waves.

No.6 set up for missile separation tests, first flown on 10 December, and aircraft No.9 instrumented for AWG-9 evaluation by Hughes Aircraft, first flown on 28 December. Two other aircraft were assigned as follows: No.3, first flown on 28 December, was to explore and qualify the defined structural limits of 6.5 g for fighter work and 7.5 g for ground attack, while No.8, first flown on the last day of 1971, was to obtain aerodynamic performance data of a production-configured F-14. Aircraft No.7 was converted into the prototype F-14B, carrying two P&W F401 engines, and would not fly for some time. By the end of the year the four aircraft destined for Point Mugu were on station ready to conduct the all-important avionics and weapons evaluation tests and the No.4 YF-14A was in the SITS having begun tests with the awesome AWG-9/ Phoenix weapon system.

One of the most enduring legacies of advanced fighter technology developed since the early 1960s was the AWG-9 radar which was, as related earlier, derived from fire-control systems for three cancelled projects: F-108, F-12 and F-111B. It was now crucial to the success of the F-14, but any similarity to the weapon system radar designed for the F-111B lay solely in the designation. The F-111B's AWG-9 weighed 1,760lb (800kg), could track eighteen targets simultaneously and was designed to fired the AIM-54A Phoenix missile. The rescoped AWG-9 for the F-14 weighed 1,235 lb (561kg), could track twenty-four targets simultaneously, controlled Phoenix, Sparrow, Sidewinder and gun and was packed into a 10 per cent smaller volume than its predecessor. Moreover, it had to be completely repackaged from the broader forward fuselage, side-by-side crew seating of the F-IIIB into the much narrower, tandem-seating fuselage and cockpit configuration of the F-14. The AWG-9 also has built-in IFF and full ECM capability and, because of the power of the transmitter, can burn through some jammers or circumvent others.

But the improvement afforded by the AWG-9 was fundamental. Until the end of 1966 US Navy F-4B Phantoms had pulse-only AN/APQ-72 radars, but the introduction of the F-4J with both pulse and pulse-Doppler AN/AWG-10 fire-control systems gave greater capability. Put simply, pulse radar works by measuring the time taken for a signal to be reflected from

A test prototype F-14A comes in to land displaying its main landing gear doors, flaps and slats and Sparrow missiles on the forward fuselage stations. Note the gun port on the side of the forward fuselage for the M61-A1 Vulcan gun retained on all variants and versions.

a solid surface and return, making it effective against the sky but not against the surface of the earth; pulse-Doppler measures the Doppler frequency of a moving target and distinguishes an object moving across the ground. The pulse-Doppler frequency is tuned to ignore objects moving at the speed of the aeroplane but to discriminate targets advancing or receding. Pulse-Doppler radar is effective at great ranges while conventional pulse radar is better at shorter ones. AWG-9 would provide the F-14 crew with an integrated system with four modes in pulse-Doppler and two in pulse giving the crew the possibility of detecting, tracking and engaging both small and large targets at heights between 50ft (15m) and more than 80,000ft (24,000m), at speeds from low subsonic to Mach 3+ and ranges in excess of 100nm (185km).

In addition, it provides four short-range automatic acquisition modes, three of which are for target designation and attack within 5nm (9.3km) of the F-14. In the Pilot Lock-on Mode (PLM) the radar projects a 2.3-degrees beam for boresight acquisition along the aircraft's longitudinal axis. Vertical Scan Lock-on (VSL) is ideal for acquiring a lock-on while pulling across to a manoeuvring target. It provides a vertical two-bar beam, 4.8 degrees in width, switched to either high or low scan. The hi-VSL mode nods up and down in elevation between +15 and +55 degrees above the aircraft's boresight, while the lo-VSL scans up and down in elevation between 15 degrees below and 25 above the boresight. In Manual Rapid Lock-on (MRL), the Naval flight officer in the back seat points the radar in the direction of the target, but this is probably the least useful mode. Pilot Automatic Lock (PAL) permits target acquisition within the azimuth scan of the radar to eight bars in elevation out to a distance of 10nm (18.5km). These short-range acquisition modes allow the pilot to keep his head out of the cockpit while the radar automatically acquires a target and displays the firing options for a selected weapon.

The AWG-9 set works through a lightweight, 24-bit, 5400B digital computer processing at 550,000 operations a second. Early sets used a thin-film memory of 24,000 words of non-destructive software and a core memory of 8,000 words of destructive read-out thin-film devices to store incoming computational results. Approximately 35,000 of the 70,000 words in the bulk storage memory are stored routines for built-in test functions. During the 1980s this 32K memory capacity was increased to 64K with four memory modules with reduced weight, volume and cooling requirements for the computer system. As new sets became available, they were integrated with Tomcats during assembly but older aircraft received retrofits when production allowed. In further planned upgrades, the Navy wanted to fit a Target Identification Device/Programmable Signal Processor (TID/PSP) able to address targets beyond the visual range. It would have discriminated between different engine types on hostile aircraft and skin

The forty-fifth Tomcat sports the garish colours of VF-1 which would carry the aircraft on its first cruise in late 1974. This aircraft would move later and end up with VF-111.

shapes for positive identification at extreme range but the programme was cancelled in 1983.

With the greatest range of any comparable radar, the AWG-9 can detect a small fighter with an RCS (radar cross-section) of 54.5sq ft (5sq.m) across a 135nm (250km) breadth of sky. The AWG-9 is configured to transmit in pulse-Doppler search signals on nineteen transmission channels, using a broadband, gridded travelling-wave-tube (TWT) amplifier. Six channels are reserved for Phoenix missile guidance and five for the semi-active guidance for AIM-7 Sparrow missiles. The large number of discrete channels from the TWT allow flexibility to prevent interference from friendly aircraft and in the face of ECM as well as giving good frequency margins for semi-active missile guidance. As well as operating in pulse or pulse-Doppler, the radar can operate in both high and low

repetition rates. A separate TWT is carried to supply guidance signals to the AIM-7 Sparrow when operating in continuous wave.

As installed in production F-14A aircraft, the AWG-9 weighs 1,307lb (594kg), of which the radar accounts for 712lb (324kg), the computer for 152lb (69kg), the controls and displays for 151lb (69kg), the auxiliaries for 199lb (90kg), and the racks with antennas for 93lb (42kg). Apart from the radar and its associated antenna, all AWG-9 equipment is stored either in the cockpit, below it or to the rear below the pancake. The antenna itself is a 36in (0.92m) diameter flat-plate unit with the IFF dipoles attached to the front. The powerful 10.2kW radar has twenty times the radiated power of the F-4B and virtually twice that of the APG-63 installed in the F-15A (the prototype of which did not fly until 27 July 1972). The maximum search azimuth is

+/- 65 degrees (65 degrees left or right of the aircraft's centreline) and up to eight bars in elevation (eight horizontal scans in sequence, each pass a notch above the previous one).

The Navy was particularly concerned about the reliability levels on what amounted to the most expensive radar and sensor package on any aircraft in the sky and took great note of the so-called mean-time-between-failure (MTBF). Rigorous test and qualification procedures were imposed on subcontractors and their electronic products. Early on, Hughes decided on 100 per cent testing of all semiconductor devices and collected altitude and thermal data to predict possible life cycles and anticipate failure probabilities down to the component level. Both Grumman and the Navy set an MTBF target of 18hr on AWG-9 subsystems delivered in 1971. That increased to 22hr a year later and to 26hr in 1973. To put meaning on those

Handlers and armourers feed ammunition to the Vulcan Gatling cannon on a VF-1 F-14A during trials. Although rarely afforded the opportunity to use the gun, lessons from Vietnam proved the folly of removing it altogether and firing trials with it are every bit as much a part of weapons familiarization as are missiles.

figures: in a typical 3hr mission an MTBF of 16hr means an 85 per cent probability of success in all operating modes and a 97 per cent probability of firing a missile at a target.

By early 1973 Hughes reported an MTBF on the radar alone of 34hr when it was operated by specialists and of 19hr when it was operated by field technicians. These were important figures, for there is a big difference between the contractor's personnel working with design engineers and specialized technicians on technically sophisticated equipment in a clean room and tired line workers beavering on blackbox electronics in the hot and noisy environment of a carrier's hangar. Grumman, Hughes and the Navy wanted the AWG-9 and its Phoenix warload to operate at the edge of reliability and operability and designed the system to consist of critical Weapons Replacable Assemblies (WRAs) each filled with high-grade

components. Installation and access were critical in the extracting and replacing of faulty WRAs without disturbing adjacent equipment or other WRAs. The AWG-9's self-test (BITE) equipment is used during maintenance to check on subsystem integrity and monitored through the NFO's rear cockpit stations.

In a novel means of husbanding missile resources, technicians on carriers or flight crews in the air can check on the integrity of Phoenix missiles through the Missile-On-Aircraft-Test (MOAT) facility. As a part of the BITE function, AWG-9 computers will check and test each missile taking a mere 23sec to give details of its health and status and put it in a sequence to ensure that degraded missiles are launched last. Flight line missiles or WRAs checked on the ground or in carriers that do fail BITE tests are removed to diagnostic equipment which isolates the troublesome circuit card and directs the

technician to the appropriate Shop Replaceable Assembly (SRA). A suite of five especially built test stations, designated AWM-23, provides simulation, controls and monitoring equipment to isolate faulty components within the SRAs. To ensure that operators thoroughly understand the complex electronics and equipment and learn the wide range of simulated faults and failures that can, theoretically, take hold, Hughes built a special training aid to give technicians experience in fault-isolation and maintenance.

Notwithstanding the ability of the system to perform reliably, AWG-9 gave its crew a remarkable advantage in combat mission capability. For long-range acquisition and fire control the crew select one or other of the four pulse-Doppler modes. Long-range search and detection is conducted by the Pulse-Doppler Search (PDS) option which provides maximum

A catapult prepares to hurl a Tomcat across the bow of the USS Forrestal with reheat cans in full song to give the aircraft a getaway speed ahead of the charging carrier.

range at distances greater than 115nm (213km) with one-, two-, four- or eight-bar coverage at +/-10, 20, 40 or 65 degrees left and right of the aircraft's boresight. It tracks in both azimuth and elevation and computes range-rate and the speed at which the target is approaching or receding; but it cannot give the crew information on the target's absolute range. That information, together with range-rate and angles, is acquired in the Range-While-Search (RWS) mode which offers the greatest surveillance volume, fifteen times that acquired by the F-4J. Effective at ranges of 90nm (167km) or more, RWS does not provide the heading, speed or altitude of the target and there is a modest decay in range detection with distance.

The distinct advantage claimed by the AWG-9 is its ability to track twenty-four simultaneous targets and fire Phoenix missiles at six of them while continuing to monitor the remaining ones. This extraor-

dinary capability is realized through the Track-While-Scan (TWS) mode effective at distances of 90nm (167km) or greater. TWS is the powerful core of the AWG-9's awesome capability and once the aircraft has acquired the target the azimuth/elevation range must be +/-40 degrees at two bar or +/-20 degrees at four bar. This is necessary because the radar must sweep the target every two seconds to hand over information on the target's position for predictive computing. Because it uses the computer to predict where the target will be 2sec later and does not lock-on as other radars do, it does not reveal to an enemy aircraft that it is being tracked. The enemy pilot believes that he is being swept by a scanning beam but not yet by the beam of an acquisition and tracking radar for missile launch, lulling him into a false sense of security where he will be reluctant to illuminate the Tomcat – assuming that he can 'see' it at that distance. With TWS selected, the target

must be within 52nm (96km) for the release of the AIM-54 Phoenix. The third mode in pulse-Doppler provides extended range for a Phoenix attack and is similar in principle to the AWG-10 built in to the F-4J from late 1966. Called the Pulse-Doppler-Single-Target-Track (PDSTT) mode it has two optional tracks: Velocity Track (VT) or Jam Angle Track (JAT). Both give maximum potential range to on-board missiles and, because of the radiated power advantage over the F-4J's AWG-10, it gives the AIM-54 Phoenix a range of 63nm (117km), the AIM-7F Sparrow a range of 38nm (70km) and the AIM-9G Sidewinder a range of up to 10nm (19km), approximately 40 per cent better in each case. Although it can track many targets simultaneously, the clear disadvantage with the PDSTT is that if the NFO wants to lock-on to a single target all the other targets disappear. The acquisition range in the PDSTT/VT mode is 90nm (167km) but in PDSTT/JAT mode the range is dependent on the degree of jamming. Jam Angle Track provides range-rate and angle information on targets protected by powerful electronic countermeasures.

Short- and medium-range search and detection, as well as ground mapping, are the province of pulse radar modes. Pulse search (PS) provides the full spectrum of radar scan pattern combinations giving 10, 20, 40 or 65 degrees on both sides of the boresight in azimuth and one, two, four or eight bars in elevation. The value of pulse radar is that there is no loss of information when the target is abeam the aircraft, as there is with pulse-Doppler, which requires a relative motion in range or distance. Because of the inherent limitations with the physics of pulse radar, the nominal detection range is, at 62 versus 115nm (115 and 213km), less than the equivalent with pulse-Doppler search. Weapons control, however, is the same borseight missile mode as PDS.

Pulse Single Target Track (PSTT) has authority over the full weapons load including gun, missiles and air-to-ground stores. Like PDSTT, it is divided into Range Track (RT) or Jam Angle Track (JAT). Single-target designation gives an exclusive lock-on with a nominal radar acquisition range of 49nm (91km) in PSTT/RT but highly variable, depending on the ECM, for PSTT/JAT. The great advantage of this mode is inherent in the way pulse radar works and it is suited best for short- range engagements where the target is turning abeam and less likely to have large range rates (high speed changes in the relative distance between the F-14 and its target). In this regard it is a lock-and-leave system for very close-in combat with little or no degradation in data return at critical stages in the combat. In this mode AIM-7F(CW) has a range of 29nm (54km), AIM-7E(CW) a range of 18nm (33km) and AIM-9 of between 1.5 and 20nm (2.8 and 37km), depending on the altitude and target geometry. Again, these range capabilities are better because of the AWG-9's radar capability. Finally, although not an independent radar selection mode, Pulse Radar Slaved (PRSL) performs a similar job in pulse-only that PDRSL does for pulse-Doppler and here the range is 49nm (91km).

Apart from the usual instruments and controls for flying the F-14, several key displays in both the front and the rear cockpit are dedicated to the Tomcat's unique weapon system and the AWG-9. The central instrument panel in the aft cockpit is dominated by the Tactical Information Display (TID), a 10in (25cm) diameter cathode ray tube which provides multiple target positions and tracks, missile launch zones, data link information, test results and television camera display. It has primarily four modes of operation: ground stabilized tactical display, aircraft stabilized tactical display, attack display superimposed on an aircraft stabilized tactical display and television image display. The screen consists entirely of computer-generated symbology in map or scroll with target information or superimposed attack display. It can double as a navigation aid and has way points and

In evaluating the F-14A pilots flew the aircraft against a wide variety of in-service combat types but none gathered as much interest as mock engagements flown against F-4 Phantoms, the aircraft it was built to replace. In no situation could the Phantom hold its own and the aircraft was repeatedly outpaced by the Tomcat.

flight information due in the main to an excess of capability.

Above the TID is the cathode ray tube of the Detail Data Display (DDD) which presents the NFO with raw or processed radar, infra-red or IFF video. Targets are displayed in range rate versus azimuth for pulse-Doppler and range versus azimuth for pulse radar, but in each case the resolution of the target is enhanced by selecting a portion of the velocity or range coverage. The tube is flanked by controls and selectors for radar frequency selection, display mode, range and other options. The electronic countermeasures control panel (ECMCP) located on the right side console provides controls for the radar and missile radar warning receivers and additional switches for the F-14's ECM equipment. These are bunched into four main categories: radar homing and warning system, an electronic pulse radar for intercepting and analysing signals from ground and airborne transmitters; the chaff-flare unit, which generates false targets for tracking radars or infra-red systems; the repeater-jammer, which transmits simulated target echoes synthesized from hostile radar signals; and the infra-red warning option which was not installed on early aircraft.

Three computer-coupled visual displays in the front cockpit assist the pilot in target acquisition and attack: the head-up display (HUD), the vertical display indicator (VDI) and the horizontal display indicator (HDI). The HUD is projected on the forward screen and contains symbology generated in response to signals from the aircraft missiles control system (AMCS) and provides the pilot with all the information he needs to perform all combat and battle-address activity. It cues the pilot on target display, steering commands, permitted steering error, weapon control status and landing glide slope position. Vital data for battle management include target range, range rate, aircraft attitude, target designators and target selection for firing. The VDI is a large rectangular television screen directly in front of the pilot and provides analogue symbology on a television raster format to cue the pilot on command information, attack display and terrain clearance. The HDI gives the pilot navigation, ECM and tactical situation displays.

Early Tomcats incorporated a AN-ALR-23 infra-red detection set under the nose mounted on gimbals, which could

No other aircraft was as important to the Tomcat as the E-2C Hawkeye, another Grumman product. Designed to operate at the outer perimeter of carrier defence, the Tomcat's offensive capability gained measurably from the early warning and battle management roles conducted by this remarkable aircraft. Together, Hawkeye and Tomcat gave unprecedented mission capability, unparalleled twenty-five years after the duo first put to sea.

Fixing and Flying

On 17 March 1969 the Navy held the first Integrated Logistic Support Management Team (ILSMT) meeting at Grumman's Bethpage facility. It was a milestone in military aviation because it brought to fruition a concept originating within a small group of forward-thinking people at Naval Air Systems Command when the VFX specification was being written. In general, wars are won because of strong logistical supply routes providing equipment where and when it is needed. It seemed logical to apply that to modern combat aircraft. While technical performance and superiority over the enemy is vital, the ability to press home repeated attacks depends on the aircraft's readiness level. In turn that depends on maintenance, support equipment, spares and repairs. Keeping the aircraft in the air and minimizing down-time is a crucial element in maximizing operational capability. But more than that, the group at NAVAIR wanted to think of the F-14 as a total weapon system and the Tomcat became the first such aircraft to be seen as that.

In some respects the F-4 could be said to have pioneered the concept of the 'weapons system' approach since it was designed to carry an all-missile armament. But it did not become part of an integrated mission statement in the way the F-14 did. With the Tomcat, airframe, propulsion, avionics and armament – primarily the Phoenix – assumed equal importance and collectively supported the written

mission. For the Tomcat that mission had several envelopes each defined by a specification met or exceeded by the system as a whole. So, when the Navy wrote the Integrated Logistic Support Management plan it proposed to give the system full on-deck support from the day the first aeroplane entered the inventory. Wasted years on useless quests for commonality shortened the lead over Soviet developments and in several respects US Navy aircraft were inferior to their Soviet counterparts. It could not afford the luxury of work-up time, the Tomcat had to have claws from the outset.

At the first ILSMT meeting more than 200 people attended from the Navy, Grumman and the contractor pool to iron out difficulties and requirements. Coming just two months after Grumman got the contract it was a new way of doing business. ILSMT meetings on other programmes took place after several years not weeks. What they provided was resources for supporting system and subsystem equipment deliveries with appropiate technical manuals, maintenance instructions and spares before the finished product arrived. No longer would technicians receive a subassembly for integration without having full installation and servicing instructions on hand. That helped to compress the integration and servicing time, factors crucial to getting the Tomcat operational within three and a half years of contract go-ahead.

In full afterburner, the catapult having done its stuff, a Tomcat from VF-24 leaves the deck with the stick-to-the-stomach for maximum rotation and climb-out. Note the two fuel tanks on the outer stores positions.

either be slaved to the radar or used independently for the optical tracking of other targets. With an acquisition range of 90nm (167km) it was supposed to be useful in heavy ECM environments, providing better target elevation, azimuth and angular tracking than radar. It was advertised as being particularly useful for rocket-powered cruise missiles or aircraft in afterburner. It was incorporated into the AWG-9 control by the Pulse-Doppler-Radar-Slaved (PDRS) mode where the radar was slaved to the infra-red line of sight. Cryogenically cooled indium antimonide detectors would provide infra-red detection from the fuselage chin position but, in practice, the system was not effective. After trials aboard the *Kennedy* and the *Constellation* in 1978, the ALR-23 was replaced by the Northrop AAX-1 Television Camera Sight (TCS), a passive electro-optical sensor providing the pilot with an ultra-long-range telescope.

The development of the TCS grew out of the US Air Force Rivet Haste and Combat Tree programmes at about the same time as the F-14A was being put through its paces in the early 1970s. The Air Force adopted a device comprising a video camera connected to a stabilized optical telescope attached to the port wing of the F-4E, and during 1977 the US Navy developed its own version known as TVSU (Television Sight Unit). In tests against simulated aggressors it proved that the pilot's normal eyeball identification range of 2 to 3 miles (3 to 5km) could be extended to 9 miles (14km) with the TVSU. During the 1978 tests Navy pilots demonstrated that they could identify surface ships and proposed a mechanism to slave the optical telescope to the radar, providing the luxury of being able to identify ship type and nationality through visual means. The Navy was convinced and during the 1980s the TCS was qualified for shipboard use and retrofitted to most F-14s.

The TCS is equipped with a wide-angle (1.42 degrees) option for long-range acquisition and a narrow-angle option (0.44 degrees) for identifying the target. Images are produced through a 10x magnification telescope with a 30-degrees field of view and presented in black and white to the pilot's VDI and the NFO's TDI (see later in this chapter). It is manually operated through a small joystick in the cockpit and moves on a gimbal system on the under-nose mounting but is usually slaved to the radar. Operational use of the TCS has proved it to be a rugged and dependable asset, stable under high g loads. It may be used to confirm visually friend or foe in the air or at sea and it has been used to discriminate between separate components of a multiple target seen as a single radar fix.

At the end of 1971, with four test aircraft (Nos. 4, 5, 6 and 9) at Point Mugu and four aircraft (Nos.1X, 2, 3 and 8) at Long Island, Grumman had half the fleet on radar, weapons and guidance systems tests and the other half on aerodynamic performance and flight evaluation at the same time. The last two YF-14A prototypes were Nos.10 and 11 (No.12 had been assigned to replace the first prototype). Aircraft No.10 took off for the first time on 29 February 1972 and on 6 April it was delivered to the Naval Air Test Center at Patuxent River, where it went through a structural validation programme with Grumman pilots. Then it went for carrier suitability trials and tests with the catapult and arrestor gear of the Automatic Carrier Landing System (ACLS). That aircraft was followed by the last YF-14A, aircraft No.11, which made its first flight on 6 March and was delivered to Point Mugu eighteen days later when it was used for non-weapons systems testing.

Aircraft no.13 (BuAer No. 158612), officially the first production F-14A in an initial batch of eight comprising Block 60 but in reality a series of development aircraft, took to the air for the first time on 2 May 1972. It went to the anechoic chamber for avionics and electromagnetic tests and for radio-frequency interference calibration. Aircraft no.14 took off on 6 June and went for maintenance and reliability demonstrations to Patuxent River. On the last day of June test pilot Bob Miller, who had piloted the first YF-14A when it crashed, lost his life when aircraft no.10 hit the water during rehersals for a charity air show at Patuxent Naval Air Test Center. On a murky day with few visual cues the pilot may have been momentarily distracted and was too late in pulling up from a shallow dive at 350kt (650km/hr). As the tail hit the water the aircraft exploded. Miller was alone in the cockpit. The aircraft had just 88 flight hours on the clock.

Aircraft nos.15, 16, 18 and 19 were delivered between August and October 1972 and given over to pilot training, the last three aircraft going to VX-4 at Point Mugu. Aircraft no.17, delivered in November, replaced No.10 in carrier compatibility trials while No.20, the last of the development aircraft, was delivered on 15 December 1972 to be used for weather and climatic testing. VX-4 had been formed in 1952 to test the air-to-air rockets that would soon form the primary armament on Navy fighters and rapidly became the primary Navy test and operational evaluation unit, taking Tomcats from the Naval Air Test Center and honing them into weapons of war. VX-4 received the aircraft and its Phoenix and Sidewinder missiles and worked up operational procedures and combat tactics. Not for nothing were they known as the 'Evaluators'. Meanwhile, VF-124 was given the not inconsiderable task of training pilots and NFOs to go to sea and operate their Tomcats as fleet air defence fighters. Established in August 1948 as VF-53, based at Miramar from 1961 and designated as a jet-fighter training squadron, VF-124 relinquished its F-8 Crusaders in 1970 but did not receive the first Tomcat until 8 October 1972.

Beginning with aircraft no.21 (BuAer 158620), the first of eighteen procured under Block 65, F-14A Tomcats were

Specification – F–14

Power plant:	Two Pratt & Whitney TF30-P-414A (F-14A) Two General Electric F110-GE-400 (F-14B/D)
Thrust rating:	TF30-P-414A: 20,900lb (9,480kg/93kN) F110-GE-400: 23,100lb (10,478kg/102.8kN)
Engine weight:	TF30-P-414A: 4,251lb (1,928kg) F110-GE-400: 4,400lb (1,996kg)
Fuel quantity:	Outer wings 1,117 litres (246gall) each Rear fuselage 2,453 litres (539gall) Forward fuselage 2,616 litres (575gall) Combined feeder tanks 1,726 litres (380gall) External tank 1,011 litres (222gall) each
Total fuel capacity:	11,051 litres (2,430gall)
Armament:	AIM-54 Phoenix; AIM-7 Sparrow; AIM-9 Sidewinder 1 x General Electric M61A1 Vulcan cannon with 625 rounds
Dimensions:	Span wings swept forward 20 degrees, 64ft 1.6in (19.5m); wings swept back 68 degrees, 38ft 2.5in (11.6m); (oversweep) 33ft 3.5in (10.1m); length 64ft 8in (19.1m); height 16ft (4.9m); tailplane span 32ft 8.5in (10m); fin tip separation 10ft 8in (3.3m); wheel track 16ft 5 in (5m); wheelbase, 23ft 0.5in (7m)
Surface areas:	Wings, 565sq ft (52.49 sq m); leading edge slats, 46.2sq ft (4.29sq m) total; trailing edge flaps, 106sq ft (9.87sq m) total; horizontal tail, 140sq ft (13.01sq m) total; fins (85sq ft (7.9m) total; rudders, 33sq ft (3.06sq m)
Weights:	Empty 40,104lb, (18,191kg); loaded, 59,714lb (27,086kg); maximum, 74,349lb (33,724kg); fuel internal/external, 20,000lb (9,072kg); landing weight 51,830lb (23,510kg)
Performance:	Maximum speed 1,544mph (2,484km/h) or Mach 2.34 at 40,000ft (12,190m) and 912mph (1,468km/h) or Mach 1.2 at low level; cruising speed 610mph (981km/h); carrier landing approach speed 154mph (248km/h); stall speed 132mph (213km/h); ceiling 55,000ft (16,765m); initial climb rate 32,500ft/min (165m/sec); unrefuelled range 2,400miles (3,860km); minimum take-off distance 1,400ft (427m); minimum landing distance 2,900ft (884m)

configured as post-development production models and would be variously divided between evaluation, crew operational conversion and squadron assignments. All but one of the first thirteen aircraft from Block 65, delivered between December 1972 and September 1973, were assigned to VF-124 at NAS Miramar. The last Block 65 aircraft was delivered on 12 October 1973, by which time the Tomcat was going into operational service. A year earlier, on 14 October 1972, the honour of being the first front-line Naval fighter units to be assigned as F-14A squadrons went to VF-1 and VF-2. VF-1 was formally commissioned on that date with the call-sign 'Wolfpack' but its sister squadron, the 'Bounty Hunters', had a history dating back to 1922 when VF-2 became the first unit to be deployed aboard an aircraft carrier, the USS *Langley* (CVA-1). In 1927 they became known as the 'Fighting Chiefs' when they were manned entirely by enlisted men. They too would not get their aircraft until July 1973, but both squadrons would take their Tomcats to Vietnam in time to cover the retreat of American forces and government officials from Saigon.

Operational Deployment Nears

By 1973 the F-14A was nearing operational deployment, but the fate of the aircraft was threatened on two fronts: persistent financial problems dogged efforts to arrive at a workable cost deal with Grumman and opponents to what was fast becoming the most expensive fighter of all time tried to get it cancelled and replaced by a 'common' fighter for both the Air Force and the Navy. Financial problems felt by Grumman as their corporate base shrank in 1969 and 1970 were mirrored in the United States at large by monetary policies that restricted growth in the space and defence sectors. Grumman was affected in both its work on the Lunar Module and subcontract work on the F-111 ending in 1971. For the previous two years turnover had been falling and in 1970 profits fell 8 per cent to $20.2 millions. Early in 1971 Grumman gathered together a significant amount of financial information and cost projections to support its case that the contract it had signed was too tight on total price for the decline in defence spending and the general downturn in the economy experienced since the F-14 deal had been signed in 1969. A serious problem existed which extended to the company as a whole.

In the week beginning 15 February 1971 key Grumman personnel briefed senior officers at the Naval Air Systems Command and explained the nature of the problem. Grumman admitted that, given the trends since 1969, it had been unwise to cut projected costs to the bone in efforts to get the F-14 contract in the first place. Fearing that the company would collapse if they failed to get the deal, Grumman executives had given themselves too little margin in unpredictable times. After a

Flying off carriers on coastal patrol or operating from shore stations, Tomcat exercises frequently take in low flying across rough terrain. Increasingly, the F-14 is asked to take on a wider range of roles from fleet defence to ground attack and familiarity with flying through mountains is essential.

week of meetings and several days of questioning to refine the summary, NASC's Assistant Commander for Contracts was formally notified by letter from Grumman at the end of March. In it the company said that, by binding itself to a total procurement package concept it became prey to excessive inflationary pressure, sluggish growth in the economy and a downturn in defence spending. The company was quick to point out that the escalating unit cost of the Tomcat was due in part to changes made by the Navy in certain requirements and in a reduction in the sales potential for this advanced aircraft. Perhaps unwisely, Grumman had looked at past orders for Navy production fighters, seeing a potential for more than a thousand aircraft where none existed in fact.

To date the company had accepted the contractual obligation for completion of thirty-eight aircraft in Lots 1, 2 and 3, defined in production terms as the first twelve YF-14A prototypes, the eight F-14A development aircraft of Block 60 and the eighteen F-14A production aircraft of Block 65. It wanted a change in the contractual terms of Lot 4 and sought government approval to renegotiate the arrangement. But the government was not listening. It wanted to keep defence spending under tight constraint, seeing a potentially disastrous situation if each one of the new procurement programmes escalated, or if each contractor felt that it could squeeze a better deal by pleading poverty. McDonnell Douglas was cranking up the F-15 programme and an influential lobby in Congress, the 'Peace Through Law' group, wanted the cancellation of the F-14 at the least or cancellation of both that and the F-15 programme at best. It envisaged a new, lightweight F- X/2 fighter that could substitute for the F-14 (sic) and support or replace the F-15. There was even support in the White House.

An important plank in the 'Nixon doctrine' was for a greater share of the defence burden to be met by those nations in Europe and the Far East to whom the US had pledged military aid. As early as September 1969, in what was referred to as the 'Free World Fighter', Deputy Defense Secretary David Packard asked Congress for approval to fund what quickly became known as the International Fighter Aircraft, or IFA, a low-cost combat aircraft that would be sold throughout pro-Western countries in the Far East. This sent shivers through the F-15 lobby which had known about a 'Fighter Mafia' in the Pentagon for more than two years. What this group challenged was the notion that a few sophisticated, highly capable but expensive 'silver bullets' were preferable to a larger number of cheaper, less sophisticated fighters. Backed by the Defense Secretary Melvin Laird, Packard pushed ahead with the notion that a small, low-cost fighter could do most of the jobs claimed for a big, expensive, super-fighter like the F-15, not only for the IFA role but

A fine head-on study defining the asymmetric form of matching lines from the Tomcat's engines, upper fuselage and wings.

The superb view from the driving seat forward and down is self-evident as a Tomcat prepares for let down. The aircraft has a lower landing speed for its weight than any other carrier-based type, due largely to its variable-geometry wing and high lift devices.

for the USAF Tactical Air Command as well.

It was an idea that seriously threatened the F-15 and it was to result in the Lightweight Fighter which went to tender on 6 January 1972, just one day after President Nixon had authorized development of the NASA Shuttle. For a government pledged to cut spending, the Nixon administration was dangerously close to opening up too much procurement for the economy to handle. But the Lightweight Fighter, and the F-16 that would emerge from that idea, was still in the future as Grumman sought to have its contract changed for F-14 procurement with Lot 4 and subsequent orders. The Navy had cut back on the number of aircraft it agreed to buy in Fiscal Year 1972 (the twelve months beginning 1 July 1971) as part of a belt-tightening process to get the federal books balanced. From a surplus of $3.2 billion in FY 1969, the fol-

lowing two years had seen the government budget deficit grow from $2.8 billion to $23.0 billion and projections for FY 1972 were grim; in fact, it would top $23.4 billion.

As a possible way out of Grumman's problem the Navy persuaded the Pentagon to ask for a procurement commitment of forty-eight Tomcats in FY 1972 and in July 1971 David Packard went to Congress with that request. Instead of changing the contract, the Navy, and Congress, sought to restore some of the lost business and give Grumman a better financial turnover from which to sort out its problems. But expanding the production rate and increasing Grumman's turnover did not get to the heart of the matter. Nevertheless, despite the loss that would result, Congress sought, and received from Grumman, a commitment to build forty-eight F-14s in FY 1972. Dated 27 July 1971, a letter to that effect was sent from

Grumman to Packard. Efforts to reduce costs all round were made throughout the year. The company cut 14,000 from a work force of 36,500 in May 1969, leaving just 22,500 by December 1971, reduced its facilities floor space by 500,000sq ft (45,900sq m) and planned on a further reduction of 250,000sq ft (23,000sq m) by mid-1972.

In the month that Grumman received the letter from Packard, the Naval Air Systems Command Cost Review Team arrived to inspect the company's procedures. They looked at operations management, policy implementation, industrial management practices, cost control in all phases of the programme and the entire range of internal corporate functions. Seeking to improve cost control and efficiency, the team identified some areas where improvements could be made and Grumman readily accepted their help and attention, if secretly fuming at the

Positions of the two variable ramp doors on the starboard engine inlet duct can be seen as a Tomcat from VF-1 reaches for the deck, tailhook trailing. Here too the superb down view from both the front and the rear seat is apparent.

presumption of their political overlords. Across the corporation, Grumman was badly hit as gross sales fell by 20 per cent and dipped below $800 millions and the group lost $18 millions, the first in its forty-one-year history. The company millstone was the very programme on which it had pinned its hopes three years earlier. The Tomcat programme alone posted a deficit of $65 millions on the year. Matters reached a head.

On 20 January 1972 Grumman advised the Navy that it could not make Lot 5 of the production programme under the terms of the original contract and the Navy began earnest talks with the company to prepare battle lines for a fight in Congress. It was a timely move as the defence budget hearings on FY 1973 were about to get under way. The Chief of Naval Operations E. R. Zumwalt prepared a memorandum for the Navy Secretary John H. Chafee (about to be replaced by John W. Warner) on 18 April summarizing the position. In early 1972 the Grumman President

Llewellyn J. Evans had a heart attack and stood down, his position being filled by the Chairman E. Clinton Towl, the last of the active Grumman co-founders. As luck would have it, in early 1971 Towl had recruited John Bierworth to the Board of Directors for an injection of business expertise in global operations. In mid-1972 Bierworth accepted the position of Vice-President of finance and within a few weeks had been promoted to President of the company. His first big challenge was to sort out the F-14 contracts issue.

Through 1972 the hard-headed Bierworth ground away at stubbon Pentagon resistance and fought Grumman's case in Congress and in the defence committees. Lew Evans died in July with the company heading for its worst year on record. There seemed to be no way out. Not only was the F-14 carrying more than its fair share of the company's losses but it was likely to bring Grumman down too. From $799 millions in 1971 sales dropped to $683.5 millions in

1972 and the company loss increased from $18 to $70 millions. It was bad news all round. In July the company's bid to building the NASA Shuttle orbiter failed against North American Rockwell and work on the Orbiting Astronomy Observatory programme came to an end. Seeing the writing on the wall and fearing that it would be left baling out essential work from a bankrupt company, the Pentagon finally agreed to talk about rene-gotiating the contract. What it wanted was to hold Grumman to the original terms through to the end of Lot 5, with the option of negotiating separate contracts each year after the first 134 aircraft had been built. This would give Grumman a net loss of 20 per cent on each aircraft and a cumulative loss of $235 millions, with the promise of more realistic deals on the remaining 256 aircraft the Navy intended to buy.

The deal was struck in March 1973, but, although it gave Grumman a light at the end of its tunnel, it would continue to lose money on F-14 production for a further two years. Under the terms of American defence contracts the government gives out progress payments that cover 80 per cent of their total value, leaving the contractor to find the remaining 20 per cent from bank loans. No one wanted to come to the aid of the company that had certain losses for at least two years and no signed agreement yet in hand for profitability after that. Bierworth set about the business of restoring faith among the aerospace finance markets by spreading the corporation's deposits among nine separate banks and keeping them unusually well informed about progress and cost cuts. In addition, injecting a sense of determination into aggressive marketing, the company extended its base into civilian aviation and, in addition, obtained a contract from NASA for production of five set of wings for the Shuttle orbiter. At the year's end on a turnover of $1.1 billion the company made a profit of $28.2 million.

Commonality Resurgent

Meanwhile, another battle had been fought and won. Although the lightweight fighter lobby had failed in its attempt to get the F-14 or the F-15 cancelled, the Peace Through Law group held to their cause in criticizing the Pentagon for spending public money on two air superiority fighters instead of one. The old 'commonality' cry was heard again and lobbyists wanted to know whether one aircraft could serve the needs of both services. In early 1971, just when Grumman's financial woes were a matter of Congressional debate, the staff of the House Appropriations Committee released the findings of an internal analysis which said that, while the F-14 could carry out the separate missions of both the Navy and the Air Force, the F-15 could not. The Air Force reacted quickly and claimed that the F-15 was a manoeuvring fighter while the F-14 was a

missile-launching platform and that its protégé could be adapted for carrier use. It was at this time that the lightweight fighter lobby was pushing hard for money to develop the F-X/2 (to become the F-16) and in a report entitled 'Report on the F-14 and F-15 Tactical Fighters' claimed that the lightweight substitute could save money for the Pentagon.

The two heavyweight fighters were too entrenched in Pentagon commitments to be levered out by the lightweight lobby, but on 8 July 1971 Secretary of Defense Laird asked the Navy to investigate the plausibility of a navalized Eagle known as the F-15N. He wanted to know what that aeroplane could be stretched to. It was slightly faster than the Tomcat and had a better dogfight potential, but it was more of a gunfighter and less of a platform for missiles and could simply not perform the naval air superiority role. McDonnell Douglas proved that the F-15N could, with a little latitude, operate from carrier decks

Operating off the USS America, a Tomcat of VF-142 comes to a stop. Note the red-tipped fuel dump nozzle on the trailing edge of the rear fuselage wedge.

and reach out as far as the F-14 but it was less flexible on loiter and not nearly as good at picking out the bandits beyond visual range. To adapt it to carrier use the F-15 grew 2,300lb (1,045kg) in weight and comparisons were made between the two aircraft equipped with Sparrow or Phoenix only.

Not to be outgunned, Grumman did its own, parallel study of a navalized F-15 and showed that, with Phoenix missiles attached, the fixed-wing Eagle would be heavily overweight – and that resurrected shivers over the F-111B fiasco. Some favoured cancelling the Tomcat, buying the Eagle for the Navy, boosting production and cutting unit price – which all sounded very laudable – but the suggestions came from the Eagle's nest and not from the objective viewpoint of dispassionate analysts who failed to see the advantages as clearly as McDonnell Douglas. Nevertheless, the Navy performed a study which penalized the F-15N, but under pressure from the Secretary of Defense it formed the basis for Navy Fighter Study III.

For more than a year, as the Tomcat slipped into production and the Eagle made its first flight, the contest between these two subsided only to arise again in early 1973. Throughout much of 1972 Grumman had prepared for the worst and defined several alternative Tomcats, cheaper to produce and less costly for the already strained defence budget. There was the F-14D, not to be confused with the Tomcat variant that appeared in the mid-1980s powered by the General Electric F110, proposed as a cutback F-14 with fewer weapons and a reduced price tag. There was the F-14 'Optimod' with a cheaper computer for the AWG-9 and the F-14T with even more radical surgery. Offering little beyond the capabilities of the by now dated F-4 Phantom II, the F-14T would have had Sparrow and Sidewinder but no Phoenix and the AWG-9 would have been replaced by simpler fire control systems.

Not content to put all its naval options on the F-15N, McDonnell Douglas also proposed an upgraded F-4 and it was against both types that the F-14T competed. A stripped-down F-4E, designated F-4T and optimized for the air superiority role, would be put up again in the late 1970s in unsuccessful attempts to keep the Phantom II production line open. But the F-14T was downgraded into the limited capabilities of the period the Tomcat was intended to succeed and a less austere family of alternative variants, designated F-14X, was proposed. These would have a reduced capability Hughes APG-64 radar, with no Phoenix missiles, simultaneous target tracking cut from twenty bogies to twelve, and the automatic direct-lift control (DLC) and approach power compensation (APC) autoland throttle control eliminated. None of these alternative proposals made any sense at all

An F-14A from VF-32 shows its long-range warload as it cleans up and prepares to dash but, with the CD-iris exhaust nozzle still in non-afterburner shape, the pilot is in no hurry.

A VF-1 Tomcat flies out to rejoin a carrier task force. Note the bleed air dump doors on top of the separate nacelles.

and Grumman was able to show through these options packages that the standard F-14 was, after all, the optimum way to achieve the Navy's mission.

However, it was not over yet. Concerned at the parlous state of Grumman's finances, the Senate Armed Services Committee began an investigation in March 1973 to see whether the F-15 really could replace the F-14. Deputy Secretary of Defense Clements proposed a lengthy and intensive series of tests to compare the austere F-14D with the F-15N in a fly-off that left some sceptics claiming that the only way to settle it once and for all was to send them both up with live ammunition! Within the Pentagon, Air Force officials produced brochures and briefing materials on a navalized F-15 while the Navy came up with similar products offering the opposite view. Both services lobbied Congressional members heavily in what each saw as a fight for the survival of the 'silver bullet'. Fortunately for the F-14 there was sufficient justification in both aircraft for logic to prevail, although the competition between the Tomcat and the Eagle had one more race to run.

Traditionally the US aerospace industry takes its land-based fighters on the global sales road, marketing them to friendly air forces around the world. Aloof from the foreign sales potential inherent in land-based fighters, Navy fighters have rarely sold in similar quantities. After all, there are few maritime forces capable of operating the large carrier battle groups for which US naval combat aircraft are usually designed. With the F-14, however, Grumman was convinced that the naval air superiority fighter had at last reached a level where it was a valid alternative for land-based air forces. The single, pervading advantage of the F-14 over land-based models was its ability to spot the enemy and throw a deadly punch across a greater range than any other aeroplane in the sky. Countries with long borders had special needs clearly met by the Tomcat, albeit at a price. But Grumman found one customer for whom the price tag was not as important as the aircraft's combat potential.

The Shah to the Rescue

As early as May 1972, in a visit to Tehran by President Nixon, the Shah of Iran had expressed interest in buying a number of modern, high-performance combat aircraft from the United States, capable of deterring Soviet intrusions into Iranian air space. Iran policed the longest border with the Soviet Union of any country in the Middle East and had for twenty years played host to sophisticated US electronic surveillance equipment spying on Soviet weapons tests. There was a mutual interest at stake and Nixon gave permission for the Shah to go shopping. For some time the Soviets had been sending their MiG-25 Foxbats over Iran, but in 1972 the combat capability of the Imperial Iranian Air Force (IIAF) comprised two fighter-bomber squadrons with F-4Ds and six with F-5s in a total force of 160 aircraft. Foxbats were oblivious to the Sparrows and Sidewinders of outdated fighters. However, with a defence budget of $915 millions the Shah could afford the best.

Of the two contenders the F-14 was the obvious choice. It had the capability of operating autonomously where the F-15 required support from radar and battle-management on the ground. There was a greater need for infrastructure with the F-15 than there was with the Tomcat. Grumman had a strong advocate in the form of Vice-Admiral Robert L. Townsend, who had joined the company as head of its international sales team. He went to town on the Navy people at the Pentagon and explained the advantages of getting foreign sales which would expand the order book and ease the upward pressure on the aircraft's unit cost at home. Worried that the Air Force would put up

Extending the message, carrier battle groups have an increasingly vital role to play in policing the seas and preserving the passage of commodities. The Tomcat has had to adapt to a changing world order and refined threats, exhibiting flexibility and role-change to keep ahead of the competition.

toward the purchase of both types.

But the real contest came several months later when the Shah visited Washington and the two contenders were let loose to give of their best in the skies above Andrews Air Force Base. Grumman pulled out all the stops and provided an air-conditioned trailer in which the Shah could don an especially tailored flight suit complete with royal crest, which he was given as a memento of the day. Not as far into its flight certification as the F-14 and so prohibited from revealing its true potential, the Eagle failed to dislodge the Tomcat from prime position and the Shah was ecstatic when the F-14 thundered around the sky, turning nimbly into flick rolls and high g pull-ups. As a pilot he could appreciate the true performance of the Tomcat and went away convinced that this was the aeroplane for Iran. It suited the US to allow Iran to purchase the sophisticated AWG-9/Phoenix combination and it served notice on the USSR that there was a new challenge to unwarranted incursions into Iranian air space.

By the end of the year the preliminary details had been completed and in January 1974 the Iranian government signed an order for thirty aircraft virtually identical to the standard US Navy F-14A, except for some highly specialized suites of ECM equipment and a couple of technical equipment changes. Yet Grumman was not out of the financial wood and in August 1974 Congress voted to cut funds to Grumman because of an implied misdemeanour, claiming misuse of government money. Because Grumman had been unable to raise the 20 per cent balance between the Navy progress payments and the manufacturing cost through domestic banks, the government had agreed to advance the sum as a loan. In that way the production line would remain open and the company would continue to build Tomcats. Although commercial interest rates for large loans were quoted at 5.2 per cent, on the loan it extended to Grumman, the government charged a rate of almost 6.9 per cent.

To relieve the financial strain Grumman put extra cash into short-term government securities and recouped $2.8 million that was deducted from the amount the company borrowed from the government. Everyone benefited but the government objected and stopped the loan, plunging Grumman into a new crisis. It was a case of the wrong move at the wrong time. The

solid support for McDonnell Douglas to market the F-15 to Iran, John Bierwirth ordered a full F-14 sales presence at the 1973 Paris Air Show to brandish it before the customer. The F-15 had made its first

flight less than a year before the Paris Show when the Tomcat impressed visitors with its expanded flight envelope, more than two years after it had first taken to the air. The Shah too was impressed, leaning

The first of eighty Tomcats ordered by the Shah of Iran leaves the Grumman test facility at Calverton from where it will be delivered to the Navy, thence to Spain from where it will fly to Iran.

Congress was tired of bailing out big business and drew a line in the sand beyond which no more help was to be given. No appeal was allowed; it was sink or swim. There would be no lifebelt. Grumman needed $200 million to honour Navy orders but the news came with such swiftness that one of Bierwirth's senior men had to be called from a round of golf with bankers to help to handle the crisis. Senior Grumman executives had already tapped the Iranians for possible help if financial problems with the F-14 contract worsened. Only later would it be known that someone told the Office of Management and Budget, which triggered the move to stop loan aid going to Grumman.

Now it was time to call in the offer of help and Bierwirth put together a package which had Iran's Bank Melli at the centre with a loan of $75 million Some of this money was used to clear the debt to the Navy and that brought a further $125

million from revolving credits at nine domestic banks including Citibank and Morgans. At a stroke, Grumman had shed the government shackles, received sufficient money to proceed through Lot 5 on the F-14 production line and come to successive procurement batches with agreement to negotiate in-profit deals with the Navy. The Iranian loan came without strings, as it had to in US law since it was a foreign bank dealing with a US registered company, and there were no imposed directorships on the Grumman board. From the domestic banks, however, came the standard imposition preventing mergers without approval and limiting cash dividends to 20 per cent of net income. But that mattered little, for Grumman was on the way back up. By the end of 1974 the company had achieved a net profit of $32.9 million.

In June 1974 Iran signed a contract for an aditional fifty Tomcats bringing to

eighty the total number scheduled for delivery to its Air Force. At first the Shah had wanted both Tomcat and Eagle squadrons but settled for additional orders of F-16 fighters. Designated F-14A-GR, the first Iranian aircraft (BuAer No. 160299) from the first batch of thirty took off on 5 December 1975 and was delivered by way of Spain to Mehrabad Air Base on 27 January 1976 where it was inducted in the IIAF with the serial number 3-942. Deliveries were arranged by the US Navy, which added a 2 per cent management charge, bringing the price of each F-14A-GR to $30 million plus training fees; aircraft were completed at the rate of about two a month. Grumman sensed that there were more orders waiting to be won in the Middle East and put on an impressive commitment, basing a thousand personnel in Iran for training and familiarization.

Much impressed by US Navy training

Almost the same as a standard F-14A, devoid of only the most sensitive elements in its avionics and AWG-9 systems, the Shah's Tomcats helped to deter Soviet overflights by MiG-25 Foxbat photo-reconnaissance aircraft. Only one was not delivered, retained in the US when the Shah was deposed.

techniques and the Top Gun school at Naval Air Station Miramar, the Iranians duplicated this with a purpose-built base 20 miles south-east of Isfahan. There, a complete air base was built with two 14,000ft (4,240m) runways, hardened aircraft shelters and accommodation for all necessary personnel. By May 1977 the Imperial Iranian Air Force was sufficiently familiar with the aircraft to stage a splen-

did display for the Shah's birthday when twenty F-14A-GRs flew past, two hooked up to a KC-135 tanker. A few months later, during an operational sortie, an IIAF Tomcat tracked a Soviet Foxbat transiting the country at 65,000ft (19,700m) and a speed of Mach 2. During August, no longer content to accept unannounced Soviet overflights, the Shah authorized live firing at targets and in August two

drones were downed by Phoenix missiles. The Soviets got the message. The last aircraft was accepted by the US Navy on 19 July 1978 and retained in the US as a test vehicle for the modifications planned for all Tomcats. It would never be delivered for revolution was boiling to the surface and on 16 January 1979 the Shah fled Iran.

CHAPTER FOUR

Tooth and Claw

Long-Distance Punch

Having established the precedent of a foreign sale through its deal with Iran, Grumman looked elsewhere, seeking markets in Japan and Saudi Arabia. The Middle East in particular was a potentially lucrative market. Saudi Arabia had a similar defence profile to Iran's: a big country with long borders and little in-depth infrastructure for the long-range interception of intruders. Rugged and independent, the Tomcat carried the range and the weaponry to suit the defence requirement. But it was not to be. The F-15 was backed by a more energetic, certainly more experienced, sales team on loan from the Pentagon and Eagles made nests in Israel, Saudi Arabia and Japan with exports amounting to more than 400 aircraft. A legacy of the F-14 versus F-15

contest for the US Navy's procurement in 1973 was to spawn Navy Fighter Study IV, in which a wide variety of alternatives were discussed. From this came the Naval Air Combat Fighter, defined through the VFAX requirement, which resulted in the F-18 Hornet resurrected from the ashes of the Lightweight Fighter competition won in late 1974 by General Dynamics with the F-16.

Ironically, it was the F-18 Hornet that won foreign sales where once Grumman executives had tried hard to sell the F-14. Among several countries in the early 1970s that expressed interest in the Tomcat was Australia, seeking a replacement fighter for its ageing Mirage IIIO. In some respects it was a similar geographic challenge to that presented by Saudi Arabia and Iran and twin-engine safety was a strong requirement. But the sale would come at a cost to the seller because the Australian

government wanted work for its own aircraft industry. Responding to this, Grumman put together a comprehensive package whereby Australia would buy the proposed F-14B with the more powerful Pratt & Whitney F401 engine and provide materials, forgings, control surfaces, panels, doors, missile racks and some avionics subsystems. The first five Tomcats for the Royal Australian Air Force were to have been assembled and tested by Grumman in the USA but the final assembly of subsequent aircraft would take place in Australia. In all, domestic offsets would amount to 90 per cent of the airframe purchase price. After a protracted and lengthy deliberation, the F-14B was turned down largely on a question of cost and Australia purchased seventy-five F-18 Hornets in the early 1980s.

Notwithstanding determined efforts to get foreign sales, by 1974 the principle worries of the Grumman Corporation were those concerned with the improving of efficiency on the production line, cutting costs and building sales orders. Those of the Navy were concerned with getting the Tomcat operationally deployed with the first two F-14A squadrons, VF-1 and VF-2. Flight-test activity had gone well, although a third YF-14A prototype, aircraft No.6, was lost during a weapons test on 20 June 1973. During trials with a Navy crew flying the aircraft off the coast of California, an AIM-7E Sparrow missile fired from the far aft centreline station tipped up and struck the aircraft, rupturing a fuel tank in the fuselage. Almost immediately the F-14 caught fire but the crew ejected safely and were picked up from the water 40min later. The accident investigation board recommended more powerful ejector cartridges to push the missile away from the aircraft and the problem was never experienced again. Yet this was just the sort of problem test pilots are paid to uncover and weapons tests are the final

Towed to a parking spot on the USS Eisenhower, a F-14A with drop tanks operated by VF-32 is towed to a parking spot during operations off the coast of Puerto Rico.

hurdle for an aircraft cleared across the flight performance envelope.

Qualifying and matching superb design and engineering in the F-14's remarkable combination of high-performance aerodynamics and effective variable-geometry wing and engine inlet, the real teeth of the Tomcat lie in its unique combination of air-to-air weapons. None of those is more advanced than the truly remarkable combination of AWG-9/AIM-54 Phoenix. As related in Chapter 1, the radar system evolved from the ASG-1B of the late 1950s, while the Hughes Phoenix arose from the ashes of the Bendix XAAM-10 Eagle designed for the cancelled Douglas F6D-1 Missileer. For much of the time TFX was evolving into VFX (F-14) for the Navy and FX (F-15) for the Air Force, Hughes made remarkable strides in adapting a heavy and cumbersome weapon system into a lean and relatively light air-to-air missile with great range, devastating accuracy and reliability. In merging the successor to Eagle and bringing both AWG-9 radar and missile in-house, Hughes effectively produced a weapon tailored to the VFX requirement.

Hughes began work on the Phoenix in 1960 as a replacement for the AIM-47A, the most potent Falcon family member with a prospective range of 100 miles (160km) and a speed of Mach 6, which was designed for use with the ASG-18 on YF-12A interceptors. Hughes was selected as the Phoenix prime contractor in August 1962. Unguided flight tests began in 1965, when the missile was firmly matched to the F-111B, and guided tests took place during 1966 using a couple of Douglas A-3 Skywarrior aircraft as launch platforms. The first successful intercept took place in September 1966 and further test missiles were procured during 1968 and 1969. A strong feature of the AWG-9/Phoenix is its ability to deal with more than one target and this was demonstrated in September 1969 when two drones were hit by missiles fired from an F-111B. Although the Naval F-111 had been formally cancelled on 10 July 1968, seven prototypes and pre-production F-111Bs were built and it was with one of those that Phoenix was tested fourteen months later, albeit with little public acknowledgement. Hughes received a pre-production testing contract in December 1970, just as the first YF-14A was nearing its first flight, and flight trials from the Tomcat began in April 1972.

As designed for the VFX requirement,

Hook on, wheels in the air, an F-14A from VF-74 sinks to the deck of the Saratoga as deck-landing crew look on. From this vulnerable position arrester crew operate the steam- driven winches capable of reconfiguring the wires in seconds.

the AIM-54A Phoenix is a single-stage, solid-propellant rocket utilizing semi-active radar working through the AWG-9 for mid-course guidance and active-radar in the terminal homing phase of flight. The forward section of the missile has a completely clean exterior and accommodates (front to back) the planar array seeker antenna, the transmitter/receiver, AD/DSQ-26 digital electronics guidance package, inertial sensor, target detecting device and the 132lb (60kg) high-explosive warhead. The rear section consists of the single, solid-propellant Rocketdyne (now Boeing-Rocketdyne) MK47 rocket motor which propels the missile to Mach 4+, a steel-cased unit with four fixed, stub wings running almost the entire length of the section and four tail-mounted control surfaces at the rear. The forward face of the rear section carries the warhead's Mk 334 proximity fuse. To the rear of the motor, surrounding the neck of the exhaust nozzle, are located the power supply, servo control unit and position drives and the data link.

Phoenix has clear lineage from the Falcon series of radar-guided, air-to-air missiles which emerged from development work that began in 1947 to become a long series of successful AAMs, some 60,000 of

which were produced in total. The slender body and stub-wing shape has low drag and high manoeuvrability, the tail fins giving Phoenix 17g sustainability. The steel missile case is covered with a phenolic ablator for thermal insulation. Phoenix has a total length of 13ft (3.9m), a diameter of 15in (38cm), a maximum width of 3ft (0.92m) and a tactical weight of 1,008lb (458kg), making it one of the biggest and heaviest of all AAMs. With wide antenna scan angles and long flight time – it can take between two and three minutes for the Phoenix to reach its target – the missile takes in a large area of sky. When fired at distant targets toward the edge of the AWG-9's capability, Phoenix flies a preprogrammed course under autopilot, switching to the integral seeker in semi-active pulse mode for the second phase. In Track-While-Scan the AWG-9 gives the Phoenix samples of target position data from which it sets its homing equations.

If fired to its maximum range, the Phoenix lofts to high altitude for the autopilot phase. This reduces aerodynamic drag but is done primarily to minimize interference between the AWG-9 and the missile's own radar. At extreme altitude the speed exceeds Mach 5. As the Phoenix nears its target the guidance switches to

Flight tests with in-flight refuelling temporarily mate Tomcat with a KA-6D tanker. F-14s are capable of taking on a partial or full load of fuel, giving them great ferry range when coupled to drop tanks on stores points.

the third flight mode, the active homing phase, which begins from 9 to 11nm (16.7 to 20.3km) from the target, whereupon the missile flies on its own homing signal to impact or proximity detonation. Under circumstances where Phoenix is launched within this range of the target the missile goes immediately to the 'fire and forget' mode and homes in on the target without the autopilot or the semi-active AWG-9 phase. Efficient aerodynamic design and performance inherent in the generous rates of axial acceleration possible through the missile's high g turn capability gave it the advantage over any air threat in being when it entered service or postulated for the next century. But it was the extensive series of tests and operational simulations it went through in the early 1970s that proved its capabilities.

The first AWG-9 was delivered in February 1970 and just over two years later, in April 1972, the first missile tests began with the seconded YF-14A proto-types. In that year Grumman fired eleven

missiles with an 80 per cent success rate. The following year the Navy launched thirteen with a 91 per cent success level and Grumman launched eight with 100 per cent success. Of the Navy's twenty-two launches in 1974 83 per cent hit their target and three of the four Grumman rounds were successful, a 75 per cent rate. In 1975, the final year of evaluation and development, the Navy achieved an 82 per cent success rate on thirty-five launches. Of the ninety-three rounds, seven were live and the average success rate was a creditable 85 per cent. Given that these results were of a development programme they are all the more remarkable. Yet the really significant aspect of the tests and operational training phases that followed was in the missile's mission, significantly more advanced and demanding than that of any other AAM operated by any air force in the world. Moreover, when the missile went deep-blue and the Phoenix put to sea, non-specialized crews got the same success rates as the engineers and test

crews that fired off the flight evaluation rounds.

At the outset, the Navy put astonishing demands on the test programme, setting up eight separate target categories to simulate a wide range of threats. It used AQM-37A targets to represent fast, highly manoeuvrable cruise missiles, suitably augmented to adopt the radar profile of real weapons, subsonic BQM-34A and supersonic BQM-34E targets to simulate large targets, CQM-10, converted Bomarc missiles, to represent large cruise missiles and four remotely controlled aircraft to pose a broad range of air threat simulations. These included the 'Q' designated, pilotless, F-4 (known as QF-4), F-86 (QF-86), F-9 Cougar (QF-9) and T-33 (QT-33). Patterns of simulated threat spreads were set up to test the AWG-9/AIM-54A combination in action and single as well as multiple targets were configured. From the outset it was clear that the radar had an excess of performance, typically F-4 size targets were routinely

The Soviet Maritime Threat

Havoc wrought by German U-boats and the stranglehold on Britain's lifelines in World War II was lesson enough for the United States to be aware of an expanding Soviet challenge. Since the end of hostilities in the Pacific in September 1945 the US Navy has retained a firm hold on the concept of deterrence through force and this has been a pillar of security and peace-keeping ever since. In the 1960s, when first the TFX and then the VFX requirement were written, the prime Soviet naval threat came from its air forces, comprising long-range bombers with extended-range cruise and stand-off weapons. The USSR had only a few client states dotted around the world from where it could operate with impunity. But the fall of South Vietnam in the early 1970s and the wars in Cambodia and along the Chinese border that ensued, added vital port and harbour resources to the Soviet Navy.

Throughout the 1970s the Soviet Navy expanded in size and capability, threatening the sea-lines of communication and poised to prevent the consolidation and resupply of NATO forces should war with the Warsaw Pact break out in Europe. By the end of the decade the Soviet naval presence in the South China Sea had increased and in the first half of the 1980s a steady build-up of naval and air forces at Cam Ranh Bay, the port of the former South Vietnam, expanded the air threat throughout south-east Asia, with reconnaissance bombers operating at will throughout the South China Sea. Tu-16 Badgers had a combat radius from Cam Ranh Bay that extended almost as far south as Australia, across to eastern India, over to encompass the Philippines and up to Formosa. After a half-hearted intervention by China, Vietnam welcomed Soviet aid and 2,500 troops moved in to wave the flag. In return, the Soviets transformed Cam Ranh Bay into the largest Soviet naval forward deployment base outside the Warsaw Pact.

The last twenty years of the Cold War, the years that saw the F-14 from first flight through the entire period of its production, brought an intensity in the perceived Soviet threat that did much to spur the upgrade programme finally authorized in 1984. Against the justifiable expansion of the Tomcat programme, mission managers and Grumman executives were continually strained to gain approval for performance improvements that should have been introduced to this remarkable aircraft long before. With the collapse of the Soviet regime and the fragmentation of the Communist empire, the installed threat metamorphosed into a disparate set of new challenges, each a potential hot-spot with the capacity to break into a brush fire. But the old enemy had gone, perhaps not for ever, and the Tomcat had new bullies on the block against which to sharpen its claws.

spotted at an extreme range of 135nm (250km).

Inevitably, bugs appeared in the system and the vigorous test and trials sessions helped to iron out the problems and illuminate areas where changes to software were necessary and improvements made. There were some weaknesses in the communications link with the fire-control system and confusing signals caused some failures so that changes were made and reconfigured and the system retested. Changes too were needed in the missile autopilot, allowing it to discriminate between separate targets in close formation and that proved successful when Phoenix was retested and found capable of picking out a single target only 300ft (91m) away from another. At extreme range, Phoenix demonstrated that it could lock-on to, launch and hit a target across a range of 110nm (204km) and at an altitude varying between less than 50ft (15m)

The AIM-54 Phoenix is the teeth of the Tomcat's long-range air-defence potential and is seen here with its principle components (from left to right): seeker head, receiver–transmitter unit, electronics unit, electrical conversion unit, autopilot, hydraulic power supply, rear antenna mixer unit, battery and one of four hydraulic actuators for the four all-flying tail fins; behind the row of equipment are the shroud cable assemblies.

In repeated tests the Hughes AIM-54A has been proved a formidable and highly reliable missile system. Never yet fired in anger, the combination of AWG-9 radar and AIM-54 missile has been impressive in all tests and simulated combat scenarios.

above the waves to more than 82,000ft (24,850m) and travelling at a speed between 400kt (740km/hr) and Mach 3.

Specifically, in simulated attacks on MiG-25 interceptors, a Tomcat attacked a targeted Bomarc at Mach 2.7 and at more than 80,000ft (24,250m) to prove that this fastest of all Soviet combat aircraft could be defeated by Phoenix. In another test a simulated Soviet Tu-22M Backfire bomber, by the early 1970s a panic-maker in Western defence circles, was duplicated by a pilotless drone fitted with a noise jammer. It was flying at Mach 1.5 and 50,000ft (15,150m) when the Tomcat engaged and launched its Phoenix from 115nm (213km). Defined by an optimum energy management trajectory, the Phoenix lofted to 103,500ft (31,360m) and dived upon the target achieving a hit. A low-altitude hit was achieved on another flight against a simulated wave-hugging, anti-ship, cruise missile duplicated by a BQM-34 drone flying at 50ft (15m). From a distance of 22nm (41km) and a speed of Mach 0.72 at 10,000ft (3,030m) a Phoenix

was successfully launched to intercept and destroy the target.

In another test, a Tomcat flying at Mach 0.7 and a height of 10,000ft (3,030m) launched a Phoenix against a QF-86 which, just 16sec later, began a series of aggressive manoeuvres to wrestle free from the radar lock of the AWG-9. At 15,300ft (4,640m) and Mach 0.8 it pulled a tight 5 g manoeuvre, then entered a vertical dive and followed through with a 6 g pull-up to resume level flight at 9,100ft (2,760m) just seconds before the missile destroyed it. In yet another test a QF-9 flying at Mach 0.8 and 36,000ft (10,910m) was screened by a BQM-34A equipped with jammers flying 25nm (46km) behind and 500ft (152m) lower. Launched at 25nm the first Phoenix went for the QF-9 while the second, launched 9sec later, headed for the drone. Both were hit and destroyed. By the end of 1972 the test team was ready for a group shot and in December four drones were destroyed by a single Tomcat on one flight.

In a demonstration of simultaneous tracking and multiple launch against

selected targets, six Phoenixes were fired from a Tomcat, flown by Cdr John R. Wilson and his NFO Lt Cdr Jack H. Hawver, for the first time on 21 November 1973. Acquired when at distances of between 85 and 115nm (157 and 213km), all six targets were addressed with the Tomcat at a speed of Mach 0.8 at 28,000ft (8,500m) and all six missiles were fired in 37sec. The first three targets were chosen by the crew and the last three by the AWG-9 for their threat potential. The first missile was fired at a drone 30 to 50nm (56 to 93km) away and all six maintained satisfactory radar lock through flight. One drone malfunctioned and one Phoenix had an internal failure, but the remaining four targets were hit and destroyed.

Throughout the protracted sequence of flight tests and operational evaluation of aircraft, AWG-9 and Phoenix missile, thirteen multiple target attacks were conducted with eight demonstration attacks against two targets simultaneously, two demonstrations of attacks on four targets at the same time, and single demonstrations of attacks on three, five and six targets simultaneously. Against manoeuvring targets, three were from behind and three were from head-on, and in eleven low-altitude attacks, five were conducted against targets flying below 490ft (148m). In twelve attacks on high-altitude targets five were above 59,000ft (17,880m) and in fifteen attacks on long-range targets four were at ranges greater than 50nm (93km). To counter ECM threats, thirteen tests were performed under varying electromagnetic conditions with the AWG-9 breaking through or providing radar contact at all times.

A Harder Hit

From the outset, Hughes knew that, like the AWG-9 and all other missile families, the type would be updated, upgraded and modified as technical developments and Congressional budget-cutters allowed. During the early 1970s a series of improvements were identified and the engineering

development of what would emerge as the AIM-54C began in October 1976. The area of greatest improvement was in the guidance system, driven by newly-defined threats from Soviet cruise missiles and manned aircraft. The new Phoenix would get a strap-down, inertial reference unit, digital autopilot, programmable digital signal processor and a solid-state transmitter/receiver unit for the active radar terminal guidance seeker head. The areas of significant improvement included the greater range or altitude over which the missile could operate, thus enabling it to cope better with agile and highly manoevrable targets, and the enhanced electronic counter-ECM. AIM-54C has the ability to lock-on to and hold chase with small, low-flying targets and to discriminate between chaff and the real thing.

The first AIM-54C engineering development models were delivered in August 1979 and the last of fifteen for qualification and evaluation were handed over by the end of the following year. Results were

excellent, particularly with the deadly Motorola DSU-28C/B target-detecting proximity fuse which detonates the warhead when the missile arrives at the optimized distance from the target for the maximum effect of the charge. By early 1982 the Navy had received thirty pilot production rounds and technical evaluation began in 1983, followed a year later by operational trials. No sooner had this programme passed muster than Hughes began flight tests with a 'sealed' AIM-54C compatible with both the F-14A and the F-14D, featuring among other improvements internal heaters that relieved the F-14D of the need for the thermal conditioning of the missile's electronics before launch. Concern to get the AIM-54C into operational use followed the collapse of the Shah's reign in Iran and the possible migration of at least one Phoenix to the Soviet Union.

But Phoenix alone does not make a Tomcat and missiles costing more than $300,000 a shot (in 1970s money) are wasted on close-in threats. Medium-range

All stores stations are occupied by AIM-54 Phoenix missiles in this superb shot of an armed Tomcat. Rarely would an F-14 not carry self-defensive armament. The high-speed cruise configuration of the aircraft, seen from this angle, illuminates the variable ramps in the engine inlet which here are set to close for subsonic or transonic flight.

Clean for speed, this splendid underbody shot of an F-14A shows the Phoenix six-pack. Partly because Phoenix missiles are in the hands of an Iranian regime that professes hostility to the West, a considerably improved Phoenix, the AIM-54C, emerged in 1982 for flight trials at the Pacific Missile Test Center, Point Mugu.

targets are addressed by the AIM-7 Sparrow, a missile which, despite its vintage, had a growth potential which would keep it at the heart of the inventory. As related in Chapter 1, in a noteworthy precedent to the selection of six Phoenix missiles as the prime long-range weapon for each Tomcat, six Sparrow III (AIM-7C) missiles had been chosen in the mid-1950s as the long-range missile for what became the F-4 Phantom II. But of course the Tomcat had a gun from the outset! Sparrow was much bigger than any contemporary US air-to-air missile and spanned three generations of design and contractors. Developed in the 1940s by Sperry Gyroscope, the AIM-7A Sparrow I was powered by a solid-propellant rocket motor built by Aerojet and flew down a beam projected from the launch aircraft. It was in service by 1956 but already in need of a redesign and Douglas Aircraft had

funding to produce the AIM-7B Sparrow II.

Taking a leap into the future, Sparrow II had fully-active homing radar built by Westinghouse and a guidance pack from Bendix, but a year later it and the F5D Skylancer it was designed for were cancelled. There was a brief sequel when Canada took it over for the ambitious Avro Arrow but that too was cancelled in 1958 taking the missile with it. Enter AIM-7C Sparrow III, which began three years earlier in a design initiative at Raytheon, the last and enduring home of the family name. Sensibly opting for the more modest semi-active radar homing, AIM-7C set the design radar and guidance style for the next decade when it first entered service in 1958. Powered by an Aerojet solid-propellant rocket motor it was quickly replaced by the AIM-7D powered by a Thiokol storable-liquid-propellant motor giving a range

of 8nm (15km). It was selected in 1960 for the (eventually designated) USAF F-4 Phantom II. But it was the AIM-7E that would take off as the missile of the decade, despite its shortcomings.

The AIM-7E was powered by a Rocketdyne solid rocket motor had a range of about 14nm (26km) and, unlike its predecessors which had a high thrust, short burn time and glided most of the way to their targets, it had a lower thrust and longer burn duration to cut the period of unpowered flight. Yet it suffered from a heritage that defined the threat as a high-flying, subsonic bomber. Against fast, agile and highly manoeuvrable threats it was seriously outclassed and Vietnam proved its undoing. Convoluted excuses were forthcoming as to why Air Force and Navy pilots were not achieving the predicted kill levels with a missile useless below 5,000ft (1,520m) and against relatively slow but sporty aircraft. AIM-7E was not short on paper performance, achieving a terminal velocity of Mach 3.7 and carrying a 66lb (30kg) fragmentation warhead, but it lacked sophisticated guidance and a truly effective radar for rapidly moving targets changing direction in snap manoeuvres. Against relatively low-performance targets, it was easily outmanoeuvred and for the new generation of combat aircraft it was both aged and dated. Accordingly, some improvements were made in the E2 derivative by reducing its range and enhancing the manoeuvrability.

When the Tomcat came along its successor was in the Raytheon corporate plan and, against a challenge from General Dynamics, this stalwart Sparrow-builder received a contract to produce the much improved AIM-7F. More than merely an upgrade yet relegated by designation to merely a subvariant of the AIM-7, the new

model had a dual-thrust, Hercules-Aerojet Mk. 56 rocket motor with a continuous burn, solid-propellant charge, shaped and chemically structured to produce a high-thrust boost phase followed by a reduced thrust sustainer phase. The external dimensions remained the same but the weight went up by 51lb (23kg) taking it to 503lb (229kg). With an improved radome and conical-scan slotted antenna, it incorporated solid-state electronics and more powerful hydraulics for better agility to meet more manoeuvrable air threats. For the first time the warhead was relocated from behind the all-flying fins to a forward location just ahead of the hydraulic servo controls, allowing a bigger solid propellant charge and increasing the range. The warhead too was improved, packing a 85lb (39kg) continuous-rod charge with fragmentation pellets triggered by proximity or contact fuse.

All Sparrow missiles have a length of 11ft 10in (3.59m), a diameter of 8in (20.3cm), a wing span of 3ft 4in (1m) and a tail span of 2ft 7in (0.78m). The range of the AIM-7F is nominally about 16nm (30km) but the exact figure depends greatly on the direction and angle of attack. In tail engagements the missile had a range of only 4 to 6nm (7.4 to 11km) due to the reduced velocity differential between the launch aircraft and the target. Equipped with electronics to handle signals from the AWG-9, the AIM-7F was also fitted with a processor to receive range information before firing, which allows the seeker head to obtain its own post-launch range data and punch through tougher ECM environments. Early Sparrows measured a reflected signal from the target with one received from the launch aircraft relayed to the missile via a small rear-facing antenna. AIM-7F became available to the

A standard mix of air defence and offence weaponry for a CAP or fleet defence role would see, typically, four AIM-54 Phoenixes, two AIM-7 Sparrows and two AIM-9 Sidewinders together with long-range drop tanks. In this configuration the Tomcat can look after the dogfighting aggressor, extend its range and go for an enemy coming in fast at great range, high or low. There is no other aircraft in the world that can yet duplicate this capability.

Product of a long history and much development over several decades, the AIM-7 Sparrow has stood the test of time. Originally selected as the prime armament for the Tomcat's predecessor the F-4, Sparrow continues to evolve and F-14 deployment forced a significant redesign which considerably increased its performance.

Tomcat during the late 1970s and was replaced in the 1980s by the AIM-7M, which has the added sophistication of an inverse monpulse seeker, highly resistant to heavy ECM, and a greatly enhanced look-down capability.

In tests with Tomcat units air crew routinely demonstrated that, with the powerful AWG-9 radar, the missile range was consistently about 40 per cent better than the range figures taken as standard for all other aircraft, a figure that should be added to those for Sparrow variants given earlier. So it was with the Tomcat's short-range claws, the AIM-9 Sidewinder. That missile has a long history too and its early development has been described in Chapter 1. When the F-14A began flight trials in 1971 the Navy had the second-

generation series Sidewinder typified by AIM-9G, H and J models. The first generation series perfected through the C, D and E models had progressively more advanced electronics and expanded capability. With the AIM-9G, which entered service in 1970, the missile received the Sidewinder Expanded Acquisition Mode (SEAM), comprising a much improved seeker head, and with the H model Sidewinder got solid-state electronics for the first time. The J model is essentially a reworked B model incorporating part solid-state electronics with range being forfeited for speed.

As Tomcat flight tests progressed, the AIM-9L model was undergoing final qualification as the third generation Sidewinder. It would enter service in 1976 with a more powerful motor, improved

tracking and manoeuvrability and an all-aspect attack capability, the first Sidewinder capable of attacking from any angle, including head-on. It had a more advanced optical fuse, greater resistance to ECM and used AM–FM scan pattern to increase seeker sensitivity and give better tracking stability. The AIM-9L went a long way toward the procurement of a common dogfighting missile for both the Air Force and the Navy and it helped to meet demanding·new requirements by altering the familiar triangular fin shape to improve manoeuvrability. In addition, the L model had an improved annular blast fragmentation warhead. Joint service evaluation was completed during 1975 and Tomcats began to receive the new missile through the usual Navy inventories immediately.

New performance capabilities and technical opportunities opened up by the Tomcat's air weapons systems argued for a radically new short- and medium-range missile to replace the Sidewinder. In 1968 the US Navy began development of the AIM-95 Agile AAM and in 1973 Hughes Aircraft was selected to provide the guidance package. A year later Thiokol was selected to produce a solid-propellant, thrust-vectoring rocket motor. As conceived, Agile was to have high g turn capability with greater seek angles than any other missile had, utilizing an infra-red homing head. Plans were made for growth versions incorporating electro-optical heads and even an RF anti-radiation homing system. Tests began during 1974 and in flight trials the missile and its revolutionary hydraulically-actuated gimbal nozzle performed well. More than 1.5 million simulated motor firings were successfully completed before the House Armed Services Committee cancelled the project, leaving the Navy to fall back on the further development of the Sidewinder family.

In 1978, two years after the L model entered service, deliveries began of the AIM-9P which was an upgrade on the longer-range J model but with an active optical target detector and modified exhaust nozzle and propellant base to inhibit smoke emission. Later variants of the P model incorporated better infra-red acquisition and guidance capability. Each model successively offered up for use by F-14s gained from the AWG-9 and modifications to the aircraft's radar matched improvements in the missiles carried by the Tomcat. In that way reciprocal advances were made in a seamless welding of technical and operational upgrades rarely seen in any other combat aeroplane and probably matched only by the F-15 Eagle and the F/A-18 Hornet. In the 1990s Tomcats fly with new variants of the AIM-9P family of Sidewinder derivatives which feature improved rocket motors and better radar and guidance electronics.

The sole function of a combat aeroplane is to deliver ordnance or carry armament. Nothing is more important, although enthusiasts and devotees of aeronautical design and type development would argue that the delivery system is vastly more aesthetic and probably more interesting than the stores it is built to carry. However, that is a fact of life: the combat aeroplane

More than 11ft (3m) in length the Sparrow derivative used by the F-14 has a range in excess of that available with other aircraft because the unique Tomcat radar adds 40 per cent to the missile's radius of action.

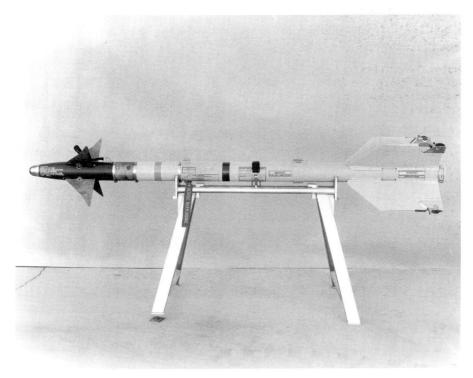

New for Tomcat too were its short-range claws, the latest version of the Sidewinder, the AIM-9L. The first of its type to have the capacity to attack from any angle, this version has improved seekers and better guidance.

are returned to the ammunition drum which eliminates the need for a separate storage case. Because they will be withdrawn in their entirety, this also prevents the gun from jamming if reject rounds find their way into the breech. With this suite of armament the Tomcat is the only fighter in the world that can address imminent threats from a distance of a few score feet to a range of more than 100 miles (160km) and perform dogfight tangles or counterair suppression missions with long-range missiles.

Computers for the Cat

Weapons system sensors, data, information and displays are all, ultimately, linked to the Computer Signal Data Converter (CSDC) which takes information from a wide range of systems and translates it into a common language. Other systems too feed into the link and provide valuable roles to make the whole package work. There is the Central Air Data Computer, or CADC, which has at its heart an AiResearch CP-1166B/A, which takes information from pitot, temperature, AoA and pressure sensors to select the optimum wing-sweep angle and sends its decisions to the Air Inlet Control System (AICS), which controls the engine inlet ramp angles. Two AICS computers are independently governed by the differences in conditions at the two separate inlet faces, fine tuning the ramp angles according to the condition in that particular box. In turn, the CADC provides information to many other systems which depend upon it for their own unique functions.

Navigation systems are particularly interbred on the Tomcat, taking data from an unusually wide range of equipments. The prime system is the ASN-92(V) CAINS II (Carrier Aircraft Inertial, Navigation System II) which comprises a ASN-90 Inertial Measurement Unit (IMU), a Litton LC-728 nav-computer, control indicators and converter amplifiers, and a link into the AWG-9 to tap some of its extra computing capability. Before flight the Tomcat's INS takes data from the Ship's Inertial Navigation System (SINS) through a microwave link and sometimes adds several waypoints. The IMU takes data on x, y and z axial velocities, primary pitch and roll measurements and true heading and consults the navigation section in the CSDC to perform

Attached to the outer stores pylon of a Tomcat, station 1A, the AIM-9L has proved itself in combat against Libyan fighters and is putting in an impressive performance record for maintainability and reliability.

is a bomb truck and a missile or gun platform and the crew are there to prevail in their environment so that those stores can get to their assigned destinations. The British at this time opted for gun armament as well as missiles on the English Electric Lightning, but McDonnell Aircraft and the Navy declined to put a gun on the F-4 Phantom II. Doomed by an edict that missiles would replace manned combat aircraft, the Lightning was the last all-British fighter while the Americans saw the error of their ways in Vietnam and put a gun on the F-4, producing a variant that outsold all the others combined. Ironically, it was the Air Force that demanded a gun

for the Phantom but for the VFX specification the Navy stipulated a gun for the F-14 from the outset.

The extremely powerful General Electric 20mm M61A1 Vulcan gun has a length of 6ft 2in (1.87m) and a weight of 265lb (120.5kg) and operates on the principle of the Gatling gun, normally firing 6,000 rounds/min at a muzzle velocity of about 3,400ft/sec (2,318 mph). The original design incorporated a linkless feed system with a capacity for 950 rounds but later this was reduced to 675 rounds. The gun is installed in the port side of the forward fuselage and, to prevent the ingestion of cases ejected from the aircraft, they

Missed Opportunity

Almost from the outset, the Tomcat fought a hard fight to retain its primary role as fleet air defence fighter against pressure from the Air Force for the Navy to buy the F-15 Eagle. Only when the aircraft began to enter service and become operational did opposition subside. In the early 1970s the direction of the attack was reversed and Grumman went on the offensive to seek a place in the Air Force inventory by putting up the F-14 as a candidate for the Improved Manned Interceptor (IMI) requirement. IMI was to serve a need that was diminishing with each passing year for a Command that would become extinct in 1980. But in the early 1970s it was a potentially lucrative market for large-volume production.

The IMI specification defined the aircraft that would replace the F-106, a mainstay of Air Defense Command formed in 1946 as one of three combat commands, the others being Tactical Air Command and Strategic Air Command. ADC was to stay at home and protect the continental USA from attack across the Arctic Circle, while TAC and SAC went overseas to fight the big one on foreign soil. Operating through a large number of air defence radars, ADC had a variety of aircraft and acquired an all-weather role in 1950. By the end of the decade the principle aircraft in Air Defense Command was the transonic F-102, modified in 1955 into the fully supersonic (Mach 2) F-106 with a wasted area-rule fuselage. It was as a replacement for the F-106 that the IMI requirement was written. Grumman

used the original Model 303E mock-up as the basis for its IMI contender, adding huge conformal fuel tanks to extend the range while retaining the awesome AWG-9/Phoenix missile combination to extend the tradition of the long-range missile intercept pioneered by the Falcon family on other jets.

Belt-tightening by the Nixon administration prevented IMI from moving into procurement. The F-14 was ideal for this role but high costs and a natural aversion to buy Navy prevented the Air Force from getting the Tomcat. The ADC replacement was redefined (in effect putting off a decision and spending money on paper studies instead of metal aeroplanes) for several years. Now known as Aerospace Defense Command, ADC wrote the requirement for a Follow-On Interceptor (FOI) and in the mid-1970s the Defense Department ordered the Air Force to consider several types including the Navy's F-14 and F/A-18 as well as the F-15 and the F-16. Not surprisingly – having already bought the Navy F-4 – the Air Force wanted to stay with landplane technology and selected the F-15, but there were dissident viewpoints. In 1977 Gen Daniel James, head of North American Air Defense Command, openly campaigned for the F-14 and quoted Air Force studies which revealed the Tomcat to be the best buy for the job.

ADC wanted about 170 interceptors to equip its F-106 wings but other studies showed that this number of F-15s would cost $3.9 billions whereas an equal number of F-14s would cost

$4.3 billions. What the Air Force did not reveal so readily was the unavoidable fact that 290 Eagles would be needed to do the job of the 170 Tomcats. When judged on the basis of getting the job done rather than costing equivalent numbers of aircraft, the total price for an Eagle-based re-equipment would be more than $6.6 billions, an increase of $2.3 billions over that of the F-14. In other studies conducted by Grumman, air kills against penetrating Backfire bombers were 50 per cent higher with the F-14 compared with the F-15's results. In a hundred four-ship attack missions against Backfires taking strong evasive action, the F-14 kill rate was 70 per cent compared with 40 per cent for the F-15.

One added capability denied to the F-15 was the way in which F-14s could be used in a datalink relay mode. Flights of Tomcats each scanning more than 200 miles (320km) from side to side could detect incoming targets and pass target information through the aircraft datalink system to others, selecting targets for attack while handing others on to Tomcats closer in. Minimal changes would have been necessary for overland, rather than over-water, radar and an Air Force flight refuelling receptacle would have been added to the wing glove. In defending the F-15 as a suitable FOI, the Air Force studied again the use of AWG-9 and Phoenix on board Eagles, concluding that they would make them overweight and under-ranged. The Air Force quickly dropped that idea, cut back on its requirements menu and bought F-15As.

---

position predictions. Access to the TACAN signal is obtained through the Gould ARN-84 operating in the 0.932–1.213 GHz region and interfaces with the CSDC to provide slant range and bearing information to beacons or ground stations.

The Aircraft Approach Control System (AACS) obtains microwave transmissions from ship or shore through the AN/ARA-63 which puts the aircraft into the azimuth and elevation signals on twenty channels. Decoded signals are displayed on cross-hairs in the cockpit. Voice communications are handled through UHF radio but coded transmissions go via a KY-58 cryptographic device, a 9lb (4kg) solid-state radio with 7,000 channels and 10W output. In the late 1980s the standard ARC-51A UHF radio was replaced by the ARC/192 combined VHF/UHF set. High-speed digital data ship-to-air are managed by linking up to the Airborne Tactical Data System (ATDS) which connects the

This close-in shot of the port underside of the wing/fuselage juncture of an F-14A displays the shape of the main landing gear doors, stores pylon, glove vane and landing gear, inboard of which is a standard drop tank.

From the outside in, stores include a weapons mix of Sidewinders, Sparrows and Phoenixes on a Tomcat operated by VF-84, the 'Jolly Rogers', who first took their F-14s to sea in December 1977 when they partnered VF-41, the 'Black Aces', aboard the Nimitz.

F-14 to a Grumman E-2C Hawkeye EW aircraft or the Naval Tactical Data System (NTDS) on the carrier. Aircraft have uniquely coded electronic addresses which allow messages to be sent from the ship to a particular aircraft within one second and this may be used to provide information on targets, which significantly adds to the aircraft's potential identification range.

Data links handled by the ASW-27B send information from the F-14 to the E-2C providing the EW aircraft with the fighter's position, altitude and speed, while data from the E-2C about targets are sent straight to the F-14's AWG-9. In this way the E-2C can manage the air threats for the individual aircraft or for a squadron, vectoring aircraft into appropriate posi-

tions to defend specific sectors. AWG-9 data on targets are also sent through the secure data link to the E-2C, enabling it to update its own target and traffic management information system. Sometimes information about threats comes from ECM and radar warning receivers on the F-14 and there is a potentially prolific array of bolt-on packs to give the Tomcat warning. Traditionally, the Air Force has favoured external packs but the Navy likes to put this equipment internally and these are linked to chaff dispensers, jammers and flares. When the F-14 first entered service it had standard APR-25 and APR-27 radar warning receivers but during the 1980s aircraft received the Magnavox ALR-50 which provide the crew with warning of hostile missile launches. As Soviet threats emerged, the electronics was updated and improved to keep ahead of the challenge and by the early 1990s F-14D Tomcats had the ALR-67.

All the computers noted so far are digital but the Tomcat came into service with three analogue computers. One is known as the Automatic Flight Control System (AFCS), also linked to the CSDC, which gives automatic commands for direction, altitude and heading. It incorporates the Stability Augmentation System, responsible for augmentation and damping in pitch, roll and yaw, and the autopilot. The Fuel Quantity Management System, also an analogue computer, adjusts the fuel levels in a number of tanks according to centre of gravity changes or shuts off selected flow routes if tanks are damaged in combat. Finally, the Aileron Rudder Interconnect (ARI) interacts with the AFCS to control rudder movements at high angles of attack and inhibit spin tendency. The AWG-9 itself is diagnostic, self-testing thirty-one black boxes that form its own functional sub-assemblies. A separate computer, the AWG-15, is responsible for firing the missiles when the information provided by the AWG-9 and the CSDC converges through pilot-selected options to authorize computer-controlled launches.

Reliability

Throughout the long and protracted period of testing, the superior performance of the Tomcat over the Phantom became evident from the flight results. As a weapon system the F-14 was only as effective as its airframe, engine and its suite of radar and electronic warfare aids. The airframe was superb, the weapons and the electronics were more than adequate, but the engine was the Achilles' heel. In fact, as related earlier, Grumman had never expected to use the TF30 throughout the programme and planned to adopt the Pratt & Whitney F401-PW-400, itself a development of the JTF-22 Advanced Technology Engine. Flight trials with the early pre-production F-14A series demonstrated how good the Tomcat was compared with the F-4, but the F-14B variant with the more powerful engine was awaited with relish. Early Tomcats utilized the standard TF30-PW-412 engine but after the first twenty aircraft had been delivered Tomcats from Block 65 had the improved P-412A and deliveries began with aircraft No.21 in December 1972.

Through the experiences of F-111 units, reliability had not been a proud feature of the TF30 but as flight time built up on the F-14 the engine seemed to perform well in this aircraft at least. All the effort put in at Grumman to come up with a better inlet ingestion tract, spacing the engines widely apart to eliminate boundary bleed, seemed to have paid off. Then, in April 1974, after about 30,000 flight hours in Tomcats, engines began to shed fan blades. As specified, the TF30 had been built without a containment casing and whirling blades cut through to the surrounding structure, endangering critical systems. By the end of the year fan blade failure was emerging as a serious problem. On 2 January 1975, F-14A No.43 (BuAer No. 158982) operating with VF-1 aboard the carrier *Enterprise* was lost when a blown engine severed critical systems and caused the pilot to eject. Twelve days later aircraft No.62 (BuAer No. 159001) from the same unit suffered an identical fate. Each aircraft had fewer than 300 hours on the clock.

Responding quickly, the Navy issued a maintenance instruction that after every 100 flight hours the engines would be completely stripped, with the compressor casings being opened and the fan blades inspected for flaws or stress. All bleed ducts

The Grumman E-2C dates back to the mid-1950s and is designed totally around the 24ft (7.3m) diameter rotodome containing the AN/APS-96 search radar, even to the extent of having four fins to get the required area while maintaining a reduced height. The type entered service in 1964 and found its perfect stablemate in the Tomcat, the only fleet defence fighter capable of using its full capability.

It had always been the Navy's intention to follow the F-14A with the F-14B and fit what it originally considered as the definitive Tomcat with the more powerful Pratt & Whitney F401 but that was cancelled. Turning to the F101 DFE engine in 1980, the original F-14B prototype (the seventh YF-14A) was fitted with that engine and named the F-14B Super Tomcat.

were to be examined and fuel lines were to be checked. *Enterprise* was in the Indian Ocean when this procedure took place *en route* to provide disaster relief to the island of Mauritius struck on 6 February by typhoon 'Gervaise'. Along with other carriers the *Enterprise* was passing through the Indian Ocean on its way to cover the American evacuation of Saigon in South Vietnam. The 100hr inspection was at best a stopgap measure but failures persisted, with two more aircraft lost by the summer and two suffering on-board fires in flight. The manufacturer protested that a subcontractor was responsible for imperfect fan blades and the Navy issued further instructions to check these critical components.

Over the next eighteen months Pratt & Whitney worked at a modified TF30 design which was to incorporate a fan

blade containment shell and new blades with increased tip radius made from a modified titanium alloy. In addition, a fire-extinguishing system was designed into the aircraft with ablative coatings applied to critical areas in the nacelle. The modified engine, designated TF30-P-414, was introduced along with associated improvements to the Block 95 production line with aircraft No.252 (BuAer No. 160396) and retrofitted to earlier aircraft. But this did nothing to help to alleviate another problem: a propensity to compressor stall which tended to be somewhat indiscriminate in its timing. The tendency was so common that special crew instructions were written up to counter compressor stalls at several places in the flight envelope. For instance, at supersonic speed the event was characterized by a loud bang, increased turbine inlet temperature and a

slow decay in the engine rpm, while a pronounced buzz gave the crew a bumpy flight. At low speeds and high altitude the stall was inaudible while at high AoA the aircraft had a tendency to slice in yaw.

While these compressor stalls were annoying they could be debilitating in combat, requiring the pilot to off-load g forces and prevent the aircraft from departing into a spin, cutting throttles to inhibit asymmetric thrust and chop the combustor flame to prevent overheating. An engine windmill restart was possible given ample height and speed or the pilot could recycle through a spooled start. Typically, pilots could expect a compressor stall on average every 500hr, but with new procedures and handling by 1980 this had dropped to one incident in 1,000hr. But still the P-414 engine introduced in 1977 did little to alleviate this tendency, which

The F-14B Super Tomcat made its first flight with the General Electric F101 DFE engine on 14 July 1981 and its performance was so good that its production derivative, the F110-GE-100, was assigned to the definitive Tomcat variant F-14D. It was also to be used for an interim variant, the F-14A+, redesignated on 1 May 1991 as a new F-14B which had nothing to do with the previous two with the same designation.

The General Electric F101 DFE engine originated when a common powerplant to replace the TF30 in the F-14 and the F100 in the F-16 was sought by a joint Navy/Air Force team. GE got the development contract for the engine when it was determined that Pratt & Whitney had a potential monopoly on the market.

was a basic TF30 family trait, responsible for as many as one in four of the Tomcats lost in training flights or operational exercises. As for the much vaunted and extremely powerful F401 engine tested in the No.7 prototype, that brought little succour to thrust-hungry members of the Tomcat club.

As early as 12 September 1973 Tomcat No.7 had taken to the air for the first time powered by two F401 turbofans, but troubles dogged the trials and the engine failed its certification tests two years later. This was not an exclusive Navy problem. The Air Force had more than its fair share of troubles with the F100, which, like its stablemate, had originated with the

JTF-22 ATE. Eventually the F100 came through and powered both principal USAF fighters, the F-15 Eagle and the F-16 Falcon. However, in the mid-1970s, coming hard on the heels of Grumman's protracted financial crisis, F-14 programme cost escalation and problems with the TF30, the Navy wisely decided that it would be better to bury the F-14B and its overrated engine quietly and stick with the TF30.

Not that the Navy had been clamouring for the new engine. As early as 1971 it told Grumman that the F-14B would not automatically follow the F-14A in a procurement option which would only be taken up if threats emerging in the 1980s

warranted the additional cost of development. This had not worked in Grumman's favour when it went on the road with its proposed F-14B, seriously considered by Australia. When work on the F401 was cancelled, the prototype F-14B was retired to storage from where it would be resurrected as a test bed for the unsuccessful General Electric F101 Derivative Fighter Engine (DFE) six years later and go on to fly with the awesome General Electric F110-PW-400, the powerplant for the F-14D.

Meanwhile, left without the power to give the Tomcat its performance potential, the Navy struggled on with the TF30, a legacy from F-111B days when Grumman

TARPS

A vital part of the US Navy mission is to project air power to places far removed from friendly airfields. To do that the carrier battle group supports attack squadrons which cannot function effectively without adequate reconnaissance information. The need for dedicated aircraft to carry out these duties grew during the Vietnam War and a new generation of sensors evolved as requirements increased. Historically, Navy aircraft built for another purpose have been adapted for reconnaissance duties and when the Tomcat began to enter service the ageing RF-8 Crusader and RA-5C Vigilante were inadequate for the job. At first Grumman proposed a dedicated reconnaissance version of the Tomcat, the RF-14A, fitted with an internal sensor suite, but the outright cost of the aircraft and the inflexibility of dedicated roles eliminated that prospect. In the mid-1970s a decision was made to develop a special sensor suite for the F-14 which could be carried on a stores point without compromising the aircraft's primary mission. Because it allowed the Navy to have one aircraft for two roles there was a certain economy in this, but

the measure was considered to be only a temporary expedient before the RF-18 entered service late in the 1980s.

In 1976 work began on a technology designed to provide optical reconnaissance in the visible and the infra-red portion of the spectrum, carried within a pod the size of a Tomcat under-fuselage fuel tank. It is known as the Tactical Air Reconnaissance Pod System (TARPS). Fitted to the rear left under-fuselage station, it has a minimal effect on aircraft performance and allows the F-14 to carry a variable assortment of missiles. TARPS is 17ft (5.2m) in length, weighs 1,750lb (795kg) and carries a KS-87B oblique camera for forward and vertical shots, together with a KA-99 panoramic camera taking strip images 180 degrees in scan. In addition, the pod incorporates a AAD-5A infra-red imager together with associated subsystems including AN/ASQ-172 data-handling processors and links to the Control Processor Signal situated to one side of the rear cockpit seat. The pod also contains a window anti-fog device. Crew equipment includes a data display link to the Tactical Information Display, providing

status information and an optical image of the infra-red field of view.

TARPS tests began during 1977. These were sufficiently successful to warrant a purchase decision in 1978 with the programme entering into full-scale production during 1979. The first TARPS pods were converted Tomcat fuel tanks but later ones were purpose-built. F-14A Tomcats began to receive the TARPS pod conversion in 1980 and were operational with this equipment from 1981. The first Tomcat to get TARPS was aircraft No.315 (BuAer No.160696), the last of the Block 100 production lot. The next was No.339 (BuAer No.160910 from Block 105) and in all forty-five F-14As were equipped to carry the pod. Seven more F-14As received the modification retrospectively. Beginning in 1986, a programme of equipping F-14A(Plus) conversions in the KB series began which resulted in a limited number of aircraft (eventually known as F-14B) having TARPS capability. As built, all F-14Ds came off the production line equipped to carry TARPS.

TF30-P-414A

Because of blade problems with the original TF30 engine, improved versions were developed culminating in the TF30-P-414A seen here with greatly improved combustion stability and much reduced compressor stall, a characteristic which blighted the original version of the engine. The Navy began to received the P-414A model in 1984, securing from Pratt & Whitney a ten-year life warranty

newly installed TF30-P-414A engines and on the first 122 engines retrofitted to earlier Tomcats.

New Engines

The desirability of an improved powerplant for Navy Tomcats and high performance Air Force fighters converged in an interservice determination to produce a new engine. After futile attempts in the mid-1970s at starting a new high performance engine programme of its own, the Navy agreed to team with the Air Force to produce a Derivative Fighter Engine (DFE). The DFE would adapt the General Electric F101 into a powerplant for the new fighters by scaling up the fan and the exhaust nozzle. GE's F101 had evolved from its GE9 demonstrator engine of 1965, through the USAF Advanced

sought to minimize the risk inherent in bringing together a completely new airframe with a totally new engine. In fact, it had been wise to do so; had it relied on the F401 the Tomcat would never have got off the drawing board. As it was, the improved TF30-P-414 brought a measurable improvement to the engine's reliability and maintenance standard when it appeared in 1977. Five years later Pratt & Whitney began a $50 million reworking of this engine into the definitive P-414A,

improving the repair interval to 2,400hr and giving it a greatly improved combustion stability and relative freedom from compressor stall. This variant of the engine produced much less smoke than the standard P-414 and gave the pilot freedom to gun the throttle and perform high-alpha manoeuvres without fear of flow problems on the compressor face. So confident was the manufacturer that when deliveries began in 1984 the Navy got a warranty of ten years or 3,000hr on the first ninety-five

Turbine Gas Generator programme, into a suitable powerplant for the Air Force AMSA, which would emerge after lengthy gestation as the B-1. For high subsonic cruise, fuel efficiency and high initial thrust, the F101 had a relatively high bypass ratio for military aircraft and a thrust level of 17,000 or 30,000lb (75.6 and 133.5kN) with afterburner. It suited the long-range bomber mission but not the high performance fighter role.

Engine testing began in October 1971 and full F101 trials got under way in April 1972, followed by qualification tests eighteen months later. Powered by four F101s, the first B-1 took off on 23 December 1974 and the engine's critical design review was held in August 1975. Product verification certificates were signed in August 1976, GE began a sustained engineering development programme and a B-1 production commitment was given three months later. The plan envisaged 241 B-1s in service by 1985. Then President Carter was elected and evinced radically different views on national defence. In June 1977, five months after being sworn in as the thirty-ninth President, he cancelled the B-1 and dashed prospects for the production of more than 1,000 F101 engines for the strategic bomber. The time was right to use this powerful base of engineering knowledge and apply it to needs elswhere in the defence programme.

Although more powerful than the TF30-P-414A, the F101 was not designed for the energy profile appropriate for modern fighters but the Defense Department was concerned that Pratt & Whitney had a monopoly on the market. Encouraged by both services and determined to exploit F101 work in the wake of the cancelled B-1, General Electric performed demonstrator tests on an F101 fighter derivative in 1977 and 1978 and released flight engine design drawings in October 1978. In March 1979 the Defense Department awarded General Electric a $79.9 million, thirty-months contract to build three F101 DFE powerplants. Up to this date, the most powerful fighter engine built by GE had been the F404 class which delivered 16,000lb (71.2kN) thrust. Its precursor, the YJ101, had been installed in the Northrop F-530 Cobra and the YF-17 Lightweight Fighter contender and the F404 would eventually power the F-18 Hornet and the F-117A stealth fighter-bomber. Much of the engineering and the technology that went into the original

F101 and the F404 engine were applied to the F101 DFE.

The basic F101 was a twin-spool turbofan with a bypass ratio of 2:1. It had two fan compressor stages and nine high-pressure compressor stages driven by two low-pressure stages and one high-pressure stage. The DFE version retained the F101 core virtually intact and lowered the bypass ratio to 0.85:1. With an additional fan stage the overall pressure ratio was increased to 30:1, giving a higher thrust at military power but approximately 10 per cent less in afterburner. Directed by Air

Force Systems Command at Wright Patterson Air Force Base, the F101 DFE moved ahead rapidly on the back of the early demonstrator work in 1977–78 with two F101-X engines. The first of the three F101 DFE engines was committed to systems testing, the second for mission trials and the third for high-altitude tests at the Navy Air Propulsion Test Center at Trenton, New Jersey. The second engine was stripped after completing 1,000 test hours in simulated ground-based fighter operations and thoroughly inspected and examined before being reassembled

A series of upgrades embracing propulsion and sensor suites characterized developments in the Tomcat programme throughout the 1980s. Upgrades to the Television Camera System, seen here as the optical sensor below the nose, coupled to an infra-red tracker of improved performance extended the mission capabilities.

A catapult officer signals with two fingers that everything is ready to cat-launch this F-14A from the deck of the Saratoga.

and rerun a further 1,000hr under simulated F-14A conditions.

For almost four years the F101 DFE was put through a rigorous and demanding series of tests and trials with extensive engineering work to refine and optimize the design around the broad performance requirements of Navy and Air Force fighters. But it need not have taken that long. In the 1978 elections the American people rejected President Carter and chose a Republican President with radically different views on foreign policy and defence issues. During 1981 the B-1 was reinstated for a modified and updated role and a hundred B-1B Lancer bombers were ordered. GE now had the orders for the F101 that would have an advantageous effect on the unit costs for the F101 DFE,

which would be redesignated F110 for its modified fighter applications.

Flight tests with the F101 DFE were to be performed by No.7 YF-14A, previously assigned to be the prototype for the aborted F-14B. Under the name 'Super Tomcat', it would perform a thorough programme of flight trials with the new engine. That path was cleared by flight tests in an F-16 which began on 19 December 1980 and were completed at the end of May the following year. In fifty-eight flights lasting 75hr a group of twenty test pilots flew the first full-scale development F-16 (FSD F-16A, 75-0745, rolled out on 20 October 1976, the third F-16 following two YF-16 prototypes), designated F-16/101, to demonstrate the engine's performance and integration qualities.

Comprehensive performance testing uncovered some vulnerable areas of the envelope but these were plugged by tweaking the technology. Infra-red signature readings, re-lights from altitudes as low as 5,000ft (1,515m) and sustained climbing turns drew a profile of engine performance that gave great promise for the Tomcat. In reality, the new engine did not do as much for the F-16 as it would for the F-14, and in anticipation of putting it through its paces, the Navy dusted off the No.7 YF-14A and brought it out for trials.

With two F101-DFE engines installed, the 'Super Tomcat' took to the Calverton skies on 14 July 1981 at the start of a short flight-test programme that lasted ten weeks. Grumman pilots flew the YF-14A during twenty-nine test missions and Navy

The 'Wolfpack' Squadron, VF-1, shares deck space with an EA-6B Prowler and a Corsair. Squadron markings reflect the period, these bright colours getting a tone-down during the late 1980s and the early 1990s.

pilots flew a further five flights logging 70hr. Apparent from the outset were the significant advantages brought by the more powerful engine. Rated at 20,900lb (93kN) thrust with reheat the TF30 had a specific fuel consumption of 2.78lb/hr/lb while the F101-DFE with augmented thrust of 27,400lb (122kN) has a comparable figure of 2.011lb/hr/lb. At an intermdiate throttle level of 12,350lb (55kN) thrust the TF30 has an SFC of 0.69lb/hr/lb, while the F101 at the same percentage setting has a thrust of 16,400lb (73kN) and an SFC of 0.66lb/hr/lb. These figures translate into mission examples of comparative capabilities. With a standard CAP load of four AIM-54 Phoenix, two AIM-9L Sidewinders and two AIM-7F Sparrows and with two 280 US gall (1,061 l) fuel

tanks, the F101-DFE powered Tomcat would have an endurance of 90min at a radius of 300nm (555km) from the carrier, compared with 48min for a TF30-powered Tomcat.

Performance enhancement was spectacular in six ways: specific excess energy was increased by 22 per cent over the TF30 (combat manoeuvring energy was raised by that amount); afterburner SFC was reduced by 30 per cent; carrier take-offs could be made at military power without afterburner, thereby reducing night glare and intense infra-red signatures from a great distance; time to altitude was cut by 61 per cent; the combat air patrol radius was increased by 35 per cent, making the aircraft a much more effective air superiority system; and fuel consumption was

dramatically reduced giving the Tomcat a 62 per cent increase in deck launch intercept radius. Another gain was the ability to execute a single-engine climb at maximum gross weight using intermediate power, a feat calling for full reheat with the TF30. At least of equal interest, reliability was very high. Of 445 test reheat light-ups 432 were successful the first time and of the remaining thirteen only seven failed to light at the second attempt. In emergencies the F-14 proved that it could be equally reliable. In thirty-three attempts at cross-bleed relights from a simulated failed engine the procedure failed to get the engine going only once.

It was just what Grumman had always wanted and thus powered a derivative Tomcat would outpace even the original

F-14B with the F401. But the Pentagon is nothing if not cautious. While ground and flight tests proved the engine's worth, engineering evolution to transform the F101-DFE into a production engine potentially fit for large-scale procurement had yet to take place – as had a commitment to buy the engine. Full-scale development began in October 1982 but a competitor emerged in the form of a developed and more powerful variant of the F100, the PW1128 from Pratt & Whitney. Bearing the military designation F100 EMD, this engine had an increased output delivering an augmented thrust of 27,400lb versus 23,800lb (122 and 106kN) for the standard F100 selected for the F-15 and the F-16. Pratt had started work on the PW1128 in 1980 and by 1983 four engines had notched up 1,200hr of sea-level testing when tests in a USAF F-15 got under way.

By this time the Air Force had decided to split propulsion procurement for the F-15 and the F-16 between manufacturers and in mid-1982 announced that they were in the running for around a thousand engines between 1985 and 1987. The US Navy followed with a commitment to competitive evaluations in its selection of a successor engine to the TF30 and considered the idea of using late production Tomcats for fit-check and engine mock-up evaluation of the F110 and the PW1128. On 18 May 1983 the USAF formally asked both Pratt & Whitney and General Electric to come up with proposals for the competing engines. The Navy decided that it would save money and go with the Air Force choice and on 3 February 1984 the decision was made. General Electric received an order for 120 F110-GE-100 engines for F-16s, 75 per cent of an order which also included Pratt & Whitney F100 engines.

It took the Navy just five months to decide on a F-14 upgrade programme, including procurement of the F-110-GE-400 series engine and an announcement to that effect was made in July 1984. This variant of the F-110 was almost identical with the Air Force equivalent but tailored to the F-14. Grumman was given approval to develop the next generic step in Tomcat evolution with the F-14D, incorporating the new engine and other upgrades and improvements to enhance the production aircraft considerably. As an interim measure a subvariant of the F-14A, known as the F-14A(Plus), would be deployed, bringing together the standard airframe with the new engine and some basic, low-cost changes. The two-tier upgrade programme would ensure that fleet fighters received the more powerful engine more quickly than if they waited for the F-14D, a pressure brought on by concerns at an escalating Soviet maritime challenge from an expanded warm-water navy. The Reagan administration was in no mood to compromise on the defence of the sea lanes. The Navy intended to retrofit all F-14A(Plus) aircraft to F-14D standard when production of the latter was in full swing.

Central to the new generation of Tomcats was the installation of the F110-GE-400 which was almost interchangeable with the TF30-P-414A. The most notice-

A VF-102 'Diamondback' Tomcat turns swiftly to port on full reheat as it climbs away from the catapult.

able feature of the new engine was its compact size and reduced length, 15ft 2in (4.6m) compared with 19ft 8in (6m) for the TF30. This brought special problems because of the mechanical mismatch between the two engines. If the exhaust nozzle were placed in the appropriate position for the basic design of the airframe the engine would be too far to the rear and upset the inlet flow geometry and adversely affect the aircraft's centre of gravity. In the No.7 YF-14A engineers installed the engine aft of its nominal position, adding forward ballast to maintain balance, a method acceptable for tests but totally unsuitable for operational aircraft. The solution was obtained by adding a 4ft 2in (1.3m) long adapter between the engine and the afterburner section, thus extending its length. The heavy sections of the engine were moved forward only 3ft 3in (1m) because the nozzles were 11in (28cm) aft of the position of the afterburner on the TF30.

The adapter comprised a core exhaust section with annular fan airflow channel, but the repositioning of the exhaust nozzle helped to improve the boattail aerodynamics over those of the F-14A design with the TF30. Mounting lugs for the F-110-GE-400 had to be repositioned on the Navy's 400 series engine to make pickup points compatible with the structural demands originally engineered for the TF30. Advantages in switching to the new engine included an integral gearbox thus eliminating the need for the Tomcat's engine accessories pack built into the airframe on the production line. This had other advantages too. TF30-powered aircraft must be manoeuvred to place their nozzles over the side of the carrier deck when running up for engine trimming. The integral digital electronics control box eliminates this pre-flight trimming. Only modest changes were necessary to adapt the airframe structure to the new engine, simple adjustments which marginally reshaped some frames and stiffeners. New ancillary systems were incorporated, including a ram-air turbine, an air turbine starter and new cockpit-mounted engine instruments and changes had to be made to the inlet ramp opening cycle.

Upgraded Cats

The new F110-GE-400 engine was bench-powered for the first time in December 1984 and Grumman prepared the No.7 YF-14 for another key role as the prototype for the F-14A(Plus) and the F-14D type. The aircraft made its first flight in this configuration on 29 September 1986 with test pilot Joe Burke at the controls. In a test

An F-14 performs a high-speed flyby close to the deck in a stunning display of automated variable sweep control. From the outset, design engineers provided an auto-sweep programmer to take control of the optimium wing sweep position leaving the pilot free to fly the aircraft in much the same way that throttle settings automatically control the engine inlet ramps.

Packed tight in between-decks hangars Tomcats rub shoulders with Intruders while drop tanks are stored at the ready on wall fitments. It takes special skill to spot Tomcats around the flight deck but the logistics of getting the right aircraft in the right place at the right time is a nightmare not shared by land-based crew chiefs.

Deck activity around a Tomcat of VF-2 typifies the attention each aircraft gets from a variety of specialized technicians. Set in calm sunny weather this view gives little indication of the harsh weather conditions under which most operations take place, in heaving seas, poor weather and also frequently at night.

Operating heavy aircraft on a rolling deck awash with rain is dangerous enough and special precautions are taken with a non-slip surface applied to large areas of the carrier. Each category of the crew is colour-coded by job allowing the deck officers to identify roles from a distance; when aircraft are operating only selected areas are open to the appropriate personnel.

flight that lasted 54min the aircraft was flown to a speed of 762mph (1,227km/hr) and an altitude of 35,000ft (10,600m). From this successful trial a vigorous development programme ensued. Initially the aircraft had no undernose sensor package but it did carry an air data set in an extended nose probe, or test boom, instrumented with pressure ports and pitch/yaw vanes. Instead of radar equipment in the nose, this aircraft had test equipment and data recorders as well as a telemetric readout system. Formerly known as the No.7 YF-14A prototype, the initial F-14B prototype with the F401 engine and the F-14B 'Super Tomcat' with the F101-DFE, this aircraft was now the first of six involved in development for the F-14A(Plus).

In the $984 million Tomcat upgrade contract awarded to Grumman in July 1984, the F-14A(Plus) would have engine and basic improvements to enhance its performance significantly, but the F-14D

would in addition provide a radical transformation in the aircraft's avionics and electronic warfare capability. Approximately 60 per cent of the aircraft's analogue avionics would be changed, with the Litton ALR-67 threat-warning and recognition system installed as well as the Westinghouse/ITT ALQ-165 airborne recognition system and the Joint Tactical Information Distribution System (JTIDS), the IRST infra-red tracker and the TCS television camera system. The ALR-67 incorporates the standard crystal video receiver and a new superheterodyne receiver hooked to a digital processor which can be reprogrammed. This permits new and enhanced threats to be countered through the use of significantly improved receivers and increased signal strength and density operating in millimetre wavelength frequencies.

The ALQ-165 jammer to be incorporated into the F-14D was one of the most

advanced and expensive pieces of electronics fitted to the Tomcat. Basic research into a radical new form of countermeasures came in 1969 when Grumman was just starting the Tomcat programme. Incorporating the result of work conducted by the Air Force, the Navy awarded competing contracts in 1979 to separate teams which duly delivered their prototypes four years later. By early 1984 the first phase of full-scale development began with flight trials taking place in a USAF F-16A and a USN F/A-18A. In what has turned out to be the most costly aircraft early warning system ever deployed, the ALQ-165 has been adopted by the F-15 as well. But compressing the many separate elements into the available space was a nightmare and achieved only through extensive miniaturization. Cost became a major obstacle and delays built up, postponing until 1986 a production commitment for the F-14D. Update

Caught in a heat haze, Tomcats line up to jump the cat. It can take nearly one hour to get a squadron off the decks but the aircraft are rarely used in such numbers. By the early 1990s the number of Tomcats on a carrier had been cut to twenty in two squadrons and then by mid decade to one squadron per Air Wing.

programmes were kept as an option, constrained only by the available budget.

The biggest asset acquired by the F-14D was the new AN/APG-71 radar which, although based on the outstanding AN/AWG-9, has considerably enhanced electronic counter-countermeasures with monopulse angle tracking and digital scan control for identifying the target and determining the post-attack result. Developed by Hughes, it was a significant advance on the original Tomcat radar by incorporating digital processing and appropriate cockpit displays. Operating modes are the same as for the AN/AWG-9 with sea-search and beyond-visual-range (BVR) capability added. It can locate and track up to ten fixed and moving targets simultaneously and engage eight targets at once. The AN/APG-71 provides a terrain-following capability as well as accepting updates from the inertial navigation system. When the Navy decided to go ahead with the F-14D Hughes was busy with the Multi-Staged

Nose down and ready to go, a Tomcat prepares to get hurled into the air as steam from the catapult flows through the trough. Exercises are maintained at a high pace and aircraft frequently operate every day for several days. Despite budgetary cuts naval aviators maintain high flying hours to prevent diminished performance.

Improvement Program (MSIP) radar for the Air Force's F-15 Eagle and immediately applied that work to the Navy requirement.

The change in designation made possible by substantial modifications and changes placed the new radar firmly in the APG series because the new F-14D stores management system now handles weapons integration where previously it was performed by the AN/AWG-9 weapons fire-control system. With a low sidelobe antenna, blocking guard channel and monopulse angle tracker, the new radar is more jam-resistant than the older AWG-9. With new digital scan control the radar does not have to follow preset scan patterns, as does its predecessor, but can focus on areas of high threat. With a unique target-identification system capable of determining the type of aircraft or the surface craft acquired through the analysis of the radar return, the AN/APG-71 is in a class of its own, albeit closely related to the F-15's equivalent. Much of

the design for the new Tomcat radar was based on work conducted during the development of the Eagle's APG-70 radar and there is a high level of component commonality.

Challenges brought about in the area of on-board data processing called for a radical transformation in computing power and options flexibility. Because the F-14D was a fully 'digitized' aircraft based on a standard multiprocessor database system used widely throughout the US armed services and NATO, the Tomcat had to have dual redundant controllers known as mission computers. These were the standard Navy AYK-14 computer, one to each databus, capable of controlling all functions of both if one were knocked out or failed. The mean time between failure is a creditable 2,200hr and the AYK-14 has become the standard general-purpose computer for the US Navy, being installed on the F/A-18 Hornet, the E-2C Hawkeye, the EA-6B Prowler and the AV-8B Harrier among others. Over time the AYK-14 was

further improved by the use of very-high-speed integrated circuitry.

Communications and data handling provided by the Joint Tactical Information Distribution System gives the Tomcat parity with the latest Navy ship/air network. JTIDS would be an important element in tying together all the separate components of the situation-awareness data, integrating flight operations with the airborne early warning and control systems. There was a determined effort to merge systems with the F/A-18 and the A-6F for maximum commonality in hardware and software and to synthesize operational roles. As a secure, jam-resistant, integrated system providing communications, navigation and identification, it provided several levels of capability and sophistication depending on the end-user. For instance, carriers are equipped with the Class 1 system which provides command and control functions of sea and airborne elements under its authority. Stand-off command, control or early warning

Combat air patrols usually involve a leader and his wingman, as here during this top-up from a KA-6B tanker version of the Intruder. The lead aircraft is from VF-84 while the other is from VF-41.

A pair of VF-41 Tomcats from the Nimitz line up for a mid-air refuelling. The probe is deployed from the starboard forward side of the fuselage adjacent to the cockpit.

functions – jobs performed by the Grumman E-2C Hawkeye – employ Class 1A systems for links to the carrier and the control of tactical aircraft in the air. The smaller decision-zones would be filled by Class 2 devices installed on tactical aircraft and ships in the carrier battle group.

Other changes for the F-14D upgrade programme included the fitting of the ASN-130 digital inertial navigation system which, like so many other Navy systems of the 1980s, had common application on several aircraft types. Later models would receive the AN/ASN-139 laser inertial navigation system while the retrofitting of GPS navigation equipment would give aircraft unprecedented navigational accuracy. Unique to the F-14D, a dual-mounted, side-by-side sensor pod beneath the nose is the only distinguishing feature of this type in contrast to earlier Tomcat variants. It comprises the General Electric Aerospace Electronic Systems AN/AAS Infra-Red Search and Track (IRST) sensor housing to port of the

centreline and the Northrop AN/AAX-1 Television Camera Sight (TCS) to starboard. Rather than replacing the TCS the IRST operates alongside the Northrop sensor and both use focal-plane infra-red detectors and signal filters to improve vision.

The F-14D crew sit on Martin-Baker Mk14 seats, the first in the world to have a microprocessor- controlled electronic ejection system, rather than the GRU-7A seats common to all Tomcats before this definitive variant. In what was certainly the most significant ejection seat programme for its manufacturer, the Mk14 was adopted by the US as the standard Navy Aircrew Common Ejection Seat and is therefore known as the Mk14 NACES. It is now standard equipment for US Navy aircraft. Eleswhere in the cockpits, the driver has the standard head-up display with two multifunction, head-down displays going some way to make it look like a modern office. Nevertheless, there are still a lot of dials and meters around

which give away the aircraft's age and the heavy frames look positively ancient by modern standards. The NFO has a single main, circular, radar screen with a large multifunctional display above and a computer panel to the right.

The only completely new weapon adopted by the F-14D was the AIM-120 AMRAAM (Advanced Medium Range Air-to-Air Missile), a replacement for the AIM-7 Sparrow. AIM-120 dates from the early 1970s when the Air Force and the Navy began looking for a 'fire-and-forget' missile with fully active guidance that could seek out a target without further attention from the launch aircraft after it had left the rail. The impressive performance of the AIM-54 Phoenix and the somewhat limited capabilities of the AIM-7 Sparrow left a performance and cost gap between relatively inexpensive, medium-range, semi-active missiles and the very-long-range but expensive Phoenix. It was in an attempt to get some of the performance of the Phoenix for the cost of

Four Tomcats aboard the Saratoga on duty in the Mediterranean await their turn for a cat-launch as deck handlers move around preparing each aircraft in turn. Operations are conducted on the basis that a full alert must be anticipated and aircraft kept at readiness for a launch-on-warning of intruders. Like no other aircraft on board, Tomcats are the first line of defence, tasked with sprinting to the outer perimeter to stop an aggressor threatening the battle group.

the Sparrow that an ambitious programme got under way following studies carried out by the Air Force and the Navy in 1972 and 1973. By modifying the Sparrow to carry a passive guidance system and homing device it was hoped to build a low-cost replacement for Sparrow. Called Brazo, it would home in on the fire-control emissions of the enemy aircraft but it could also be directed to the terrain following radar, the communications signal or, for terminal guidance, the infra-red signature.

In 1978 Brazo was abandoned in favour of the new AMRAAM design which evolved from a general trend, led by Israel, toward missiles that would home on radia-tion sources. In 1977 the Air Force and the Navy held a fierce mock air fight. Known as the Air Intercept Missile Evaluation, it pitched F-14s and F-15s against 'aggressor' units flying F-5E fighters armed with simple missiles in the skies over the Nellis Tactical Fighter Weapons Center, Nevada. What it revealed shook the air chiefs as they saw the 'aggressors' get within striking distance with their Sidewinders. By the time the big fighters equipped with long-range radar had locked on and fired their own missiles the less sophisticated aircraft were within the range capability of their own missiles. The lesson was clear. What was needed was a

missile with fully-active guidance that the parent aircraft could launch and leave. Particularly significant were aircraft such as the MiG-29 Fulcrum and the Su-27 Flanker which formed the standard against which a study was made of the next-generation threat. Fast and agile, these fighters would tangle with the 'friendlies' as they fought to keep a lock on targets.

From these lessons came the preliminary specification for a missile with Mach 4+ dash instead of the gliding flight of the Sparrow, a ripple-fire capability against multiple threats instead of all missiles heading for the same target (or one target at a time), and rapid acceleration and

VF-32 launches a Tomcat from the deck of the Eisenhower **during an exercise in Latin America during 1994. The cat-officer gives the two-fingers ready sign, the pilot lights the afterburner and the cat operators launch the F-14 – in that order.**

agility during flight. Five manufacturers responded to the call for proposals and in February 1979 Hughes and Raytheon were selected for competing designs. Within two years Hughes had emerged as the winner and development began, but in 1982 Raytheon was awarded a contract as a second source for procurement thus ensuring two production lines and separate research centres – the type of dual-source contracting usually confined to the open-chequebook mentality of the 1960s space programme. In December 1984 a series of concerted tests began on what was to have been the replacement for Sparrow. But under tight language in a price-capped procurement contract the missile ran over budget and wrangles developed in Congress while purchasing decisions were delayed. Test results brought concern about AMRAAM's reliability and

questions were asked about its effectiveness in battle.

By 1990 the estimated price for 24,000 missiles had risen 24 per cent above the price set six years earlier but concerted efforts to improve performance and reliability began to pay off when four AMRAAMs fired from a single F-15 hit and destroyed four QF-100 target drones. Then the Soviet empire imploded and procurement was chopped by 9,000 when US forces began a drawdown and production plans cut deliveries from 3,000 missiles per year to 1,500. The net effect was a further price rise of almost 40 per cent. It had been hoped that Operation *Desert Storm* would have provided an opportunity to test the missile under combat conditions, but although fifty-two AMRAAMs were delivered to the 58th Tactical Fighter Squadron for use with

their F-15s, the Iraqi forces either fled the country or took cover and not one AMRAAM was fired.

As built, AMRAAM has a length of 12ft (3.6m), a diameter of 7in (18cm) and a maximum span of 1ft 9in (0.5m) across the four wings and of 2ft 1in (0.6m) across the four tailerons. With a weight of 345lb (157kg), AIM-120 is about 170lb (77kg) lighter than the AIM-7P Sparrow and has a nominal range of almost 30 miles (48km). Powered by a solid propellant Hercules rocket motor with low smoke emission to reduce the chance of an enemy pilot seeing it coming, AMRAAM can be guided to its target by semi-active or active radar. At extreme range the pilot loads the missile with delta-velocity (the difference between the speed of the launch aircraft and the speed of the target) and bearing information at the push of a button. When

TA-3B Skywarrior to check the upgraded electronics. One aircraft would be reconfigured to fly in the F-14D development programme when its primary function supporting F-14A(Plus) work-up had been completed.

The phased introduction of the full modification programme was a timely response from a new and energetic will in the White House and a reaction to a perceived threat expansion from the Soviet Union and its client states. There was concern to get the more potent engines into operational Tomcats as quickly as possible and the first production F-14A(Plus) made its initial flight on 14 November 1987, ten days before the first development aircraft took to the sky. This aircraft was delivered to VF-101 at Oceana, Virginia, on 11 April 1988. In all there were thirty-eight new-build F-14A(Plus), the last being delivered in May 1990, but an additional thirty-two aircraft of this type were converted from old F-14A airframes. These aircraft were given the identifications KB-1 to KB-32, of which eleven were initially equipped to carry the optional Tactical Air Reconnaissance Pod System (TARPS). Paradoxically, none of the purpose-built F-14A(Plus) had this option but all F-14Ds would be engineered for TARPS.

Conversion Programme

On 1 May 1991 all but the No.7 prototype F-14A(Plus) were redesignated F-14B, thus securing in an operational Tomcat the designation once reserved for the F-14A upgrade originally intended to have the F401 engine. This did nothing to lessen confusion. Engine development for the F-14D was, of course, part of the upgrade programme that originally involved the No.7 prototype which had first flown with the F110-GE-400 on 29 September 1986. Four converted F-14As were assigned as prototypes for the F-14D variant in the most thorough shakedown of modifications and upgrades brought to the F-14 programme since the first production aircraft had been delivered in May 1972. The extensive series of electronic and systems integration testing, as well as verification trials involving ships of the fleet and other carrier-based aircraft, was performed with the assistance of a lone TA-3B.

The first converted F-14D prototype,

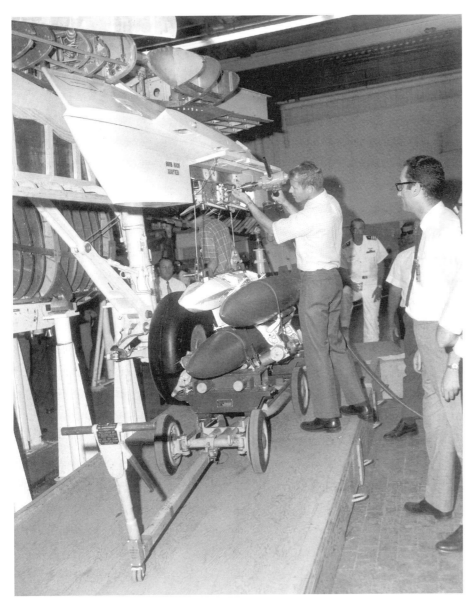

From the outset, Grumman designed a bomb-carrying capacity into the F-14 but the Navy did not want to dilute the vital role this aircraft would play in fleet defence and bomb-truck drivers in Corsairs, Intruders and, more recently, Hornets did not want any trespassers. But in the late 1990s when each aircraft must perform a variety of roles, the F-14 is getting a new ground-strike capability which has dubbed them Bombcats.

the missile is launched it uses its inertial measurement unit to steer toward the target and can be updated by the tracking aircraft if necessary for a precise long-range shot. If not, it uses its own seeker, allowing the aircraft to break away and engage other threats or protect itself from attack. If launched at minimum range the active seeker on the missile locks-on to the target before launch and flies straight in to strike.

After the No.7 aircraft had first flown with the new F110-GE-400 engines installed on 29 September 1986, a rigorous test programme followed during which the new powerplant was given a shakedown before the production of a limited number of F-14A(Plus) and F-14D Tomcats. On 15 February 1987 General Electric received a production order from the Navy and on 30 June the customer received its first engine in this series. In addition to the No.7 prototype Tomcat there were to be five F-14A(Plus) development aircraft, the first of which (BuAer No.162910) first flew on 24 November 1987. The first three aircraft performed avionics testing with a

Developed in the mid-1970s to provide optical reconnaissance in the visible and the infra-red, the Tactical Air Reconnaissance Pod System (TARPS) brings new uses to the Tomcat. Fitted to an underfuselage station, TARPS carries cameras for oblique and panoramic images.

PA-1 (BuAer No.161865), flew with the TF30 engines but it had the APG-71 radar and new avionics suite along with cockpit changes characteristic of this type. It took off for the first time on 23 November 1987 at the start of a programme in which it would test the radar system, datalinks and new display systems. The second prototype, PA-2 (161867), was the only one of the four development aircraft to have the four F110-GE-400 engines and it took to the air for the first time on 29 April 1988 before radar and avionics tests. Later it would be used for environmental trials and TARPS evaluation as well as radar fault finding. PA-3 (162595) first flew on 31 May 1988 and would validate the IRST/TCS nose sensor assembly, the ECM, the radar and the weapons management integration. It would also carry out

live firing trials. PA-4 (161623) made its maiden flight on 21 September 1988 and joined the test programme as the JTIDS trials aircraft. In May 1990 the first prototype F-14D was delivered to VX-4 ('The Evaluators') for an extensive operational work-out.

In the original F-14 upgrade plan the US Navy scheduled 127 F-14D variants for delivery beginning in March 1990, with an additional 390 F-14A and F-14B models remanufactured to 'D' standard, complete with the F110-GE-400 engine. Eventually, almost the entire Tomcat inventory was to have been either F-14B or F-14D new or rebuild variants. But this was not to be. While maintaining the F-14B new-build and rebuild programme, the Navy received funds for only thirty-seven of the planned 127 newly-manufactured F-14Ds. The first

of these aircraft was rolled out on 23 March 1990 by which date the original production plan had been cut. The last of the F-14Ds, and the last new Tomcat, passed through the factory gates on 20 July 1992 giving a total of seventy-five of new-build F-14B and F-14D Tomcats to receive the new engine and varying levels of avionics and electronics upgrade. In all, seven F-14Ds were ordered in FY 1988, twelve in FY 1989 and eighteen in FY 1990.

In June 1990 Grumman began work on converting F-14A Tomcats into F-14D variants, a job that was expected to take approximately fifteen months per aircraft. Under the plan, six aircraft would be funded in FY 1990 with twelve in FY 1991 and the work split two-to-one between Grumman and the Naval Aviation Depot, known as NADP (pronounced NeyDep), at Norfolk, Virginia. An additional 372 aircraft were to have been funded for conversion work between FY 1992 and FY 1998, twenty-four in the first year, forty-eight in the second and sixty a year thereafter until the total of 390 had been reached. The Grumman/NADP conversions were to be identical to each other and reworked aircraft were to be indistinguishable from new F-14Ds. Some limited structural modifications to reworked aircraft were made in strip-down. Changes were made to sponsons, forward and aft fixed cowls and to engine doors and wheel wells. Apart from the deletion of the wing glove, aircraft received a monolithic canopy and the new NACES ejection seat and an on-board oxygen generating system.

Aircraft selected for the conversion programme had been chosen initially from the Block 85 and the Block 110 production lot. With an eye on the 6,000-hour fatigue life, aircraft were selected according to their age. In reality the airframes were good for more than that and one structural test

article completed 7,100hr without failure. When aircraft were received for rework they were weighed and inspected with teardown preceding three crucial stages before the aircraft joined the F-14D new production assembly line, each of which stages was known as a separate station stop. In B1 station the stripped airframe was subjected to modifications with new pyrotechnic lines added and technical changes made to the engineering requirements. In B2 environmental control and hydraulic systems were fitted along with cables and new engine door hinges for the F110-GE-400. In B3, which carried the greatest work load, all the many technical engineering changes and additions before the streaming for the F-14D line were completed along with the installation of the new doors and black boxes. Approximately seven months after arriving for teardown the airframe is ready to merge with the new Tomcats about to receive the unique assets of the F-14D.

Hardly had the conversion work begun than the ambitious rework plan was

cancelled and no further conversions were approved in major budgetary cuts made by the Bush administration. The eighteen existing upgraded F-14As were designated F-14D(R) and each was given a DR series identification number in the order DR-1 to DR-18. In all therefore only fifty-five F-14D and F-14D(R) aircraft were produced, of which two were delivered to the Navy for warfare and weapons tests along with the prototypes PA-2 and PA-4 redesignated NF-14D. The ex-PA-2 aircraft served with the Pacific Missile Test Center, or the Naval Air Warfare Center/Weapons Division as it is now known, PA-4 went to the Naval Air Warfare Center/Aircraft Division (formerly the Naval Air Test Center), while aircraft BuAer Nos.163415 and 163416 went to VX-4. This unit would do the groundwork on the undernose-mounted TCS, which enabled the crew to examine the target visually at a distance of 100 miles (160km).

In 1988 the US Navy began studying ground-attack versions and by 1990 it was

At first TARPS capability was acquired through sensors stuffed in disused fuel tanks, then purpose-built pods were supplied and the first squadrons were operational in 1981. Some F-14A aircraft have been converted for TARPS as well as a limited number of F-14B and all F-14D variants.

Over the life of the F-14 several different colour schemes have been tried and applied and any detailed catalogue of squadron schemes and experimental colour trials is outside the scope of this book. This Tomcat has a hybrid scheme for overland operations with suppressed national markings. Classified surveillance and reconnaissance operations have been conducted over Iran and other Middle Eastern countries, timed to coincide with overflights from intelligence gathering satellites.

test flying Strike Tomcat F-14As. Harking back to one of the Tomcat's original roles specified in the initial RFP drawn up in 1968, the air–ground role had been squeezed from the F-14 in the mid-1970s by a Navy that insisted on a dedicated aircraft for that role. This became the requirement that specified the F/A-18 Hornet, but the logic of adapting the Tomcat to carry iron bombs and smart weapons was undeniable. Test activities concentrated first on the Mk80 series of low-drag iron bombs carried by standard BRU-10 racks, but the bombs tended to eject too slowly and to linger in the vicinity

of the aircraft, recontacting it on occasion. With twice the ejection velocity and two kick-feet to eject the ordnance, the BRU-32 rack employed for the F/A-18 improved matters, but to attach it to the fuselage-mounted Phoenix missile rails a ADV-703 adapter was necessary, a piece of equipment then in short supply.

Trials were based on four bomb racks carried on Phoenix missile rails with a nominal stores mix adding two Sparrows and two Sidewinders. In some tests aircraft released four 2,000lb (909kg) Mk 84 bombs at the Chesapeake bombing range. To monitor carriage and ejection high-

speed cameras were installed in the under-fuselage positions and sixty-five flights were performed in subsonic release trials. A further thirty test sorties provided details on weapons accuracy but the combination of range and weapon-load carrying capability gave the Bombcat, as it was dubbed, unparalleled strike potential. Few modifications were necessary, among which were changes to the ballistic equations in the computer and new symbology in the head-up display. VX-4 did much of the mission test and profile write-up, developing the tactics and the operational rule book for the strike version.

CHAPTER FIVE

The Prowling Tomcats

Operational Deployment Begins

No warplane ever emerges to full operational status in one dramatic event and the F-14 was no exception to this. It took several years to bring the programme to maturity as a funded commitment from the US Navy. It took three years from pre-concept formulation at Grumman to the announcement of a contract to build the prototype; it took less than another two years to get the aircraft into the air; and it took almost four years after that to put the Tomcat on its first operational cruise. Fraught with challenges from competing designs, cost problems and production delays, the Tomcat had a better run than most in taking less than eight years from an idea in the minds of design engineers to the first squadron deployment on a blue-water mission. It was the four years from first flight to full deployment aboard the carrier USS *Enterprise* that brought the headaches, toil and sweat on which the success of each new flat-top flyer ultimately depends.

Led by Cdr F. J. Thaubald, VF-1 got its first F-14A on 1 July 1973. The Squadron had formed up on 14 October in the previous year and made ready to join Air Wing 14, commanded by Cdr George M. 'Skip' Furlong aboard the *Enterprise*. The sister squadron VF-2, led by Cdr J. A. Brantuas, was a veteran, having been formed on 1 July 1922 as the first Navy fighter squadron put aboard a carrier. It was the second F-14 squadron to be formally named, receiving orders for its conversion to the swing-wing on 14 October 1972. VF-2 received its first aircraft in July 1973 and provided the second squadron of twelve Tomcats that would make a brief shakedown cruise beginning on 18 March 1974. With that accomplished, but with some concern still rife about the problems with the aircraft's TF30 turbofans, the first two Tomcat squadrons moved from Naval Air Station Miramar in California on 12 September

VF-1 and VF-2 were the first two squadrons to deploy at sea with F-14As in 1974 and within five years twelve squadrons had been fully equipped and completed their first carrier cruises. It had taken just ten years from inception to deployment in strength.

1974 and were flown to Naval Air Station Alameda and there were hoisted aboard the *Enterprise*.

Over the next several days the aircraft and the equipment was lifted on to the *Enterprise* and the personnel reported aboard until by the 17th all was ready for departure. In typical Navy fashion the mooring lines were set loose at precisely 1000 hrs and two powerful Navy tugs nudged the giant carrier from her moorings. Just 1hr 5min later *Enterprise*, powered by her nuclear reactor, slipped under the Golden Gate bridge and increased speed for the open sea. The first Tomcat deployment had begun aboard a warship with a historic association and flagship for Rear-Adm Owen Oberg, the commander of Carrier Group Seven. For this sailing the ship was under the command of Capt C. C. Smith and would operate with the Seventh Fleet in the Western Pacific. It was historic for more

than one reason, marking the return to sea of Grumman fighters after a gap of fourteen and a half years. Not since the last Grumman cats, the F-11F Tigers of VF-111, berthed from their last sailing aboard the USS *Hancock* had Grumman had a fighter at sea.

Engine problems had plagued the early months of Tomcat flight tests and VF-1 had already lost two aircraft (BuAer Nos.158982 on 2 January and 159001 on 14 January 1975). In both instances a fan blade had torn loose, puncturing a fuel line and causing a fire. After the second incident a major tear-down and inspection programme was begun aboard the carrier and engines with more than 100 hours of flight time were stripped. Mechanics removed compressor cases and inspected the fan sections, reassembled and put on the carrier's single test cell and trimmed. During the cruise engineers performed this inspection on fifty-five engines, all with

more than 100hr on the clock. When engineers examined the blades they looked for foreign object damage on the leading edge, the suspected cause of earlier problems. It took two months to carry out all the inspections and both squadrons did a remarkable job in keeping the aircraft in the air. VF-2 logged a hundred engine changes during the cruise.

Engine problems continued to hamper full operability during the first cruise and, with two aircraft down, VF-1 was under establishment. On 9 February *Enterprise* responded to a call for emergency aid when Mauritius was struck by typhoon 'Gervaise'. The carrier arrived at Port Louis three days later and spent 10,000 man-hours helping the island back to normality by restoring water supplies, power lines and telephone systems, clearing roads and using helicopters to transport medical supplies, food and drinking water to the stricken islanders.

Close-order spacing. With two Tomcat squadrons on each carrier to protect the battle group and the Air Wing's valuable strike assets, the commitment was considerable, in 1990s prices more than $1 billion of F-14 hardware and weapons on each carrier.

The USS America **proudly sports her charges. Tomcats of VF-142 and VF-143 occupy deck space with LTV Corsairs and Viking anti-submarine warfare aircraft.** America **was the third carrier to put to sea with F-14s, beginning her first cruise with Tomcats in April 1976.**

On 18 April a general call went out to the carriers *Midway, Coral Sea, Hancock, Okinawa* and *Enterprise* for emergency evacuation relief off South Vietnam. Contravening the terms of the agreement with United States, North Vietnam was sending thousands of troops south in a general invasion that totally overwhelmed all resistance from South Vietnamese forces. Ten days later *Enterprise* was on standby with VF-1 and VF-2 ready to cover the evacuation of American personnel and selected individuals from South Vietnam.

The plan was to evacuate 1,000 Americans but in addition some 5,300 Vietnamese were airlifted away from the capital Saigon in an operation that was extended from a planned three hours to twenty. An additional 1,800 people were also lifted from remote regions. Fifteen of the twenty-two available F-14s on the *Enterprise* flew twenty sorties, flying top cover for the helicopters. A vast quantity of American equipment was abandoned in

the haste to leave the country, with more than 1,000 aircraft belonging to the South Vietnamese left for the invaders from the North. Among these were Northrop F-5E fighters delivered only in the previous two months. It was an inglorious start to a long career and few airmen who supported the F-14 flights relished the reputation of having covered for an American retreat.

The two Tomcat squadrons were away from US waters eight months and two days, cruising the west Pacific Ocean, flying off the deck of the *Enterprise* on 19 May 1975 as it neared its home port of San Francisco. Together VF-1 and VF-2 had grossed 2,900 flying hours and made 1,600 arrested landings, 460 of them at night. During the cruise in November 1974, Cdr John R. Wilson took over command of Air Wing 14 from Cdr Furlong and affirmed that 'the addition of the F-14 to the *Enterprise*'s air wing made that carrier the world's most powerful warship'. Although a training sortie, the rigours of operational combat

flying had been pressed upon the two squadrons through a busy and intensive schedule. Gunnery, air combat tactics, interception training, escort routines and rapid turnaround were practised day and night and in all weather conditions with the active firing of Sidewinder, Sparrow and Phoenix missiles.

Before the next cruise, the first from the east coast, it was time to do a little flag waving and show off the latest member of the Navy fighter fraternity. Arguably the most important international aviation event, the Paris Air Show was the perfect venue for displaying the latest in American air power and wooing foreign customers. Selected from VF-124 at Miramar, Lts Rick Bradley and Dennis Gladfman piloted the Tomcat through eleven dazzling displays in the ten-day show that began on 10 May 1975. They did 360 degree turns at 300ft (91m) pulling 7g in the air, while in the chalets Mike Pelehach gave dazzling descriptions of the new technology, exotic

153

materials and innovative design trends represented by the F-14. Representatives from several countries including West Germany, Australia and Iran crawled all over the gleaming Tomcat.

In the USA the next two Tomcat squadrons – VF-14 and VF-32 – made ready for the first F-14 cruise to the Mediterranean. Under the command of Cdr Dwight Timm, Air Wing 1 would deploy aboard the carrier USS *Kennedy* under Capt William A. Gureck. The two Tomcat squadrons would operate closely with the E-2C aircraft of VAW-125 and the three squadrons integrated their training and preparatory schedules at Norfolk and Oceana. The F-14s first flew with the E-2C in August 1974 and between 18 and 28 March 1975 the Tomcats performed fly-offs from the deck of the *Kennedy* off the east coast. During this intensive exercise the aircraft were flown around the clock on simulated combat operations involving the firing of missiles. Next up, Air Wing 1 was to perform a predeployment shakedown cruise off the coast of Florida and the *Kennedy* departed on 6 April for Jacksonville, Florida, where the F-14A/E-2C teams participated in TYT (type training) activities, after which two days were spent in Mayort before departing on 16 April for 'Agate Punch', a tri-service, close air support operation performed off the coast of Charleston, South Carolina, to confirm the effectiveness of the team concept.

The *Kennedy* was back at Norfolk on 28 April where final preparations began for the Mediterranean cruise. There was one more test needed to qualify the integrated Air Wing component for real, live threats. While the shakedown cruise would be an important test of men and machines matched operationally for the first time far from home, the carrier was not on a training exercise and could be called upon to function in war, should conflict break out. So a simulated threat was staged to represent a typical scenario the carrier might face. The exercise required the Tomcat squadrons to operate from the *Kennedy* off Jacksonville, and in early May the carrier sailed for its preordained destination.

On 6 May the two squadrons took off and flew across the Florida peninsula to the Gulf of Mexico where they were to encounter a Bomarc missile launched from Eglin Air Force Base. The Bomarc was to simulate an approaching MiG-25 Foxbat flying at more than twice the speed of sound and a height of almost 70,000ft (21,200m). The object was to acquire and identify the target, more than 450 miles (720km) from the carrier and destroy it by using Phoenix missiles. Lt Cdr Andrews from VF-32 was only one of a large team involved in this exercise but it was his lot to kill the simulated threat. Teamed with KA-3D tankers from VA-34 at Norfolk, the Tomcats had radar range surveillance and communications relay through the

From the Mediterranean the only way to reach the Indian Ocean or the Persian Gulf is through the Red Sea. The USS America **eases her way through the narrow channel transiting between the seas.**

The dark covering on the deck of the USS Ranger, a Forrestal class carrier, provides a non-slip surface for aircraft and personnel. With water, oil, grease and aviation fuel around special materials applied to the deck cladding help to maintain grip for shoes and tyres.

E-2C Hawkeye of VAW-125. When Eglin temporarily lost track of the Bomarc the fidelity of the data from the Hawkeye was so good that they provided the Air Force with tracking data. Working through the E-2C the Tomcats had no problem locking on to the target at a range of more than 50 miles (80km) and Andrews locked on, launched the missile and 'killed' the simulated threat. Over the three days of the exercise, Tomcats from VF-14 and VF-32 launched nine Phoenix, four Sparrow and three Sidewinder missiles.

During late May and early June *Kennedy* sailed off the North Carolina coast where it took part in Operation *Solid Shield*, a ten-day mock war. The exercise involved simulated harbour blocking with A-6 Intruders and A-7 Corsairs, close air support operations and combat air patrols which were largely the responsibility of the Tomcats. Finally, all was ready for the cruise and *Kennedy* left port on 28 June 1975 for the first Tomcat patrol to distant

waters from the east coast. In addition to being on standby for operational purposes, the carrier participated in a number of NATO exercises, anti-submarine warfare work and tactical exercises with Spanish and French forces during its seven-months long cruise.

In one of these exercises, Operation *Lafayette*, the French tried to penetrate the *Kennedy*'s air-defence screen with Mirage 3s and 4s and Jaguar aircraft . In ninety-one separate attempts the penetrating aircraft were unable to break through the outer defences provided by Tomcat and Hawkeye. In most attempts the Tomcats were scrambled on warning and still destroyed the aggressors. In all VF-32 operated for 2,478 flying hours and made 1,291 carrier landings while its sister-squadron VF-14 flew 2,069 hours and effected 1,120 traps. VF-32 flew so frequently in such a short period during September 1975 that it established a new record of fifty hours of flying time in one

24hr period and 500hr in a month. On 27 January 1976 the *America* arrived home and the first transatlantic cruise for the Tomcat had been a great success. No sooner had the aircraft arrived than attention switched to the next paired squadrons to undertake a Mediterranean cruise.

In the meantime a major decision had been made about the service use of the F-14. During July 1975 a decision to deploy the Tomcat with four Marine Corps squadrons was reversed in favour of four squadrons of F-18 air combat fighters. Mobile maintenance units that would have been used by the four Marine squadrons assigned to have the F-14 would be used on carriers without installed equipment, thus allowing all twelve flat-tops to get the Tomcat. Marines would have used F-14s for top cover during amphibious landings and in conjunction with ground-based radar for early warning once ashore. Navy F-14s would now carry out that role in conjunction with Marine units.

Tomcat 21

Long before the Navy got around to ordering the F-14D, Grumman had been actively working on a broad range of improved versions that could have considerably extended the capabilities of the basic aircraft. Evolutionary progression from the F-14D would have produced the F-14 Quick Strike, a development with stand-off capability and additional radar modes which owed much to parallel improvements through the F-15E and the A-6F programme.

Next up would have been the Super Tomcat 21 and an attack version, the Attack Super Tomcat 21, leading to a further development which Grumman designated the ASF-14 as a challenge to the naval version of the Advanced Tactical Fighter. Intent upon keeping its production line open as long as possible, Grumman was, nevertheless, pitching against the trend. McDonnell Douglas had successfully manoeuvred its F/A-18 into a multi-mission slot required by the Navy at a cost much lower than the existing and growth versions of the Tomcat.

When the new Tomcat derivatives were presented in early 1991 they made impressive reading. The F-14 Quick Strike was a determined attempt to give the aircraft a true multi-mission role by enhancing its ground-attack capability. With the same wing and underbody weapon stations, wing pylons and nacelle drop tank points, Quick Strike would have the option of carrying a FLIR navigation pod and a separate targeting FLIR with laser ranger and designator. Taking software changes made to the A-6F, Quick Strike would have a suitable weapons interface card for stand-off weapons.

A major improvement was also proposed in the AN/APG-71 radar, including synthetic aperture radar for high-resolution ground mapping, Doppler beam for improving the medium-resolution mapping and a fixed target tracking mode. All these had been put together for the AN/APG-70 fitted to the F-15 and were easily taken and applied to the F-14. The AYK-14 mission computer upgrades for handling the new radar and weapon controls, together with the necessary software changes, would come from existing work on similar improvements for the A-6F. By carrying 300gall (1,350 l) drop tanks the combat radius could be improved by 92miles (147km).

The two versions that most interested the Navy were the Super Tomcat 21 and its attack derivative. These would have been the ultimate F-14, with a mission radius up to 100 per cent greater than that of the F-14D, supercruise capability (supersonic cruise without after-burner), greatly improved self-defence capability and more lift than the standard Tomcat. Except for an increase in the trailing edge of the horizontal tail, with the surface area increased to 154sq ft (14sq m), the external dimensions remained the same.

The central feature of the Super Tomcat 21, however, would be a modified high-lift system to greatly extend the aircraft's capabilities. Two-segment, extended-chord, leading edge slats with a 2,000lb (900kg) weight penalty were more than offset by the performance advantages. At the trailing edge, a single-slotted Fowler flap in three segments fabricated from composites would replace the existing flaps. A four-segment extended-chord spoiler would be mounted at the wing trailing edge forward of the flaps. In wind-tunnel tests conducted by the Navy and Grumman the new wing elements improved lift by 25 per cent all the way to maximum AoA.

Super Tomcat 21 would have had a much improved engine, based on the General Electric F110-GE-129 giving an extra 35 per cent of thrust in the mid-altitude, transonic region compared with the F110-400 used in the F-14B and the F-14D. Providing supercruise at Mach 1.3 with four AAMs, the engine could have been superseded by the Pratt & Whitney F119 with thrust vectoring exhaust nozzles, the power-plant selected for the F-22 Raptor, but since the F-14 can achieve a 77-degrees AoA that was considered unnecessary. The aircraft would also have carried an auxiliary power unit (APU) fitted, necessitating some minor relocation of the existing systems.

The biggest change in the external appearance of the derivative would have been extended inboard glove sections carrying an extra 2,000lb (909kg) of fuel. Additional fuel pick up points would include the two existing 280gall (1,260 l) drop tank mounting on the nacelle underbody and two 300gall (1,350 l) tanks on the outer wing pylons. It would be possible to mount 425gall (1,912 l) tanks on the nacelle positions taking to more than 28,000lb (12,700kg) the total aircraft fuel capacity.

A completely new multi-mode radar with double the power of the AN/APG-71 now fitted to the F-14D would incorporate two-dimensional passive radar utilizing electronic scan technology together with an inverse synthetic aperture radar adapted to indicate ground moving targets. Overall, the detection capability would have been about twice that of the AN/APG-71. The standard infra-red search and television camera systems would be carried forward to the Super Tomcat 21 with the added advantage of a laser rangefinder and target designator. Separate conformal FLIR units for navigation and attack would be installed on either side of the forward fuselage in blister fairings for reduced radar signature.

The application of radar and other sensor data would be greatly improved with very-high-speed-integrated-circuit (VHSIC) modules which would integrate all target sensor data. With an ALQ-165 jammer fitted with two transmitters, one for the low band, and 135 as against 60 chaff packets, aircraft defences would be considerably enhanced. Cockpit changes would give the aircraft more of a 1990s 'feel', replacing the framed windscreen with a single-piece unit and providing large multicolour display panels, helmet-mounted sights and displays, and a completely new and upgraded electronic control system. Information between controller and aircraft or between individual aircraft would flow through the AN/ASW-27C as fitted to all *Desert Storm* Tomcats.

All these features would carry through to the Attack Super Tomcat 21 which would also have a special suite of features for high-speed, low-altitude strike missions deep into enemy territory. These would include terrain-following and terrain-avoidance radar, navigation FLIR, digitized moving-map and wide-screen head-up display. Full GPS navigation satellite compatibility would be built in. With a full load of ground-attack weapons the strike version of Super Tomcat 21 would have a low-level speed of 600kt, or 700kt in afterburner (1,100 and 1,300km/hr). Typical warloads might be two HARMs, four Harpoons, two Sidewinder or Sparrow self-defence weapons and two 280gall (1,260 l) drop tanks or a combination of nuclear and conventional bombs. A maximum of six Harpoons could be accommodated on pylons and racks.

The final growth derivative of the basic airframe would be the ASF-14, described by Grumman as 'revolutionary rather than 'evolutionary'. This aircraft would build upon the success of existing production aircraft but take up twenty-first-century technologies developed through the Advanced Technology Fighter (ATF) programme which resulted in the F-22 Raptor. In 1990 the company claimed that it could be ready by the turn of the century but the development investment would be high and Grumman had no answer when probed about the aged, non-stealthy airframe design.

It was VF-142 and its partner VF-143 that would make the third Tomcat carrier deployment and the second east coast cruise. Commanded by Cdr Jerry L. Unruh, VF-142 had been in existence since 24 August 1948 (when it was known as VF-193) and had been designated the 'Ghostriders'. It transitioned to the F-14 at Miramar in 1974. VF-143 originated as Reserve Squadron VF-871 in July 1950 and then became VF-53 in June 1962 when it took up the F-4 Phantom, first going to sea across the Pacific in 1963. Under the command of Cdr Ruben W. Schaffer it turned in its F-4s for the Tomcat during 1974. During 1975 both squadrons continued to receive their F-14 Tomcats and moved to Oceana during April in readiness for joining Air Wing 6 aboard the carrier America.

Further difficulties were brought by engine problems with the TF30. On 24 June another Tomcat (BuAer No.159432), from VF-143, suffered an engine fire when a fan blade from the port engine ripped through the compressor case. The Squadron had been working up toward deployment aboard the America in April 1976 and the aircraft had been flying out of Oceana. All aircraft were immediately grounded and a 6hr inspection of fan blades instituted. Up to that date 145 Tomcats had been delivered to the fleet and by the second week of July the aircraft were being returned to flight status. In tests to determine the cause of these engine failures there seemed to be no correlation between wear and engine life; Pratt & Whitney claimed that it was a quality control problem from a contractor.

In preparation for their first deep-sea cruise VF-142 and VF-143 joined the Wing in November 1975 and continued an increasingly gruelling training and exercise programme involving the usual range of combat manoeuvres, gunnery and missile firing, tactics and air intercepts. They sailed for the Mediterranean on 15 April and returned on 25 October 1976.

Cat Overboard!

Meanwhile, high drama in deep water off the naval base at Scapa Flow in Scotland threatened to dump all the best-kept secrets of America's most potent naval fighter right in the lap of Soviet military experts. It happened on 14 September when an F-14A, BuAer No.159588, the 135th Tomcat built, of VF-32 ran off the deck of the carrier John F. Kennedy and into the sea, coming to rest 2,000ft (600m) beneath the surface. The cruise began 2 September 1976 and would include a patrol through the North Atlantic. In what was to have been a routine training flight, the F-14 taxied slowly toward a catapult position when the engines roared to high thrust setting and the Tomcat leapt for the side of the carrier giving no time for the crew to do anything other than eject to safety as the 27 tons of high-performance advanced engineering threw itself into the water.

As with all US carrier battle groups,

Deployed on her first Tomcat cruise in December 1977, the Nimitz displays the parallel catapults on the bow deck with blast deflectors raised. Early shakedown cruises were completed before global deployment to the Mediterranean or the Persian Gulf from the Atlantic seaboard or the Pacific and the Indian Ocean from the western seaboard.

First to put the Tomcat to sea on operational deployment, the USS Enterprise displays the ship's aircraft and personnel during her cruise.

Soviet fishing vessels close by monitored all communications traffic and probably saw the incident. But even the Soviets were not equipped for a deep-sea recovery, even though it was arguably the most valuable piece of hardware on the sea floor. Noting the spot the carrier had cruised on, a rescue attempt swung into action. It was absolutely vital to keep the valuable aircraft and its AIM-54 Phoenix missile system and AWG-9 computer out of foreign hands and a race began to beat any attempt from the USSR to get there first. Apart from which it was important to conduct a close examination of the wreckage for clues about what happened. Capt Robert B. Moss was in charge of gathering together the men and the equipment necessary to find and retrieve the hardware and his deputy Capt William N. Klorig handled the operation.

Almost immediately the Navy sent CURV 111, a special unmanned retrieval device, by air from San Diego to Scotland and put it aboard *Constructor*, a Norwegian salvage vessel. Meanwhile, Capt Klorig set out to sea on the salvage tug USS *Shakori*. By 21 September, one week after the accident, the first salvage attempt began with *Shakori* making a run of the search area, defined as a four-square miles (10sq km) area centred on the position of the carrier when the Tomcat left the deck. Using a

side-scan radar *Shakori* swept the sea floor in parallel tracks 250ft (76m) apart, but in worsening weather and heavy seas the attempt was frustrated. Technical problems beset the operation and the pitching vessel was unable to make much progress. By early October, with 90 per cent of the area swept and no signs of the Tomcat, a decision was made to change the direction sweep and on the first pass a positive reading was obtained. With the position fixed *Shakori* returned to port; but when it next went to the scene the object had moved and yielded a blurred reflection instead of the positive return.

By now another weapon in the armoury had been brought to the scene: NR-1, the only nuclear-powered, deep-sea search and rescue submarine in the world. Amid fears that fishing nets that could have snagged the F-14 might foul the recovery vehicles, NR-1 and CURV 111 were sent out to investigate. During deployment a cable flooded and CURV 111 shorted out. When it was returned to base NR-1 took over and eventually found the Tomcat, bottom up and snagged by nets, but with its precious Phoenix missing. Nevertheless, with the NR-1's mechanical arm a line was hooked around the aircraft's landing gear and on 26 October a haulage line was passed through the slip noose. The line was winched in by *Oil Harrier*, a British ship

with an open-ended stern and big winch gear, but this broke and the NR-1 had to be returned from trying to find the Phoenix missiles to placing another line on the F-14. This too failed, but when the F-14 fell back to the sea it righted itself making the retrieval job much easier, a task made more agreeable by the successful rescue of the Phoenix.

On 1 November more ships arrived, the German boats *Taurus* and *Twyford* and a British heavy trawler the *Boston Halifax*. At first it was believed that a trawling net that had caught on to the Tomcat in the first place might do the same thing again and so the trawler made an attempt to drag it up – unsuccessfully. Now it was the turn of the German salvage vessels and they succeeded in getting a heavy hawser around the landing gear. Secured by a heavy shackle the aircraft was slowly winched in as the boats moved slowly toward shore. Then, just as the Soviet spy-trawler gave up hope, the Tomcat hit an uncharted rock and the line broke. With more sonar and a diving bell the aircraft was again located and deep-sea divers secured yet another line. This time it held and the Tomcat came ashore on 11 November. Although the entire operation cost $2.4 millions it was judged to be worth every cent for had the Soviets got their hands on a Tomcat the price could have been paid in human lives and great additional expenditure would have incurred in changes to maintain the American edge in technology.

This edge was a real factor. Operational Tomcats were distinctly more powerful and capable than the aircraft they replaced. When the F-4 arrived in the Navy during the early 1960s it heralded a new age in jet combat aircraft, but when the F-14 appeared just over a decade later it forced an awesome revision of carrier air warfare. Flight test results and the aircraft's introduction to service use, as evidenced by its performance on the first three cruise patrols (notwithstanding the engine problems, soon to be corrected), revealed an outstanding aircraft with extraordinary potential. Its sheer performance was stunning: operational Tomcats had a 21 per cent increase in acceleration, a 20 per cent increase in the rate of climb, a 27 per cent increase in a manoeuvring climb and a 40 per cent increase in turn radius. The aircraft held the same outright performance band as the F-4 but its agility, dog-fighting capability and acceleration were in a different league.

Evident too was the need for special conversions to some of the older carriers to match the requirements of the F-14. The first cruise was conducted aboard *Enterprise*, which had been commissioned in 1961, and the second aboard the *John F. Kennedy*, commissioned in 1968, while the third was with *America* commissioned in 1965. None of these was more than thirteen years old when the Tomcat squadrons put to sea for the first time. The next deployments were on *Constellation*, *Kitty Hawk* and *Nimitz* in 1977, the *Eisenhower* in 1979 and *Ranger* in 1980, when VF-1 and VF-2 switched from *Enterprise*. But when the continued production and expanded deployment of two Tomcat squadrons per carrier continued it was to the older vessel that the Navy looked for assignment. None of the carriers deployed with Tomcat so far needed modifications other than special blast deflectors for the afterburners. However, when the Navy wanted to put Tomcats from VF-74 and

VF-103 aboard the *Saratoga* it had to wait until the ship had been modified.

Under what the Navy terms a Service Life Extension Program, or SLEP, carriers are periodically taken in for an extensive rework, modification, upgrade and adaptation for new generations of aircraft, equipment and operational requirements. Just as an aircraft exists to carry the ordnance that justifies its existence, so does a carrier exist solely for the purpose of deploying Air Wing elements around the globe; the carrier must always be subservient to the needs of the Navy aviator, just as the airbase on dry land must adapt to match the changing requirements of the tactical units it houses. To upgrade the *Saratoga* a SLEP was performed between October 1980 and February 1983. Built between 1952 and 1955, the carrier was subjected to a $549 million (in 1980s money) rebuild at the Naval Shipyard in Philadelphia, good value when compared with the $5 billions for a new carrier. The old flat-top received a 42ft (13m) exten-

sion to the catapult, new deck elevators with load capacity increased from 84,000 to 110,000lb (38,200 to 50,000kg) and new stores facilities and smaller lifts to handle the new ordnance coming aboard for the Tomcat.

Saratoga put to sea with its new Tomcat squadrons in 1984 and the rebuild gave it a further ten years of life until it was retired in 1994. Next in the yards for a SLEP, the *Forrestal* was laid up between January 1983 and May 1985, going to sea with her first Tomcat squadrons in 1986 when VF-11 and VF-31 sailed for the Mediterranean. Then it was the turn of *Independence*, built between 1955 and 1959 and in SLEP from April 1985 to February 1988. This carrier had already performed several cruises with Tomcats between 1982 and 1985 and, being of more recent build than others of the *Forrestal* class, it had provision for F-14s; it resumed operations in late 1988 and had a further ten years before retirement. Last in its class to receive a schedule for rework, *Ranger* was to have had her SLEP

A pair of Tomcats from VF-142 about to pass over Eisenhower, **second in the** Nimitz **series, during her cruise off the coast of Virginia close by the Norfolk naval base from where the Atlantic carriers operate.**

Operating out of the Pacific the carrier Carl Vinson **with Tomcats and a friendly message visits Australia.**
Vinson **was the third of the** Nimitz **class and is likely to remain in service until at least 2020.**

between July 1993 and August 1996 but cuts doomed her to retirement in that year.

The Iran–Iraq War

The need for an effective and highly capable carrier force was justified throughout the 1980s and the 1990s and the Tomcat served to maintain a clear edge over potential aggressors. But it came close to an embarrassing own-goal when the Iranians overthrew their Shah and installed a fundamentalist Islamic regime. For a while international relations were turned on their head. Seeing in the new extremism a potential threat to world order by religious fundamentalism imposed upon neighbouring states, Western democracies were prone to favour less dogmatic inter-pretations of Islam. For some time Iraq would be seen as a potential bulwark against the exporting of terrorism or threats to the oil fields in the Persian Gulf region and Saudi Arabia, the long-time

friend of the United States. Yet, under the Shah's reign, Iran had been a major outpost for Western interests, jammed with electronic surveillance equipment and packed with arms procured by a ruler who had put power before people. On 1 April 1979 monarchical Iran became an Islamic republic and the seventy-nine Tomcats in the country fell into the hands of political extremists.

When the Shah was deposed Iran had orders pending for approximately $9 billions worth of hardware from the US and large contracts in the offing for tanks from Britain. Not yet sent were 400 AIM-54 Phoenix missiles for the Tomcats, sixty F-16 Fighting Falcons, sixteen RF-4E Phantom reconnaissance aircraft, seven Boeing E-3 AWACS and 200 Harpoon missiles. But the switch from friend to foe was relatively slow with approximately $2.4 billions of orders going through in the first half of 1980. By early 1981 all ties with Iran had been broken as militant funda-mentalists increased their pressure on

sympathetic world revolutionaries. But Iran was ill at ease with its neighbours too. Iranians are not Arabs and tend to regard themselves as superior to them, the Shi'ite sect is not that of most Islamic countries and Iran's zealous drive to export its own brand of religion brought discontent and suspicion from across the border.

Disputes over territory and a concern that Iranian plans to export its version of Islam would undermine Iraq pushed the latter toward war. Sporadic Iranian shelling, more misplaced bravado than serious military action, in September 1980 served only to inflame Iraq. On 22 September Iraqi armed forces attacked Iran in a war that would last eight years and see both sides decline into barbaric conflict reminiscent of the Dark Ages. Seeking to find another client state and get their hands on high-tech Western equipment, the Soviet Union came out in support of the Khomeini regime in Iran and offered goods, services, technical assistance and economic aid, but the Islamic radicals would have none of it and sent aid to rebels fighting a Soviet-imposed dictator in Afghanistan. Soviet diplomats were sent back to Moscow and around a thousand members of the Iranian Communist Party were imprisoned.

When war began each side had approximately the same number of fixed-wing aircraft, around 300, but arguably the quality of the Iranian equipment was higher than that of the Iraqi. Unfortunately for them, the Iranians had already suffered from a collapse in the spares chain and fewer aircraft were serviceable or could be operated at their full potential. There had been serious concern about the Tomcats and their unparalleled kill capability at great range. Before the revolution, orders for the AIM-54 Phoenix totalled 714 rounds but of that number only 284 had been delivered, while 150 which were about to go had been embargoed and the rest were cancelled. In a remarkable volte-face, the country that had bailed out Grumman and kept alive plans for full production of the F-14 when bankers in the United States had been reluctant to help a domestic manuacturer was now in the forefront of a revolution to destroy Western influence in the region.

When American personnel left Iran around the time of the collapse, they retrieved or disabled large quantities of electronic intelligence-gathering equipment that had been used along the northern border with the USSR to monitor Soviet tests from missile sites in Kazakhstan. They left little in working order and executed an emergency plan to destroy, hide or remove anything that could define the exact nature of the work or be used by the new government. Grumman personnel made sure that items vital in operating the AWG-9 and the Phoenix weapon system were not available to the new Iranian regime. Other, less open departments of industry and government, went in and sabotaged avionics and electronics – some of them pro-Shah Iranians performing clandestine operations for the Central Intelligence Agency and a branch of the Defense Intelligence Agency that has the primary responsibility for ensuring such precautions are in place. Nevertheless, rumours leaked out that some at least of the Tomcats were serviceable.

The only foreign country to operate the Tomcat, Iran acquired seventy-nine aircraft shortly before the Shah was deposed. In a war that began with Iraq over territorial disputes the Tomcat saw service against the Iraqi Air Force with reports of patchy success. This Iranian Tomcat is camouflaged for the desert war.

In tanker trials conducted with the No.5 prototype, a US Marine Corps C-130 makes ready to top-up the Tomcat, flanked by a F-4 Phantom monitoring operations. The use of tankers based on carriers would form an important link in moving F-14s to distant locations for reconnaissance or patrol.

In 1981 the war had settled into a slugging match between two inept combatants intent on replaying the horrors of World War I on the desert sands of Iran. The few Tomcats that were flyable were employed as radar pickets, giving early warning of incoming hostiles from Iraq, the AWG-9 being particularly good in that role. Based at Meharabad, Khatami and Shiraz there were probably no more than ten Tomcats available at first, but over the next year or so that number probably doubled and there were continuous reports of Tomcats flying on US radar screens employed to pick up possible hostiles. Satellite intelligence has confirmed this while substantiating a belief that the Iranians were unable to deploy the AWG-9/AIM-54 combination in significant numbers. From the time that they discovered that the equipment had been

disabled the Iranians tried to obtain black-market parts for their Tomcats but none of these attempts was successful.

Recognizing the extraordinary tactical advantage in having several squadrons of Tomcats, Iranian intelligence attempted to obtain F-14 spares. First they tried the usual arms markets but found few spares outlets for a high performance fleet defence fighter that only the US Navy operated. Then they tried to get their covert arms traders to find the necessary equipment to get the Tomcats back into service, including Israel, which had provided large quantities of weapons to Iran, and the United Arab Emirates, which provided goods worth $1 billion. Iran even tried Pakistan and China before using very circuitous links with Moscow to see whether it could help. To the relief of the

Pentagon they could not, implying that the Soviets had no inner access to Tomcat secrets. In time that would change, thanks to the dealings of some very unpatriotic Americans.

Meanwhile, the Iranians continued to operate their Tomcats in novel ways far below the level for which they were designed and built. Still trying to maximize the F-14 fleet, the Iranians began a reverse engineering exercise whereby they tore down the component sections of the hardware and tried to manufacture their own spares from the information thus gained. They quickly realized that the technical steps necessary to engineer and manufacture F-14 spares were beyond their capability, so, with the data in hand, they went back to the Israelis and asked them to do the work. The link with Israel had been alive and well in the days when the Shah ran the country and the Islamic revolutionaries were not about to look a gift horse in the mouth. Israel has probably the most advanced electronic servicing and manufacturing industry outside the US and Europe and was well placed to trade skills for cash. Gradually, Iran began to increase the number of serviceable Tomcats and to build a modest pool of spares for those in front-line operations.

By the end of 1982 the Iranian defence ministry claimed that it was able to perform full maintenance and repair on Tomcats and that it could replicate 80 per cent of the aircraft's components. Most of this was

treated with a good deal of scepticism by Western observers, and the usual excuse that war propaganda had got the better of common sense evaporated when the Iranians put on show in October 1983 a wide range of spares for a number of combat aircraft, including the F-14. Statements affirmed that Iran was able to manufacture not only replacement parts but improved designs, citing the Tomcat's brake gear as one area where Iran had produced a superior design. Despite the exaggerated claims, there was an element of truth in these statements, although the difficulty of maintaining even simple military equipment under the circumstances in

Iran at the time denies validity to the stronger assertions.

Nevertheless, F-14s did fly against Iraqi jets and there is evidence that some were shot down. An Iranian pilot reported in March 1982 that he witnessed an MiG-21 get the better of a Tomcat, but on at least one other occasion an Iraqi MiG-29 was shot down by his own side because the pilot thought a twin-tailed aircraft must be a Tomcat. The fact that Iran was unable to use the Tomcat or integrate it into an effective defence infrastructure says much both for the state of the country's military capability and the nature of modern weapons. With inadequate training and

A Tomcat driver from VF-84, the 'Jolly Rogers', and his NFO are flanked by their wingman to starboard. Operating in pairs Red Flag exercises ensure tight discipline during engagements when the pressure of combat can strain the drills worked through in simulations and exercises.

An F-14A from VF-142 carrying Phoenix and Sidewinder with the nose-mounted Television Camera System blended by a pronounced fairing common to all Tomcats.

little expertise in optimized operations and handling, the Tomcat drivers were unable to use it effectively and Iraqi aircraft had little difficulty in pentrating all the way to Tehran. But more than that, less sophisticated types were able to get the better of the Tomcat in frequent engagements that left the swing-winger impotent not only to operate offensively but also to save itself in combat.

In September 1983 the Iranian Air Force mounted operations against Iraqi forces deep inside Iraq and used F-14s to fly cover for the strike aircraft. What was left of a declining Iranian air capability was hurled against forces on the ground, but in the ensuing combat against Iraqi fighters two Tomcats were shot down near Marivan. On 4 October the Iraqi Air Force struck an Iranian ship spotted in the north-eastern part of the Gulf and later that day fought and shot down one of two Tomcats

patrolling the area, sending the other back to base. The war was spreading outside the territory involved in the land battle and the main Iranian oil terminal at Kharg Island in the Gulf became a focus for attack. Kharg is at the northern end of the Gulf and close to Iran, but it was a key strategic target for Iraq because it was the terminus through which the Iranians continued to export oil – even to the US. On 21 November 1983, on the pretext of stopping an Iranian military force sailing from Kharg, Iraq sent fighters to attack Iranian defenders. In the ensuing melee an F-14A was shot down near Bahragan.

As the peripheral air war intensified and Iran seemingly increased the number of Tomcats it was able to put in the air, Iran fell foul of Iraq's now superior air power. Losses, it seemed, would be proportional to the engagements. On 24 February 1984 another Tomcat was shot down, reportedly

over Khafajiyah, with another on 1 July claimed by Iraq but denied by Iran. Then again on 11 August Iraq mounted a concerted air attack on a convoy of Iranian ships in the area of Khowr-e Musa, close to the Iranian shore. Several ships were sunk or left burning, but Iraq claimed three Tomcats down. In a message sent out on the following day Iraq increased the probability of an engagement between F-14s of different air forces when it announced that any ships heading for Iranian ports would be considered fair game. In response, the United States pledged to protect ships from non-belligerent states and assigned aircraft carriers to cover neutral traffic in the Persian Gulf.

News that any ship in the region would be liable to attack prompted other Middle Eastern states to enter negotiations to bring about an end to the conflict. Led by Saudi Arabia, the Gulf Co-operation

An excellent view of the rear fuselage underside of an F-14A operated by VF-84 and based on the Nimitz. The aircraft carries a pair of Sparrow missiles on underwing pylons.

Council met to deliberate but each side in the war paraded forces in a jingoistic attempt to impress the other and international bystanders. On 11 February 1985 the Iranians staged a fly-past across the capital Tehran, in which were twenty-five Tomcats reported by the authorities to be those not engaged on air-defence operations, implying that the F-14 force was strong and present. It may not have been as abundantly supplied as Iran would have wished its adversary to believe, but the fact that so many aircraft were still around was due in no small part to the clandestine traffic in parts and spares that had begun in the preceding two years.

US intelligence sources were increasingly aware that organizations in North America were implicated in international arms smuggling of major proportions. To uncover the operation US customs set up a phantom company purporting to deal in underhand arms trading. Called Ameritech, it was based in Irvine, California, and sucked in the suppliers plying their wares. On 9 January 1985 Portuguese intermediaries named Moises Broder, Eduadro Ojeda and Carlos Ribeiro were arrested by customs officers handling Hawk missile parts worth more than $619,000 and purchased from the shell company. The links between the US and Iran used several routes to move the parts and the weapons around and several went through London where dealers worked with the National Iranian Oil Company. Both goods and money were laundered through England and several British companies were actively involved in illicit trading. With the FBI, British intelligence cracked the links and on 11 July arrested an Iranian national while the FBI caught several agents across the US.

The Iranian arrested in Britain worked with Primitivo Baluyat Cayabyab, then a storekeeper on the Kitty Hawk based at San Diego; Pedro Manansala Quito, a civilian in the Navy North Island Supply Department at San Diego; and Edgardo Pangilinan Agustin, an ex-Navy New York businessman. The rings involved with these people were not traced to their source but an unusual link emerged as Kitty Hawk was preparing to sail for the Indian Ocean. An auditor with the Navy, P/O Robert Jackson discovered what he thought was the fraudulent redirection of Navy property, including Phoenix missiles, to Iranian linkmen. Totally disregarding official Navy procedure, Jackson sent a telegram direct to President Reagan claiming that he had irrefutable evidence that if Kitty Hawk sailed on schedule 24 July valuable evidence would be lost. The matter was endorsed by Congressman Jim Bates, but Defense Secretary Weinberger refused to halt the sailing but put the Inspector General on to the case.

Kitty Hawk sailed on schedule but the investigation revealed links through the carriers *Carl Vinson* and *Ranger* where more spares and weapons purportedly had been stolen. Within one week the FBI had uncovered the contacts and arrested six men in time to prevent the arms getting through. The accused included a military publisher, a Lebanese man in the import–export business, an Iranian procurement official and an arms trader. Before declaring their hand the officials had planted bogus equipment in among the shipments, but there was little evidence to suggest that any missiles reached the Iranian Air Force. Several groups tried to earn personal fortunes by clandestine trading to support the Tomcat squadrons in Iran but none was totally successful although some parts did get through. It was a case of diminishing opportunities. By 1986 the Iranians had fewer than sixty operational aircraft of which no more than nine were F-14s. But there was one chilling legacy to the ever-present menace that an Iranian F-14 could one day threaten US aircraft from carriers in the Gulf.

On 3 July 1988 an Aegis missile system aboard the US destroyer *Vincennes* shot down an Iranian Airbus A300 *en route* from Bandar Abbas to Dubai. Operators aboard the destroyer mistakenly identified the airliner as an incoming F-14 and when it failed to respond to an IFF code two surface-to-air missiles were launched, striking the aircraft at 12,000ft (3,600m) and killing all 290 people on board. In retribution for this terrible case of mistaken identity, Iranian Islamic fundamentalists arranged through a terrorist group in Palestine for a bomb to be placed aboard an American airliner. On 21 December a Pan American Boeing 747 took off from London-Heathrow westbound for New York. Shortly thereafter, while it was flying over Scotland, the bomb exploded and the aircraft fell on to the small town of Lockerbie. All 258 people on board were killed.

Dispute with Libya (I)

If the combat performance of Iranian pilots flying the F-14 was abysmal, the record struck by US Navy pilots flying the Tomcat against aggressors vindicated the aircraft's

With wings about to sweep forward, a Tomcat is moved on to the catapult just ahead of the blast doors, flanked by A-6 Intruders and A-7 Corsairs.

outstanding capability. That threat was first presented less than seven years after the Tomcat's first operational deployment. In an exercise which was to last two days beginning on 18 August 1981, the carriers *Nimitz* and *Forrestal* together with fourteen other Navy ships positioned themselves in an area of the Mediterranean due south of Italy where they would conduct live firing tests against drones and targets. The test area occupied 3,200sq miles (8,300sq km) and extended into the Gulf of Sidra. Libya had claimed that its territorial waters extended south from a line of latitude from Misurata in the west to Benghazi in the east, but the US refused to accept this unilateral claim and recognized only the standard three-miles limit as the legal division between national and international waters.

On the day the exercises began, the Libyans made thirty-five intrusions into the test area, the precise location of which had been declared through the official channels six days before. Because the exercises were being conducted in international waters, the Sixth Fleet, commanded by Vice-Adm William H. Rowden, had no right to expel overflights by foreign powers but F-14s were sent out by Adm James E. Service, commander of Task Force 60, to advise intruders visually that live firing was taking place. If the Libyan aircraft failed to divert the firing was suspended until the airspace was clear.

The *Nimitz* was stationed on the northern edge of the exercise area about 100miles (160km) from the coast of Libya and a variety of Libyan aircraft flew close to the Sixth Fleet, one about every 26min. Most flights involved two-plane elements and were generally MiG-23 or MiG-25 types together with French-built Mirages. Approaches were flown from west, south and east and six penetrated into the test area proper.

The following day, 19 August, the Fleet expected a similar pattern of disruptive intrusions as flight operations got under way at 0545 hr. The Libyans had already sent a two-plane intrusion through and a second pair were being turned away by F-14s from VF-41 when two Su-22 Fitter jets, the only ones observed during the entire exercise, were picked up on radar by another two F-14s. An E-2C Hawkeye was aloft north of the *Nimitz* when the Su-22 appeared, positioned well away from possible Libyan suicide missions dispatched with the aim of bringing it down. It was not the E-2C that saw the intruders but the radar scope on aircraft No.107 flown by Cdr Henry Kleeman (CO of VF-41) and NFO Lt Dave Venlet and their No.2, aircraft No.112 piloted by Lt Larry Muczynski with NFO Lt Steve Walker. From 20,000ft (6,000m) about 100miles (160km) south of *Nimitz* the Tomcat pair were close to but well outside the accepted three-miles limit.

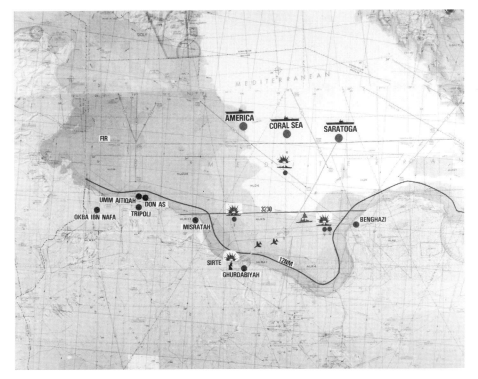

Disputed waters in the Gulf of Sidra shown by the horizontal line between Benghazi and Misurata became the location for a confrontation on 24 March 1986 when US aircraft were shot at and responded by attacking Libyan surface ships and missile installations and radar sites at Sirte. This briefing map shows the region where Tomcats flew cover and turned back two MiG-25 Foxbats.

When they observed the Libyan fighters the Tomcats contacted *Nimitz* which ordered them to intercept the aircraft and order them away. About 2miles (3.2km) apart the two Tomcats moved south as a loose pair and did not take up attack positions. The two Fitters were heading north-east in tight formation about 500ft (150m) apart and Kleeman got into visual range at 8miles (13km) when he banked 90 degrees, intending to turn 150 degrees to the left and come alongside the Libyan fighters so that he could warn them off. Kleeman's Tomcat was about 500ft above the lead Su-22 and the two were about 1,000ft (300m) apart when the Libyan fighter fired one AA-2 Atoll heat-seeking missile. Both Tomcat pilots saw the firing and broke hard left, the missile passing clean under Kleeman's wing. Muczynski then turned inside the lead Fitter and came in behind.

At this instant the second Fitter broke hard right and started to climb so Kleeman reversed his turn to the left and followed his target round until he was flying almost directly into sun. The Libyan fighter continued to pull round to the right and, as soon as his target was clear of the glare and flying south-east, Kleeman launched an AIM-9L Sidewinder from the left glove mounting which hit the Fitter in the rear fuselage 5sec before the pilot ejected. By this time Muczynski had turned inside his target and came out high and behind as the Su-22 continued on a northerly heading before coming round to the right toward the sun. Before he reached the safety of the glare the No.2 Tomcat had fired a

On 14–15 April 1986 a large strike force converged on Libya in an attempt to punish Col Qadhafi for acts of international terrorism and unwarranted attacks on American aircraft operating from international waters in the Mediterranean. With aircraft sent from Britain and carriers in the area, F-14s acted as escort flying CAP and reconnaissance using TARPS. This map shows the route flown by F-111Fs and the proximity of the carriers.

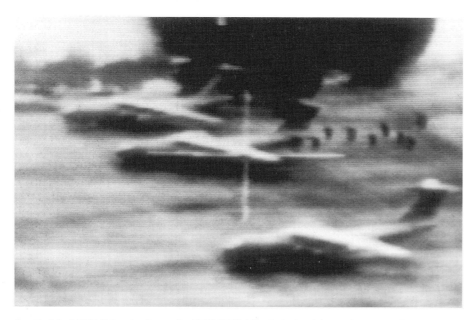

An attack by F-111F fighter-bombers using 500lb (228kg) bombs in the night attack on 14–15 April was imaged by a Pave Tack laser-guided tracking system used to place the bombs accurately on target. The picture shows a line of Il-76 transports about to receive a direct hit. Operations such as this are made possible by the defensive screen laid by F-14s.

were attacked by batteries of anti-aircraft fire and up to ten SAMs but without success. Next day the US attacked and VF-142 flew top cover for the strike aircraft hitting Syrian gun positions. Just hours after this attack the US Marines at Beirut Airport were fired on by rockets and artillery and on 6 December ten Tomcats roared over Beirut heading for the mountains beyond. It was on this day that the director of the CIA, Adm Stansfield Turner criticized the use of high-value Naval aircraft to tease out the aggressors, claiming that reconnaissance information could be obtained more safely by using more appropriate aircraft – such as the SR-71. But the flights continued and were stepped up throughout the month. On 13 December more overflights brought the usual rounds of anti-aircraft fire and an almost immediate offshore shelling by warships. Repeated five days later, the carrier *Independence* sent Tomcats over Syrian positions with the predictable responses in sequence by each side.

By the end of December the routine overflights were running into increasing opposition and special countermeasures were felt to be necessary to avoid the increasingly intense anti-aircraft measures. Low-level overflights drew heavy gunfire and missiles and the F-14s employed heat balloons to deflect infra-red weapons. Through January and into February 1983 the F-14s kept up the pressure until both the US and Israeli forces decided that it was time to go home. In the event the major clash between US and Syrian air elements never took place and the carriers withdrew. Yet the psychological effect produced by the F-14 was every bit as great as any land-based fighter and testifies to the aircraft's reputation so that it was regarded by friend and foe alike as a weapon of awesome potential.

Action Over Lebanon

The F-14 did not have long to wait to see more action. On 6 June 1982 Israeli forces launched an attack into Lebanon to clear enclaves used by the Palestine Liberation Organization (PLO), destroy artillery positions used to bombard Israeli settlements and to flush out springboards for terrorist raids into Israel. While the Israeli Air Force shattered SAM sites up the Bekaa Valley and fought off Syrian MiGs, 35,000 Israeli troops poured into the cities of Tyre, Sidon and Damour. After much effort and several weeks of siege the PLO were driven from Beirut and a multinational force moved in. On 18 April a terrorist group bombed the US embassy in Beirut killing forty-nine people, fighting broke out between rival factions and President

Sidewinder which homed on the Fitter, swept straight up the tailpipe and blew the back off the fuselage. The pilot ejected but his parachute failed. Within minutes the Libyans had a well co-ordinated search and rescue operation under way for the downed airman, using a C-130 to command activities. The engagement had taken place about 50miles (80km) from the Libyan coast, and was notable as the first engagement between variable-geometry aircraft.

Reagan ordered US warships to shell positions in the hills beginning on 8 September. Next day the *Eisenhower* sent out Tomcats to conduct reconnaissance missions but they were more a show of intent than tools for intelligence gathering.

With TARPS aircraft to deploy, VF-143 sent Tomcats out regularly over the next several days and during the morning of 19 September flew over Beirut. Just two days later F-14s streaked over the southern Lebanese mountains as Syrian MiGs flew up the Bekaa Valley. Tension was high and a major clash of arms was in the offing. On the ground suicide attacks continued to take a heavy toll in human life as a truck full of explosives took the lives of 239 US soldiers and fifty-eight French paratroops on 23 October. On 10 November Syrian air defence units based in Lebanon fired surface-to-air missiles on F-14s from the *Eisenhower* flying over the central mountains close to the Lebanese capital. Sensing a flagrant provocation, Syria ordered general mobilization and Israel prepared for the worst. As US forces stepped up the pressure of F-14 overflights, the drama implicit in using such a high-profile combat aircraft for 'reconnaissance' flights was not lost on Syria or Lebanon.

Additional overflights by formations of Tomcats increased toward the end of November and on 3 December two F-14s

Dispute with Libya (II)

Further to the west, Libya took an increasingly active role in mobilizing international terrorism and the United States was equally determined to put that down. As if to send a warning to Col Qadhafi, Tomcats were again used to press home the willingness of the US to use force if necessary. On 25 July 1984 they flew over the disputed territorial boundary in the Gulf of Sidra without first giving notice of intent. Qadhafi was furious and the Soviets

Carrier support with F-14 CAP flights allowed the precise targeting of military installations and individual combat aircraft at Benina airfield. The quality of these images is as good as those obtained by reconnaissance Tomcats; the use of dual-purpose aircraft such as the F-14 brings flexibility to mission planners and in operational tactics.

complained that the United States was engaged in unprovoked aggression of a minor power. The following year international terrorism took on a new form as the cruise liner *Achille Lauro* was hijacked and an American killed. In an operation with the PLO, Qadhafi had further extended his hand of intervention and within his own borders the number of training camps for terrorists increased. In early 1986 the US declared that any PLO terrorist action would meet with an immediate military response and Qadhafi announced that the latitude he claimed as the true boundary of Libya's territorial waters (32 degrees 30min N) was a 'line of death' within which any intruders would be attacked.

In March 1986 three US carriers, *America*, *Coral Sea* and *Saratoga* were deployed for exercises in the Mediterranean, operations that would take place in the Gulf of Sidra below Libya's 'line of death'. Although the presence of the warships had been notified through the appropriate channels Qadhafi took matters into his own hands and on 24 March fired several SA-5 surface-to-air missiles at Navy aircraft flying in the area claimed as Libyan territorial air space. Later the same day two MiG-15 Foxbats, pride of the Libyan Air Force, entered the Gulf of Sidra and were turned back by two F-14s. Other SA-5 launches followed, together with one SA-2 and the US retaliated by firing a Harpoon at a fast Libyan missile patrol boat and sinking it. Next day the guided missile cruiser USS *Yorktown* fired another Harpoon at an unidentified ship behaving in a threatening manner and closing on the US warship. Later, when the Libyans continued to fire at US aircraft in international air space, A-7 Corsairs hit missile and radar sites at Sirte. Throughout, F-14 Tomcats flew cover for the attack aircraft and CAPs to keep the air clear of Libyan aircraft.

When Libya was suspected of complicity in the bombing of a discotheque in Berlin where one of its serviceman was killed the US decided to apply its 'inherent right of self-defence' and a combined US Air Force and Navy operation was mounted against Qadhafi. From bases in the United Kingdom and warships in the Mediterranean a major strike was mounted against targets in Libya during the night of 14–15 April. Hailed by one commentator as the 'first opportunity for US air forces to apply many of the technologies incorporated since the end of the Vietnam War', the strike involved about a hundred aircraft, key among which were eighteen F-111F fighter bombers and some EF-111 Raven electronic warfare aircraft. The F-111Fs came from England, routed round France, which had refused an overflight request, while Navy aircraft were launched from the *America* and the *Coral Sea*.

Under Operation *Prairie Fire* the Navy was assigned targets near Benghazi, including the Benina airfield, two miles from the town. Under cover of EA-6B Prowler electronic jamming aircraft, F/A-18s, A-6Es and A-7Es conducted strikes while F-14s of VF-33 and VF-101 flew CAP and top cover. VF-101 aircraft were fired on by Libyan SAMs but no aircraft were lost and none was engaged in combat. The Tomcats picked up the transiting F-111s as they appeared in the Mediterranean, the first time the two

aircraft – one the product of the other's failure to satisfy Navy needs – had operated in such close co-operation on a major military action. With the extensive use of 'smart' weapons and several laser-guided bombs employed for the first time, the post-attack bomb damage assessment was of especial interest. No sooner had the strikes been completed than an SR-71 departed for a high overflight, its mission confounded by cloud.

Tomcats were again involved in Mediterranean action less than three years later, this time further east, well away from the 'line of death' and about 70 miles (112km) north of the coastal city of Tobruk. On 4 January 1989 Air Wing 3 was operating in the Mediterranean, flying screen for the carrier USS *Kennedy*. At 1155hr local time the carrier's airborne E-2C reported two MiG-23 Flogger Es

airborne from Libya's Al-Bumbah airfield and two Tomcats from VF-14 at 20,000ft (6,000m) patrolling south of the carrier were notified. At first the MiGs flew approximately north-east and then turned to a heading of 340 degrees to intercept the Tomcats. Two minutes later the lead Tomcat reported a radar contact at 72 miles (115km) descending from 10,000 to 8,000ft (3,000 to 2,400m). One minute later the two MiGs were due south at 8,000ft on a heading of 330 degrees and seconds later still the two Tomcats began a 20-degrees left turn to avoid contact. Almost immediately the Libyan fighters turned on a heading of 360 degrees, toward the F-14s, and descended to 5,000ft (1,500m). It was at this point that the Tomcats knew the Libyan fighters were intent on engaging them.

The Tomcats reacted by descending to

This page and opposite: Tomcats flying **TARPS** missions in the 1990s have the range and the flexibility to pursue intelligence-gathering objectives far beyond those made available to reconnaissance aircraft of previous decades. In-flight refuelling provides extended sea legs for long-duration flights across hostile territory in pursuit of reconnaissance imagery or surveillance conducted on a repetitive basis. Note the extended refuelling probe and the 270gall (1,215 l) drop tanks.

3,000ft (900m) and turning again, once more to avoid confronting the Libyans but 30sec later, with the range now down to about 45 miles (72km), they turned once again to head for the F-14s. At this the Tomcats accelerated and took avoiding action for the third time, but at a range of 35miles (56km) and a height of 7,000ft (2,100m) the MiGs turned on to a collision course. At this the carrier battle group commander gave the order 'Weapons hold' and the Tomcats turned away a fourth time. Just 7sec on the F-14 wingman reported a radar lock on to the second MiG and another 5sec later both MiGs turned to a head-on course. Again the F-14s turned away and again the MiGs turned head on. At 12:00:57 local time the lead F-14 switched the master armament on as the MiGs got to within 20 miles (32km) and 23sec afterwards the lead Tomcat fired

an AIM-7M Sparrow at the lead bogie at a range of 12 miles (19km) followed 12sec after by a second Sparrow at 10 miles (16km). Both locked on initially but missed.

At 5 miles (8km) range the Tomcats split, but the two MiGs turned sharply and went for the lead F-14 just as the wingman spotted the bogies and launched a Sparrow at the MiG wingman; this destroyed the Libyan fighter as the Tomcat broke away and climbed fast and to the right. Exactly 30sec later the lead Tomcat reversed back across to the right after the split and rolled on to the tail of the lead MiG. The pilot fired an AIM-9M Sidewinder at a range of 1.5miles (2.4km), which hit and destroyed the Libyan aircraft. Both F-14s turned north and dashed for the carrier at low altitude while the pilots of the downed MiGs, floating to the sea on parachutes, were

soon to be retrieved by Libyan ships. With four kills to its credit, once again the Tomcat showed itself as superior in the hands of professionals.

To date the F-14 had been involved in sporadic engagements, committed to flying top cover or CAPs for other men's missions or patrolling unfriendly sea looking for aggressive intent. As the product of a Cold War stand-off, the F-14 was too late to see the last of the intermediate-generation jet wars – the conflict in south-east Asia. Yet, just as it first flew operational CAPs at the last retreat from south-east Asia, so would it fall to the F-14 to participate in a war of liberation, returning a sense of accomplishment to an American military machine badly scarred by the withdrawal from Vietnam.

The pairing of the extended eyes of the E-2C Hawkeye and the AWG-9 or AN/APG-71 radar of the F-14 receives added effectiveness with the new AN/ASW-27C data link system which allows groups of four Tomcats to operate independently of an airborne early warning and control system. Aircraft deployed to Desert Storm in late 1990 were equipped with this system which significantly enhances sensor data and autonomous control of the air battle.

The Gulf War

The Persian Gulf had been the prowling ground for the Tomcat on several occasions but previous engagements were as nothing compared to the force that would be unleashed upon an aggressor playing bully to an unprotected state. The prelude to a mighty coalition of armed force unprecedented since World War II began when troops of Saddam Hussein's Republican Guard invaded Kuwait on 2 August 1990. It came after he had failed to get a political agreement to Iraqi territorial claims and a demand that Kuwait should write off $5.5 billions in loans it had made to Iraq during its recent war with Iran. The United States and its NATO allies had been concerned about Iraq's military build-up and intelligence indicating its nuclear,

biological and chemical (NBC) weapons development. When Saddam Hussein asked the US Ambassador in Baghdad how the US viewed the dispute with Kuwait he was told that the US had no opinion on internal Arab matters. Later, others would comment that the Ambassador knew full well that Iraqis are not Arabs but Saddam Hussein missed the point.

When Iraq invaded Kuwait the US froze Iraqi assets in America and within four days Saudi Arabia had invited foreign troops in for a consolidated defence against further aggression. Under Operation *Desert Shield* the US would help to deter an invasion of Saudi Arabia, leading a coalition of forces to eject Iraqi troops from Kuwait and destroy key weapons, disable Saddam Hussein's military machine and eliminate R&D and manufacturing plants supporting his NBC warfare programme.

The carriers would be key elements in asserting an early US presence in the region. The *Independence* had sailed on a west Pacific/Indian Ocean cruise on 23 June and passed through the Straits of Hormuz and into the Persian Gulf on the very day Iraqi troops had poured into Kuwait. Like other squadrons on the carrier, VF-21 had its Tomcats at full alert, flying screening missions at the perimeter while the coalition forces gathered and plans were made to strengthen naval forces in the region. However, it would be the lot of *Independence* to have to leave the area before action began and on 20 December the carrier was back home.

As scheduled before the invasion, on 7 August the *Saratoga* had sailed for the Red Sea carrying Tomcat squadrons VF-74 and VF-103 equipped with the new F-14B (at this date known as the F-14+). It was to

Tomcats from VF-32 aboard the USS Kennedy **cruise in loose formation during a patrol. Traditionally, F-14s hunted in flights of four but engagements with the enemy have shown that two aircraft operating together are a more efficient mix and achieve similar results.**

relieve the *Eisenhower*, at sea with Tomcat squadrons VF-142 and VF-143 since 8 March. *Eisenhower* was home on 12 September and missed the action that was to come but it was there when it was needed most – at the invasion of Kuwait. No sooner had that taken place than Pentagon planners threw away their well-laid plans for cruises, training patrols and the like for a new blueprint that would put firepower on deck in the Persian Gulf/Red Sea area. Command of Desert Shield would be in the capable hands of Gen Norman Schwarzkopf.

Since the debacle over Desert One in 1980 and the disastrous attempt to free American hostages in Tehran the Pentagon had set up a Rapid Deployment Force (RDF), for each of several selected global regions. To each region a commander was appointed with the remit to specialize in the people, places and political nuances that could involve American action. Schwarzkopf was the commander for the Persian Gulf. At first the RDF was to have been a specialist, elite unit capable of being dispatched to any brushfire on the

planet; but that was seen as inefficient: with a Naval presence in most oceans all the time, indigenous, local forces would be appropriate. So the RDF became a plan rather than a separate armed force which could be implemented in extreme emergency and triggered by extraordinary events. In that regard, the Tomcats aboard the carriers were as much a part of the RDF as the troops that poured into Saudi Arabia from August 1990.

With the *Eisenhower* scheduled to be relieved by *Saratoga*, the first carrier to sail specifically for the Middle East in response to the invasion was the *Kennedy*. It slipped its moorings at Norfolk on 15 August carrying F-14A Tomcats in VF-14 and VF-32 of Air Wing 3. Its destination was unclear because the plans for *Desert Shield* were still evolving; but the giant carrier sailed first for the Mediterranean where it performed some exercises to complete qualification, an operation which flexed all elements of Air Wing 3 and included the demonstration of activities conducted in a simulated chemical and biological warfare environment. Few were under any illusion

about the possibility of Saddam Hussein's employing these methods or worse. From the Mediterranean the *Kennedy* was sent to the Red Sea to support the *Saratoga*, passing through the Suez Canal in September. By this time plans were well in hand for consolidating the carrier force.

Plans for ejecting Iraqi forces from Kuwait evolved in the closing months of 1990. Where once there had been hope that a massive show of force would convince Saddam Hussein to comply with United Nations' resolutions there was now a firm conviction that war was inevitable. Concern grew that the size of Iraq's Army and the potential threat from missile and chemical attack were too great for the size of the response in the original plans that had been drawn up. So, further consolidation was to lead to a delay during which more troops were dispatched to the region along with more aircraft and a stronger naval presence. Between August and October 1990 considerable progress was made in reaching final decisions about the right way to eject the Iraqis. A massive air campaign was inevitable, to destroy C3I

Tomcats overfly the Kennedy, this time in tight formation. Note the degree of overhang on the two F-14s parked on the aft port aircraft elevator.

(command, communications, control and intelligence) facilities, demolish AAA batteries and SAM sites, gain control of the skies over Kuwait and southern Iraq, blunt as far as possible the ability of the Republican Guard to operate and destroy a considerable part of the Iraqi war machine. Beyond that was a menu of targets for doing long-term damage to Iraqi work on weapons of mass destruction.

Plans were set and stalling moves by Irqai politicians and Russian intermediaries were swept aside. Saddam Hussein was given an ultimatum to get out of Kuwait or be ejected by force. War plans involving the US Navy revolved around the use of battleships and submarines to launch large numbers of cruise missiles against high-value targets in Iraq, sweep the sea lanes of mines and Iraqi shipping, conduct air strikes launched from carriers and provide cover for Navy and Air Force operations. The Red Sea Battle Group was to be supported by four carriers with the

Persian Gulf Battle Group comprising two carriers. Half of the US Navy's flat-top force was to be concentrated in one region to support the biggest military operation involving allied forces since 1945. But this was to be no Vietnam. The politicians agreed to hand over management of the assault to the military and, once unleashed, the coalition forces would have a free hand within the constraints of international codes governing the use of force by states. As Saddam Hussein would correctly predict, it was to be the 'Mother of all battles', but not in the way he believed.

On 8 December 1990 the carrier *Ranger* moved out toward the Persian Gulf carrying Air Wing 2, including VF-1 and VF-2 with F-14A Tomcats as well as A-6E Intruder, EA-6B Prowler and E-2C Hawkeye squadrons. It would take up station with the carrier *Midway*, which had sailed on 2 October. *Midway* was the oldest carrier in the Fleet, supporting Air Wing 5 also with F/A-18 Hornets, Intruders,

Hawkeyes and Prowlers. It was the only carrier in the Gulf not to have F-14 squadrons on board. On 28 December the *America* and the *Roosevelt* weighed anchor for the Red Sea Battle Group, there to join the *Saratoga* and the *Kennedy*. *America* housed Air Wing 1, with the F-14A Tomcat squadrons VF-33 and VF-102 while *Roosevelt* conveyed Air Wing 8, including the F-14A squadrons VF-41 and VF-84. In all there were eight Tomcat squadrons in the Red Sea and one in the Gulf.

Just before the Tomcat squadrons deployed for *Desert Storm*, the military action to oust Iraqi forces, all F-14s were fitted with the Harris AN/ASW-27C tactical data link. The equipment was a development of the ASW-27B, which allows each F-14 to link information back to an airborne controller – in most cases the E-2C Hawkeye – which then relays it to other aircraft. The AN/ASW-27C is a fighter-to-fighter link which provides

The carrier Nimitz **reaches the Suez Canal, greeted by fire hoses and small boats. US carriers are frequent visitors to the region and battle groups serve a diplomatic purpose, hosting VIPs from countries whose waters they pass through, acting as representatives of the US government and generally carrying the flag on goodwill missions. All too frequently the carriers turn-to when disaster strikes.**

a tactical display in the cockpit to show the relative location of other F-14s in the strike and their individual radar targets. Each net was assigned a common frequency but in the fighter-to-fighter mode the multiplexing was limited to four aircraft. In one big step it took the handling of real-time situations out of the hands of remote controllers and into the decision structure of the flight element leaders. In effect, it allowed the pilots involved to link together and prevent data loss from a distant controller should the UHF hook-up fail due to the range or obscuration at low altitude. F-14s would operate over Baghdad and communication links via the E-3 Sentry 250miles (400km) away were sometimes spotty. By switching to the AN/ASW-27C the pilots had a clear picture of the air situation and could mark 'bogies' from 'friendlies'.

However, when the Tomcat force went to war along with the rest of the coalition

air forces on the morning of 17 January 1991 the result was to prove disappointing. The Iraqi Air Force was loath to come up and tangle, consigning air defence to ground units operating through AAA or SAMs. More than one pilot hoped to confront the best Saddam Hussein could throw at them and show what the Tomcat could do. Still, there was work to be done. Tomcat missions were broken into three primary types: target combat air patrol (TARCAP), barrier combat air patrol (BARCAP) and MiG sweeps. Aircraft were given separate missions. TARCAPs were assigned to protect strike aircraft over the target and would rendezvous at that location or escort strike aircraft some or all of the way across hostile airspace. BARCAPs would have Tomcats positioning themselves between the strike force and potential hostile air threats, using their powerful AWG-9 radars to provide early warning and their own target

designation. MiG sweeps were the most demanding because they actively hunted down the enemy; they were also the most frustrating for aforesaid reasons.

It was in the heat of downtown Baghdad that the AN/ASW-27C was most useful, however. Each pilot had his own address and in fighter-net mode he would set his own assigned frequency; the system would then maintain track of all the aircraft in his net, because each aircraft transmitted all the AWG-9 targets to the other Tomcats and these were continuously updated. Back-seaters could extract additional information by painting a specific target symbol on the display. Information down to heading and the speed of friendly or enemy aircraft or even the fuel quantity remaining in a wingman's aircraft could be obtained through this system. By extracting friendly aircraft from the skies of a crowded region the Tomcat drivers were able to get a coherent picture, creating a map showing where other F-14s were and where the bogies were. By accessing systems information from other aircraft, element leaders could make tactical decisions without having to revert to a distant controller. Best of all, the AN/ASW-27C was almost impervious to jamming and by sensing and then countermanding ECM signals the data link was secure.

Just four days into the war and with no success in finding combat, Tomcat crews were itching for a fight with the might of the Iraqi Air Force. But the tables were turned and it was the Iraqis that made the first kill. From the *Saratoga* F-14B BuAer No.161430, piloted by Lt Devon Jones with NFO Lt Lawrence R. Slade and equipped with TARPS, took off shortly after 0600hr to escort an EA-6B Prowler on a single strike with one HARM (high-speed anti-radiation missile) near the heavily defended airfield of Al Asad. After

refuelling they formated and flew out at between 26,000 and 30,000ft (7,800 and 9,100m), reached the target and covered the Prowler as it released its HARM, pressing on to a target of opportunity. When they reached it there was no chance for a strike so they turned for home, just as a SAM started snaking up from below. Conforming to the simulated response, Lt Jones rolled into the SAM to throw it off track but the missile retained its lock and came at them from behind. It was a Soviet SA-2 modified by the Iraqis with optical tracking; it detonated with a bright flash that threw the Tomcat into a roll from which it degraded into a flat spin.

The violence of the explosion tore the mask from Jones's face and threw in large negative g loads making it almost impossible to see the instruments. In the back, Slade could see the altitude tumbling and at 14,000ft (4,200m) both men reached for

the ejection handle. Jones got to it before his NFO and both men punched out leaving the doomed Tomcat to a desert grave. The two crew members parachuted to the desert but were separated. Jones started walking toward some cover, seeking to put as much distance as possible between himself and the wreckage, and radioed to say where he thought he was. Coming upon some bushes he continued walking in the hope of finding cover or some alleviation to the rock hard surface, anything into which he could dig a small burrow. After more than two hours he spotted what turned out to be a cylindrical tank and, short of reaching it, decided that he would scratch out a hole for cover.

It took Lt Jones one hour to claw sand and compacted rocky material from the surface, making a trench 4ft long by 3ft deep. By mid-morning, wondering whether he had done more harm than good by

An F-14 from VF-32 operating with Air Wing 3 aboard the *Kennedy* performs a joint patrol with a Royal Air Force F-4 deployed to the Red Sea during Operation Desert Shield, the defence of Saudi Arabia and the Gulf States against further Iraqi aggression.

With flaps and slats reconfiguring the wings of this F-14 as it drops toward the deck of the carrier Roosevelt, **another Tomcat returns from a patrol over southern Iraq in support of Operation** Provide Comfort **during May 1991.**

disturbing the ground and making a visible change in the surface texture, a truck rolled up to the cylinder and Jones mused over the prospect of using his .38 revolver to hijack the vehicle and make a dash for the border. It soon moved off. Around noon he tried to call search-and-rescue through his radio and this time, to his surprise, got a reaction. It was from an A-10 Warthog piloted by Capt Randy Goff of the 354th Tactical Fighter Wing with his wingman Capt Paul Johnson close by. Putting out flares from 18,000ft (5,500m) and getting a reflection from a mirror flashed by Lt Jones, the A-10s were able to plot his location and call in a pair of MH-53J helicopters from a special

operations unit. While that was happening the Iraqi truck reappeared and the A-10s came down and destroyed it. It took about an hour for the big Pave Low helicopters to bridge the 140miles (220km) back to Saudi Arabia.

Lt Slade did not have such luck and was destined to spend six weeks as a prisoner of war. He managed to survive the day but was picked up by a couple of dishevelled Iraqis driving a white Datsun truck. Since they were armed with a shotgun and an AK-47, Slade had little option but to go with them. They took him to an Army camp outside Baghdad from where he was moved to a number of other camps, blind-folded and frequently beaten up. After

being shifted into buildings close to targets and narrowly escaping death from coalition bombs the fighting stopped and he was repatriated to Saudi Arabia and from there home. Lts Jones and Slade were the only Tomcat crew shot down.

When the F-14 went to war in *Desert Storm* the type was familiar to Iraqi airmen. They had encountered Iranian Tomcats before and knew the aircraft's capabilities. From the outset coalition pilots discovered that Iraqi aircraft would turn and run the instant they were illuminated by an AWG-9 radar. Constantly frustrated, the Navy pilots went hunting for prey that eluded them as a result of their reputation. At first, when air cover was essential, flights of four and the great range of the Tomcat was favoured for these reconnaissance and bomb-damage assessment flights. The F-14 was effective in these long-range operations and many times an F-15 Eagle was vectored in to attack a stray Iraqi aircraft where the Tomcat pilot would have had all the aids he needed to down the bogie. But that day did come – only once. On 6 February an F-14A (BuAer No.162603) from VF-1, piloted by Lt Donald S. Broce with NFO Cdr Ron D. McElraft, the Squadron Commander, fired an AIM-9M Sidewinder at an Iraqi Mi-8 helicopter and brought it down: the only kill to a Tomcat in *Desert Storm*.

Extending the Tomcat's Life

Even as Saddam Hussein was planning the invasion of Kuwait, Grumman was putting the final touches to a major programme for extending the life of the basic airframe. Through a series of derivatives, each more sophisticated than its predecessor, Grumman wanted to maintain the existing production line and give the aircraft a new lease of life well into the twenty-first century. The Grumman chairman Renso Caporali took the proposals to the Pentagon and in a letter to Defense Secretary Cheney, dated 24 April 1991, argued the cost-effectiveness of buying upgraded Tomcats rather than a developed version of the Hornet, the F/A-18E/F, for a combined fleet fighter and attack aircraft, which was the Pentagon's preference. The Navy was caught between needs and desires as budget cuts slashed the money available for aircraft procurement. The F-14 was not cheap and, while wanting the best aircraft it could get, the Navy had to settle for the most cost-effective package. The Hornet was a strong contender for the multi-role mission specification combining fleet defence and attack; but Grumman was not about to give up without a fight.

The niche that opened up for the F-14 Tomcat derivatives and the F/A-18E/F Hornet was brought about by the cancellation of the A-12 advanced attack aircraft. In January 1988 General Dynamics and McDonnell Douglas had been contracted to develop a delta-shaped successor to the A-6 Intruder, incorporating stealth and performance improvements for a development price of $4.8 billion. Two years later, on 4 May 1990, they came back to the

A new lease of life for the Tomcat opened up when the A-12 Avenger stealth attack replacement for the A-6 Intruder was cancelled in January 1991, leaving that slot wide open. This artist's view shows the remarkable triangular planform with recessed engine inlets.

Tomcats would go out on CAP or escort, but the effect of an F-14 in the area was unprecedented and unmatched by that of any other aircraft in the conflict. Quite soon, and as a direct result, it was possible to put only two up and commit more aircraft to other work. For Tomcat pilots the most frustrating part of the job was resisting the temptation to light off after Iraqi aircraft. Their job was to fly shotgun on strike aircraft and undefended ECM or AEW types and a radius limit was applied outside which they were forbidden

from going in pursuit of the enemy.

Tomcat crews had long days, building up to a mission with two hours or more briefing and preparing, four to seven hours in the air with several mid-air refuellings and another two hours in post-flight debriefing. The downing of an F-14B with all its superior electronics, avionics and more powerful engines was both a blow and a shock. Only four of the twelve Tomcat squadrons had the F-14B and feelings ran high after this loss. Many operations called for TARPS runs deep into Iraqi territory

Pentagon with estimates up by $1 billion and a programme schedule beyond the times agreed in the contract. During the sesond half of the year the Pentagon learned of numerous difficulties with the A-12 and Cheney served notice on the Navy to show cause why the aircraft should not be cancelled. The Navy could not and on 7 January 1991 Cheney axed the A-12, opening prospects for an interim replacement, or AX, expected to cost $63 millions a copy. Top of the Navy's selection list for the interim aircraft were derivatives of the F-14, while McDonnell Douglas pushed for the selection of a hybrid Hornet incorporating elements of two existing F-18 versions already in development: the F/A-18E single-seat version of the C model and the F/A-18F, a two-seat version optimized for attack.

Under Cheney, the Department of Defense was already committed to cancelling the Tomcat and in February 1991 the remanufacturing of the F-14A into the F-14D version was ended because the Pentagon denied funds essential for the continuing of that work. For Grumman as a company the future looked bleak without the F-14 programme. Total aircraft production had fallen drastically in the 1980s although gross sales were well up.

The company was vulnerable and with the Navy deciding to terminate A-6 production in 1991 and E-2C production in 1995 it was ripe for take-over. With the F-14, these three programmes alone accounted for 35 per cent of sales and to maximize investment Grumman proposed three new successive variants of the Tomcat: the F-14 Quick Strike, the Super Tomcat 21 and its attack derivative, and the ASF-14 (see Box). The Quick Strike version was a modified F-14D which Grumman said would cost around $200 million to develop and be available three years from the go-ahead.

In his letter to Cheney, Caporali quoted a unit price of $31 million for each of twenty-four Quick Strike versions, less engines, for delivery in 1993, compared with $43.8 million for an F-14D. Prices would fall progressively each year with successive batches of twenty-four, falling to $27.8 million by 1997 (all in 1990 dollars). Super Tomcat 21 was a completely reworked aircraft with an estimated development cost of almost $2 billions and a fly-away cost initially of almost $50 million. By comparison, the competing F/A-18E/F advanced version of the Hornet for the same mission objectives as those more than met by the Super

Tomcat 21 would cost $4 billion in development and $30 to $40 million per copy – according to Navy estimates. Grumman fought back hard using these figures to consolidate an argument: that the Hornet was, and never could be, the equal of the upgraded Tomcat. Weight was added in a letter signed by fifty-nine naval aviators, led by Lt Steven E. Harst of VF-111, that 'the Hornet will never be an adequate replacement for either the A-6 or the F-14, and falls considerably short of the mark as a replacement for both.'

The intransigent attitude of the Pentagon was all the more surprising given McDonnell Douglas's figures about F/A-18E/F performance and economics. It admitted that the Hornet was 'not an aircraft that is specifically designed for fleet air defense or as a medium-attack aircraft...It is a compromise.' The exacting Navy requirement for a fleet air defence mission asked that the aircraft should take-off and cruise at best speed to altitude, loiter for 90min, accelerate to Mach 1.35 for combat, spend up to one minute in afterburner during engagement, break off, return to the carrier at best speed and land with 20min of fuel reserve for sea-level loiter plus a 5 per cent margin. Carrying similar weapons and with drop tanks, the

Seeking to fill the slot for an attack aircraft left by the A-12, Grumman brought out proposals for a range of upgrades for the F-14D and advanced attack versions based on a concept it called Super Tomcat 21, affiliating it with a next-century identity. The Navy wanted to pursue this but Defense Secretary Cheney had already decided to stop the production of the aircraft and the last new feline was not a Super Tomcat 21 but an F-14D completed on 20 July 1992.

The aircraft selected by the Defense Department to replace the A-6 is an F/A-18 Hornet derivative. An outgrowth of a failed bid to be a land-based lightweight fighter, the Hornet evolved into a light naval fighter and attack aircraft from which base it has now evolved into a strike aircraft.

F/A-18E/F would have a combat radius of 299 miles (480km) compared with 403 miles (645km) for the F-14D and 495 miles (790km) for the Super Tomcat 21. In attack requirements, where eight Mk83 bombs and two AIM-9 Sidewinders are carried, complex high g evasive turns are programmed into the flight profile and set combinations of altitude and speed are adhered to, the F/A-18E/F has a strike radius of 305 miles (490km) compared with 460 miles (740km) for the F-14D and almost 600 miles (960km) for the Attack Super Tomcat 21.

Independent financial analysts noted that the $4 billion cost of developing the F/A-18E/F, compared with the $2 billions for the Super Tomcat 21, did not include money for an improved radar, infra-red search and track equipment or television camera systems for long-range detection. All these elements are in the F-14D now, with six times the average peak power of the current AN/APG-65, the F-18 radar, twice the detection range and fourteen times the search volume. The arguments were convincing but Cheney was determined to kill the F-14, and with the production line gone there could be no derivative. By early 1992 the message was clear and Tomcat was winding down. The last F-14B had been delivered in May 1990 and the last new airframe, the last of thirty-seven F-14Ds, was delivered on 20 July

1992. Just before that event the Navy examined possible F-14 upgrade programmes as the F/A-18E/F ran into cost overruns.

Of the many options available, both

Grumman and the Navy reviewed ways in which the F-14 could be given a stiffer ground-attack role than that available through the Bombcat programme. Of the programmes that were on option, steps had already been taken to improve the attack capability. A Navy avionics centre in Indianapolis had already developed the ADU-703 general-purpose bomb adapter and the Fleet began to receive the new equipment in July 1992; further reworking of the software broadened the weapons suite to include Rockeye and CBU-59 anti-personnel cluster munitions. By December 1992 the Strike Aircraft Test Directorate at the Patuxent River Naval Air Station had conducted drop tests with GBU-16 laser-guided bombs using a F-14A and plans moved quickly to give the aircraft a smart weapons capability. Added to this was the desirability of providing the Tomcat with the ability to deliver precision-guided munitions at night. Such a capability would broaden and extend the ability of the aircraft to fill mission needs in an era when no one aircraft on a carrier deck could be dedicated to a single role. It was acquired through the unique marriage of a Lantirn pod to the F-14B.

Lantirn (Low Altitude Navigation and Targeting Infra-red system for Night) was

The warload of the Hornet is substantial but the platform is not nearly so capable as the F-14 and many experienced naval aviators have risked their careers by breaking rules and writing to the Pentagon with that view. As it is, the reason why the F/A-18E/F was selected may have more to do with Northrop's takeover of Grumman than the technical or operational reasons by which all such judgements should be made.

VF-171 Tomcats turn for the carrier, as they will be doing until at least 2015 when the type will be replaced by a new generation of super-stealthy Joint Strike Fighters.

developed for use by single-seat F-15 and F-16 aircraft and contains a wide field of view FLIR with terrain-following radar, allowing the pilot to operate at low altitudes. It is particularly effective when used in conjunction with precision-guided munitions and the first production models were delivered in 1987. Beginning in 1994, a team led by Lockheed Martin Electronics and Missiles began to integrate a Lantirn system with GPS satellite receivers, inertial measurement units, a hand controller and associated electronics. By March 1995 the Lantirn system was available for demonstration sorties of which forty were conducted with laser-guided weapons before a contract for production was signed in November that year. A joint fleet exercise flexed the new system in carrier trials between 26 April and 17 May.

In June 1996 the carrier *Enterprise* sailed on cruise with F-14 Strike Fighters of VF-103, equipped to operate with precision-guided munitions at night. Of the fourteen Tomcats that put to sea nine could carry a single Lantirn, similar to Air Force pods of the same type but greatly improved thanks to the satellite navigation and inertial measurement unit. The Navy worked to a tight timeline to put F-14 Strike Fighters on deck by mid-1996 and saved money in the process. As uniquely configured for the Tomcat, the Lantirn gets information from the AWG-15 weapon control system and the AWG-9 radar, putting video and guidance symbology on the cockpit displays in an efficient and less costly manner. The Navy plans to modify 212 Tomcats to carry the ninety Lantirn pods that will be eventually produced. Aircraft selected for their adaptability will have sufficient flying time left to remain operational until at least 2005. Each squadron will receive between six and eight pods.

Somewhere around the end of the end of the first decade of the next century, the F-14 will be replaced by a Joint Strike Fighter that looks very different to the Tomcat. With stealth technologies and greater engine efficiency and performance, it will be a worthy successor if it works. Like the failed TFX that spawned VFX which metamorphosed into the F-14, the Joint Strike Fighter is the ultimate 'commonality' machine designed to serve the needs of the Navy, the Air Force and the Marine Corps, replacing the F-14, F/A-18, A-6, AV-8B, F-16 and A-10. In addition, variants will replace the Harrier F/A2 with the Royal Navy and the Harrier GR7 and Tornado GR4s in the Royal Air Force. At least TFX sought only to provide a common fighter for the US Navy and the Air Force. According to received wisdom, sometime around 2010 the JSF will begin to replace all these nine different types of aircraft and thus conjure a remarkable feat even denied to the Wizard of Oz. And so will the Tomcat finally go into retirement, with the last aircraft lingering on perhaps until 2015? By then the design will be more than forty-five years old, but the aircraft will be as capable as anything in the sky for the mission it had been designed to fly.

US Navy Tomcat Units

VF-1 'Wolfpack'

The first Navy unit to become operational with the F-14A sailed from San Francisco for the west Pacific aboard the USS *Enterprise* (Air Wing 14) on 17 September 1974 along with VF-2. The Squadron had been commissioned on 14 October 1972. Tomcats had been with VF-1 since 1 July 1973 and had embarked on cruise training on 18 March 1974, but when they went operational it was to go to a war – of sorts – to participate in Operation *Frequent Wind*, the humiliating evacuation of Saigon which marked the inglorious end of the Vietnam War which had seen the defeat of the French and now the Americans.

On 9 February 1975 the *Enterprise* diverted to the aid of the citizens of Mauritius in the Indian Ocean which had been struck by typhoon 'Gervaise' just three days earlier. Arriving on 12 February, the carrier personnel spent 10,000 man-hours rendering assistance, restoring power and airlifting medical aid and food supplies to the distressed island. Then, on 19 April, it was off to the waters off Vietnam as thousands of North Vietnamese troops moved south to support the Viet Cong. But the response was token and the South was left to its fate. Operation *Frequent Wind* was a standby effort to airlift American citizens to safety. The carrier was back in US waters on 19 May 1975 and, with VF-1, undertook a second cruise to the west Pacific and the Indian Ocean between 30 July 1976 and 28 March 1977 and a third between 4 April and 3 October 1978.

On 10 September 1980 VF-1 sailed aboard the USS *Ranger* in service with Air Wing 2 when it went to the Indian Ocean in response to crises in Iran and Afghanistan, returning on 5 May 1981. It had a second tour with the *Ranger* between 7 April and 18 October 1982, a year in which it received a safety award from the Chief of Naval Operations for five years and 17,000 F-14 flying hours without an accident. VF-1 sailed with the USS *Kitty Hawk*, also with Air Wing 2, between 13 January and 1 August 1984 before returning to the *Ranger* later in the same year. Two north Pacific cruises were completed in 1986 and early 1987 before two west Pacific and Indian Ocean tours during the second half of 1987 and between 24 February and 24 August 1989.

In dry periods, between cruises, VF-1 showed its mettle against USAF F-15s and three crew teams got through the Top Gun school at Naval Air Station Miramar. VF-1 went to war for real on 8 December 1990 when it sailed to the Persian Gulf region aboard the *Ranger* for a confrontation with Saddam Hussein, becoming the only F-14 squadron to score an air-to-air victory in Operation *Desert Storm*, albeit only an Mi-8 helicopter with an AIM-9 missile. As a matter of policy the F-14s were restricted to escort work.

With VF-1 on board, *Ranger* returned to the US on 8 June 1991 but went back to the Gulf region between 1 August 1992 and 31 January 1993 supporting Operations *Southern Watch* and *Provide Relief* – again in the escort role. The 'Wolfpack' Squadron was in the vanguard of Navy cuts, reducing from two to one the number of F-14 squadrons deployed aboard a carrier. Hopes for a conversion to F-14D aircraft were dashed when VF-1 was disbanded on 30 September 1993, some of its crew going to the sister squadron VF-2.

VF-2 'Bounty Hunters'

Arguably the oldest squadron in the US Navy, VF-2 was formed on 1 July 1922 and became the first to see service aboard a carrier, the USS *Langley*. Little more than fifty years later, on 14 October 1972, it was established as an F-14 squadron along with VF-1 and received its first Tomcat in the following July. The unit's deployment and cruise history follows that of VF-1 – the two squadrons operating together as they switched between carriers – but VF-2 acquired a TARPS role in 1981. In that year also the Squadron won several awards and logged its ten-thousandth accident-free flying hour.

TARPS gave the Tomcat a tactical reconnaissance role, shaken down during its 1982 cruise aboard the *Ranger*, which lasted from 7 April to 18 October, in company with VF-1. Throughout this cruise and in evaluation trials the following year VF-2 wrote many of the procedures that would be adopted by subsequent TARPS Tomcat squadrons. The Squadron accompanied VF-1 on its 1991 tour of the Gulf region and one of its pilots lodged a record 744th tail-hook landing – 126 in one year. Also in 1991 a VF-2 F-14 conducted trials in the Bombcat role by carrying and dropping two Mk83 bombs. After the late 1992 cruise with VF-1 aboard the *Ranger*, the 'Bounty Hunters' parted company with their sister squadron and went to Miramar for conversion to the F-14D and the F-14D(R). With a greater diversity of roles and applications, VF-2 survived the purge that deactivated VF-1, and with its new Tomcats the 'Bounty Hunters' performed their first patrol with F-14Ds aboard the *Constellation* between 6 May 1994 and 30 June 1994.

VF-11 'Red Rippers'

For long paired with VF-31 flying F-4s, the 'Red Rippers' converted to the F-14 in 1980 and began their first cruise patrol on 4 January 1982 aboard the USS *John F. Kennedy* with Air Wing 3. Back in port on 14 July, another cruise followed in the

Atlantic between May and June 1983 to support Operation *Ocean Safari*, a NATO exercise involving several countries. VF-11 sailed with the *Kennedy* on 27 September 1983 for a visit to Latin America and joint exercises with the Brazilians before moving to the Mediterranean and a full-scale air operation against Libya on 4 December.

During 1984 VF-11 received several well-earned honours and on 1 April 1985 moved, with VF-31, to the carrier *Forrestal* under Air Wing 6, where the two squadrons had operated F-4Js for many years. Cruises to the Mediterranean and the North Atlantic followed between 2 June and 10 November 1986 and between 28 July and 9 October 1987 and a brief tour to the Gulf took place from 8 to 20 April 1988. Following a five-day turnaround, the *Forrestal* took VF-11 to the Indian Ocean, returning on 7 October that year. Ever active, a cruise tour of the Mediterranean was conducted between 4 November 1989 and 12 April 1990, and during the following winter some F-14s went to Luke Air Force Base for air-combat practice against F-15s and F-16s of the 58th Tactical Fighter Wing.

VF-11 was deployed to the Caribbean between 29 November and 23 December 1990 before sailing for the Mediterranean on 30 May 1991 in support of Operation *Provide Comfort*. Denied a role in the Gulf War, it was to play a part in flying top cover for Kurdish refugees and dispatch one of its number to fill a static display slot at that year's Paris Air Show. After the *Forrestal* returned to the US – and into retirement as a training carrier – on 21 December 1991, VF-11 and VF-31 migrated to California where they converted to the F-14D via three months at Miramar, being the first operational squadron with this Tomcat variant in July 1992. Deployed to Alaska late in 1992, VF-11 was moved aboard the carrier *Carl Vinson* for its West Pacific cruise between 18 February and 15 August 1994.

VF-14 'Tophatters'

Getting its name from the logo that showed a grinning cat with top hat and white tie, the 'Tophatters' got cats for real when they received their first F-14s in July 1974. With Air Wing 1 aboard the carrier USS *John F. Kennedy*, VF-14 sailed for its first Tomcat cruise on 28 June 1975, a Mediterranean

visit ending on 27 January 1976. After VF-1 and VF-2 paired for the first deployment in September 1974, VF-14 and its partner squadron VF-32 became the second paired Tomcat units to go on operational deployment. As one of the oldest Navy combat squadrons, the 'Tophatters' had a reputation to uphold; their pedigree went back to September 1919 and they were the longest surviving squadron.

VF-14 made a North Atlantic cruise aboard the *Kennedy* from 2 September to 9 November 1976 and then set off for the Mediterranean on 15 January 1977, returning on 1 August that year. On 7 November it began a cruise round the Caribbean which ended on 13 December and little more than a month later, on 20 January 1978, it set off on an Atlantic cruise returning on 22 March. Three months later, on 29 June, the *Kennedy* sailed for the Mediterranean, getting back to its home port on 8 February 1979. After a lengthy stay there the *Kennedy* took VF-14 for a Mediterranean and Indian Ocean cruise beginning on 4 August 1980 and ending almost eight months later on 28 March 1981.

Now the squadron moved from Air Wing 1 to Air Wing 6 and deployed with the carrier USS *Independence* for Mediterranean duty from 7 June to 22 December 1982, cruises to the Caribbean from 6 June to 21 July and from 15 August to 16 September 1983. From there it went on a combined tour of the Caribbean, the Mediterranean and the north Atlantic between 18 October 1983 and 11 April 1984 during which it flew combat air patrols over the invasion of Grenada (23 October–5 November 1983) and escorted TARPS-equipped F-14s over Syrian positions in Lebanon. VF-14 conducted two more cruises, one through the Atlantic and the Caribbean (20 August–9 September 1984) and one through the Mediterranean (16 October 1984–19 February 1985) before the *Independence* was put up for a life extension programme.

On 1 April 1985 VF-14 moved to Air Wing 3 and a slot aboard the *Kennedy* which took it back to the Mediterranean for a long cruise between 18 August 1986 and 3 March 1987 and a return tour from 2 August 1988 to 1 February 1989, interspersed with a visit to the Caribbean from 2 August 1988 to 1 February 1989. The Mediterranean cruises provided the opportunity for a NATO exercise with the Egyptian Air Force in Italian airspace and

later with the Moroccan Air Force which, with their diminutive F-5Es, nevertheless proved a formidable 'opponent'. During January 1990 VF-14 had a Caribbean tour before *Desert Shield* pulled it to the Red Sea on a tour from 15 August 1990 to 28 March 1991. Later that year the squadron helped with post-life extension shakedown trials aboard the USS *Kitty Hawk*.

When next VF-14 went to sea its F-14s had become Bombcats and it used its cruise to the Mediterranean between 7 October 1992 and 7 April 1993 to practise ground attacks. It also performed combat air patrols over Bosnia-Herzegovina in support of Operation *Provide Promise* after which the squadron moved to the USS *Eisenhower* for a short cruise to the Caribbean between 7 May and 1 July 1994.

VF-21 'Freelancers'

Another ex-Phantom unit, VF-21 was paired throughout its Tomcat era with VF-154 with which it had shared deck space during its F-4 days. Those ended in November 1983 when it began to receive Tomcats, reaching establishment status on 15 March 1984 only three days before it sailed for an east Pacific cruise aboard the carrier USS *Constellation* with Air Wing 14. Returning to port on 15 November, a short second cruise to the region was conducted between 6 and 16 December. It had been a good year for the stand-up Tomcat unit, receiving an award for best PacFleet fighter squadron missile readiness record. An extended Pacific and Indian Ocean cruise was performed between 21 February and 24 August 1985, but a short north Pacific cruise between 4 September and 20 October was the only wet duty in 1986 for VF-21.

The west Pacific and Indian Ocean region was the destination for the *Constellation* between 11 April and 13 October 1987, repeated more than a year later between 1 December 1988 and 1 June 1989 and followed by a north Pacific patrol from 16 September to 19 October that year. Not because of the invasion of Kuwait but in time to support the build-up of *Desert Shield*, VF-21 was moved to the USS *Independence* during 1990 for a cruise to the west Pacific, Indian Ocean and Gulf regions between 23 June and 20 December. As it passed through the Straits of Hormuz at the southern end of the Persian Gulf on 2 August, it was the first

US carrier on the scene but in consequence it was withdrawn from the region before hostilities began; it was compensated by an award for excellent safety records.

The next assignment for VF-21 aboard the *Independence* was to replace the USS *Midway* at its home port. It sailed on 5 July 1991, via Pearl Harbor, where it transferred to Air Wing 5, arriving on 28 July. The carrier remained on cruise until 11 September, followed by three short west Pacific tours before it started a lengthy patrol through the west Pacific, the Indian Ocean and the Persian Gulf region on 15 April 1992. While in the Gulf the *Independence* supported the no-fly zone over southern Iraq and returned to port on the last day of 1992. Preceded by four short patrols in the west Pacific, VF-21 began a long cruise through the region and on into the Indian Ocean between 17 November 1993 and 17 March 1994, returning to police the no-fly zone and assist at the crisis in Somalia. VF-21 lost its Tomcats and was disestablished in 1996.

VF-24 'Fighting Renegades'

Honour goes to VF-24 as the first squadron to log 3,000 Tomcat flying hours, but the unit was denied a role in *Desert Storm*, becoming one of the select Bombcat squadrons and conducting reconnaissance runs before its demise in 1996. Teamed with VF-211 in Air Wing 9 from 1 March 1976, VF-24 had been flying F-8J Crusaders until it began converting to F-14As in November 1975. When the USS *Constellation* sailed for the west Pacific on 12 April 1977 the two units became the fourth paired Tomcat squadrons to deploy. Back in port on 21 November, the Squadron received a flight safety award in July 1978 and on 26 September sailed for the west Pacific/Indian Ocean region to provide a presence during the Yemen crisis, returning to the US on 17 May 1979.

It fell to VF-24 to fly cover for the unsuccessful and misconceived attempt to rescue hostages in Tehran. To support Operation *Eagle Claw*, as it was called, the *Constellation* sailed for the west Pacific and Indian Ocean region on 26 February 1980, returning to port on 15 October. During air cover operations the F-14As had black and red identification stripes painted on their wings but the carrier was replaced by the *Midway* on 27 June. *Constellation* began a

patrol of the west Pacific on 20 October 1981 and was back in port on 23 May 1982, after which Air Wing 9 – and VF-211 – moved to the USS *Ranger*, sailing for the Indian Ocean on 15 July 1983 and returning on 29 February 1984.

Another move shifted VF-24 to the USS *Kitty Hawk* in time for a west Pacific/Indian Ocean patrol from 24 July to 21 December that year. Finally, a round-the-world cruise from 31 January to 29 July 1987 was completed before the *Kitty Hawk* was laid up for a life extension programme and VF-24 shifted to the *Nimitz*. Another west Pacific/Indian Ocean cruise took place between 2 September 1988 and 2 March 1989 during which the squadron flew tanker-protection duty in the Gulf under Operation *Earnest Will*. Getting the new F-14B from spring 1989, VF-24 sailed aboard the *Nimitz* for a north Pacific cruise from 15 June to 9 July before shaking down in the Bombcat role, becoming the first front-line Tomcat unit to drop bombs, on 8 August 1990. Another Indian Ocean cruise between 25 February and 24 August 1991 afforded the opportunity for air exercises with Thailand and Malaysia.

During the last few months of 1991 the Squadron worked up operational procedures for Bombcat F-14s and qualified as the first Pacific coast Tomcat squadron to complete the Advanced Attack Readiness Program. During the first half of 1992 VF-24 switched back to F-14As, the F-14Bs being assigned to Atlantic Air Wings. The *Nimitz* carried VF-24 to a west Pacific and Gulf tour beginning on 4 February 1993 during which it cruised no-fly zones over southern Iraq on TARPS reconnaissance runs before returning to home port on 1 August. In 1994 VF-24 was in the Red Flag competition against the USAF at Nellis Air Force Base, Nevada and was disbanded as a Tomcat squadron in 1996.

VF-31 'Tomcatters'

As the second oldest US Navy air squadron, the 'Tomcatters' began F-14A conversion on 8 September 1980, received their first TARPS-capable aircraft on 22 January 1981 and became operational with VF-11 in Air Wing 3 aboard the USS *John F. Kennedy* on 4 June. From the first Indian Ocean patrol that began on 4 January 1982, operational deployments and cruises matched those for VF-11. The squadron saw action in 1983 when it flew support

missions against hostile forces in Beirut, two TARPS aircraft coming under fire on 3 December which incited a retaliatory US strike against Syrian ground positions. Again in the Mediterranan three years later, along with the entire complement of the USS *Forrestal*, VF-31 Tomcats stood at a constant state of high alert as the carrier stood off the coast of Lebanon within sight of the shore.

During the second half of 1991 the squadron conducted low-level exercises with the Israeli Air Force and took advantage of the Mediterranean deployment to run up a strenuous sequence of tests and exercise operations before returning to the US. Along with its partner squadron VF-11, VF-31 went to the West Coast while the *Forrestal* was retired and received its first F-14D aircraft in early 1992. While VF-11 went to Alaska, VF-31 joined Air Wing 14 aboard the USS *Carl Vinson* and began training with its first five F-14Ds on 8 July 1992. VF-11 rejoined VF-31 for a patrol aboard the *Vinson* that began on 18 February 1994.

VF-32 'Swordsmen'

As part of the second deployed pairing of Tomcat squadrons, VF-32 joined VF-14 with Air Wing 1, converting to the type from early 1974 and sailing with the *John F. Kennedy* on 28 June 1975. All subsequent movement dates correspond with those given for its sister squadron VF-14. During 1979 VF-32 became the first Tomcat unit to participate in the combined forces Red Flag exercises staged at Nellis Air Force Base. In October 1983 the squadron flew air cover in Operation *Urgent Fury*, the US invasion of Grenada, and from the end of the year through early 1984 it flew reconnaissance missions over Syrian positions in Lebanon on bomb-damage assessment missions following US strikes on unfriendly positions in December 1983.

To VF-32 goes the distinction of downing the type's third and fourth air victims, achieved on 1 January 1989 when two F-14As destroyed two Libyan Air Force MiG-23s beyond visual range.

VF-33 'Tarsiers'/'Starfighters'

The first Tomcats began replacing F-4J Phantoms with VF-33 in December 1981 and the unit was declared operational in the type a month later. Along with its sister squadron VF-102, the 'Tarsiers' went cruising with Air Wing 1 on the carrier USS *America* in the Atlantic and the Caribbean from 30 May to 8 July 1982 and in the north Atlantic and the Mediterranean from 23 August to 4 November. This was followed by an extensive cruise of the Mediterranean and the Indian Ocean from December 1982 to June 1983 and in the Caribbean from November to December 1983 supporting Operation *Just Cause*. A three-week Caribbean cruise was conducted in February 1984 before a seven-weeks patrol from Central America to the Mediterranean and the Indian Ocean between April and November 1984. The whole of September 1985 was taken up with the north Atlantic exercise *Ocean Safari*.

Along with VF-102, VF-33 sailed for the Mediterranean on 10 March 1986 and fourteen days later began operations off the coast of Libya against Col Qadhafi's Air Force from the Gulf of Sirte, a region declared by the Libyan leader to be territorial waters and a 'zone of death'. VF-33 flew cover during Operation *Prairie Fire*, air strikes on Libya on 15 April. The USS *America* was back in port on 14 September 1986. Between 6 January and 19 February 1987 VF-33 participated in shakedown trials in the Caribbean with the carrier USS *Theodore Roosevelt* and in late 1988 the squadron paired with VFA-82 flying F/A-18 Hornets in exercises against USAF F-15s, F-16s, F-111s and A-10s and flew practice attacks against VF-45 .

By now the 'Tarsiers' had changed their name to 'Starfighters' and resumed normal patrols when they sailed for the north Atlantic and the Caribbean on aboard the USS *America*, along with VF-102, on 11 May 1989. They returned to port on 10 November that year. But the squadron was the only F-14 unit on the *America* when it sailed with composite Air Wing 9 between 12 February and 7 April 1990. By the end of the year VF-33 was paired back with VF-102 for a cruise to the Gulf in support of Operation *Desert Storm* between 28 December 1990 and 18 April 1991. The 'Starfighters' were employed on strike escort and combat air patrol while the *America* was based in the Red Sea. When it moved to the Persian Gulf the F-14s operated in their more traditional fleet air defence role.

Between 21 August and 11 October 1991 the *America* took the paired squadrons to the Atlantic for participation in Exercise *North Star* before sailing for the Mediterranean on 1 December where VF-33 flew practice air combat against F-5Es of the Tunisian Air Force and AV-8Bs of the Spanish Navy. Returning on 6 June 1992 from its last patrol, VF-33 was disbanded on 1 October 1993; its surviving sister squadron VF-102 remained the sole F-14 unit aboard *America*.

VF-41 'Black Aces'

The 'Black Aces' began receiving Tomcats in April 1976 and the squadron was declared operational in December 1977 when it sailed aboard the USS *Nimitz* on an eight-months cruise as part of Air Wing 8. Returning on 20 July 1978, VF-41 embarked on another cruise with the *Nimitz* beginning on 10 September 1979 and ending on 26 May 1980. During this period it visited the eastern Mediterranean, passing through the Suez Canal to the Indian Ocean. It was followed by another cruise beginning on 14 May 1981. Just twelve days later a Marine Corps EA-6B crashed on to the deck of the *Nimitz* and destroyed three F-14s. A cruise to the Mediterranean began in early August 1981 and on the 19th two F-14As from VF-41 scored the first two combat kills of the aircraft's career when they shot down a pair of Libyan Su-22s using Sidewinders. VF-41 was back home in February 1982.

In the following year the squadron sailed for the Mediterranean, being away from November to May 1983 and receiving three well-earned awards for safety and readiness as well as for the best Navy fighter squadron. VF-41 went back to the Mediterranean between 8 March and 3 September 1985 and sailed aboard the *Nimitz* on a north Atlantic patrol between 15 July and 16 October 1986. Air Wing 8 moved to the carrier *Roosevelt* and departed for a round-the-world cruise on 30 December 1986, returning on 26 July 1987. A tour of the Caribbean was conducted between 8 March and 8 April, followed by an extended north Atlantic cruise between 25 August and 11 October 1988. It was on this cruise that the Navy tried a more flexible disposition of forces, reducing to twenty from twenty-four the number of F-14s in the Air Wing, carrying twenty F/A-18s instead of twenty-four A-7s and reducing the number of A-6s from twenty to ten. In this way the Navy could redirect the balance between strike and air defence according to requirements; it would become the pattern until later changes slimmed the inventory even further.

A return to the Mediterranean took place on 30 December, ending on 30 June 1989, and between 19 January and 23 February 1990 VF-41 participated with the rest of Air Wing 8 in a shakedown cruise in the Caribbean for the new carrier USS *Abraham Lincoln*. On 28 December 1990 the *Roosevelt* sailed for the Mediterranean and the Persian Gulf. A day later nine Tomcats from VF-41 joined the carrier as it sailed in support of *Desert Shield*. On station on 19 January VF-41 joined VF-84 in several patrols over southern Iraq without making contact with the enemy. VF-41 transferred from the *Roosevelt* to the *Kitty Hawk*, joining Air Wing 15 for a Pacific patrol beginning on 22 June 1992, followed by a west Pacific cruise between 3 November 1992 and 3 May 1993. VF-41 subsequently rejoined Air Wing 8 and was with the *Roosevelt* when it performed an Atlantic patrol between 19 May and 29 June 1994.

VF-51 'Screaming Eagles'

Paired with VF-111, the 'Screaming Eagles' formed up on F-14As in 1978, taking on its first Tomcat on 16 June and sailing with Air Wing 15 aboard the carrier *Kitty Hawk* on 20 May 1979. The squadron was plunged full tilt into two international crises when it was called upon to stand off Korea after the assassination of the South Korean President General Park Chung Hee, and to position itself close to Iran at the seizing of sixty Americans by the Revolutionary Council. Flight crews were called upon to perform unusually high flying hours, making 785 hours in twenty-two days during bad weather in the Far East. VF-51 returned home on 15 February 1980.

A second cruise was conducted between 1 April and 23 November 1981, this time to the west Pacific and the Indian Ocean region, before Air Wing 15, including VF-51 and its sister squadron, moved to the USS *Carl Vinson* for a round-the-world trip beginning on 1 March and ending on 29 October 1983. *En route* back to Alameda the carrier visited Australia and put in some time off the coast of Iran, showing the flag to a turbulent and unpredictable country and flew practice attacks against Tunisian F-5Es.

In 1984 VF-51 followed two short Pacific tours (14 May–28 June and 31 July–22 August) with an extended west Pacific cruise from 18 October 1984 to 22 May 1985. In that time VF-51 became the first Navy unit to intercept and escort a Tu-22 Blinder, an event which took place on 2 December. Using the TCS nose sets, F-14s intercepted a variety of Soviet aircraft and VF-51 performed the first day and night automatic carrier landings.

In 1985 the unit's pilots became anonymous film stars when they were employed to fly for the film 'Top Gun', a fictional story based on Naval Air Station Miramar. Back to business in 1986, the *Vinson* carried VF-51 to the west Pacific from 12 August to 5 February 1987, followed by another visit between 15 June and 14 December 1988. In a busy sequence of cruises, the *Vinson* took the squadron through north Atlantic and Pacific patrols between 5 September and 8 November 1989, followed between 1 February and 31 July 1990 by a combined tour to the west Pacific and the Indian Ocean.

It had been planned to deploy the paired squadrons as the first F-14D unit but cuts cancelled this and Air Wing 15 shifted carriers, moving to the USS *Kitty Hawk* for an east–west passage of Cape Horn during a cruise that began on 18 October 1991 and ended on 11 December. In that period the Tomcats flew exercises with aircraft from Venezuela, Chile and Argentina. Next came a long tour embracing the Indian Ocean and the Persian Gulf between 3 November 1992 and 3 May 1993, during which the Tomcats flew patrols during Operation *Provide Relief*. On 24 June 1994 the *Kitty Hawk* began another cruise, to the same area, and in March 1995 its sister squadron VF-111 was disestablished leaving VF-51 as the sole F-14 unit with Air Wing 15.

VF-74 'Bedevilers'

Twenty-one years after it became the first Navy squadron to go operational with the F-4 Phantom II, VF-74 relinquished its fixed-wing fighters between June and October 1983 as it converted to Tomcats. Between 26 January and 21 February 1984 it partnered VF-103 in Air Wing 17 aboard the carrier *Saratoga* for a shakedown in the Caribbean and then sailed for the

Mediterranean in a cruise which began during April and ended on 20 October 1984. In November the carrier came under 7th Fleet control and spent from January to March 1985 conducting patrols off the Libyan coast. A return cruise to the Mediterranean and the Indian Ocean followed between 25 August 1985 and 16 April 1986. F-14s flew shotgun on attacks against Libyan missile sites. Again the carrier returned to the Mediterranean between 5 June and 17 November 1987.

The *Saratoga* carried VF-74 to the Gulf region for Operation *Desert Storm* in a cruise that began on 7 August 1990 and ended on 28 March 1991. Between 6 May and 6 November 1992 VF-74, now equipped with the F-14B, made another cruise with the *Saratoga* as it participated in Operation *Provide Promise*. Only one final cruise remained, a post-life extension programme shakedown for the carrier USS *Constellation*. As part of the reduction in F-14 squadron assignments to carriers, VF-74 was disbanded on 28 April 1994.

VF-84 'Jolly Rogers'

The 'Jolly Rogers' began to convert to the F-14 in October 1975 and became operational in April 1977. Assigned to Air Wing 8, VF-84 made a cruise aboard the USS *Nimitz* with its sister squadron VF-41 between December 1977 and 20 July 1978. Subsequent sailings are described under the diary of VF-41. The squadron was unable to match the success of its sister in the 1981 operations against Libya, but high flying hours were accumulated in 1982 as the *Nimitz* cruised within sight of the Lebanese coast and personnel stood at maximum readiness to deflect possible suicide strikes.

In late 1986, during a cruise to the north Atlantic, VF-84 carried out some exercises with aircraft of the Royal Norwegian Air Force. In 1989 the unit did mark a notable achievement when one of its aircraft became the first from the fleet to make an arrested landing on the new carrier the USS *Abraham Lincoln*. Between 11 March and 8 September 1993 the squadron was the sole F-14 unit aboard the *Roosevelt* during a cruise to the Mediterranean.

VF-101 'Grim Reapers'

This squadron has an auspicious role in the

history of the Tomcat, being the sole unit responsible for training East Coast F-14 crew. Operating from Key West and Oceana the 'Grim Reapers' had been training pilots and air crew since 1958, but in 1975 they received Tomcats and structured a training programme for pilots, backseat drivers and ground crew. It was the crews for VF-41/VF-84 that came through the squadron first during 1976 and by 1977 the 'Grim Reapers' had discharged their first stand-up squadrons. VF-101 made frequent flights to carriers for training activities but rarely stayed. The unit received the F-14B in 1988 and for a while trained crew on this type for both the Atlantic and the Pacific Fleet, until the F-14B was consolidated on the East Coast. Reciprocally, the sister-training squadron VF-124 did a similar job with the F-14D.

In 1990 VF-101 acquired Bombcat training responsibilities and, to lead the way, the commanding officer became the first pilot to drop a bomb, on 12 September 1990. The squadron was tasked with developing ground-attack procedures for operational units and then applying them in training programmes. Uniquely, VF-101 also accepts exchange pilots from the Royal Air Force, temporarily swapping their Tornadoes for the F-14. With the demise of the Soviet Union and the subsequent end of the Cold War, the Navy decided that two training units were a luxury the slimmed down Navy could not justify, and when VF-124 was disestablished in September 1994 the 'Grim Reapers' became the sole F-14 training squadron.

VF-102 'Diamondbacks'

Partnering VF-33, the 'Diamondbacks' acquired the F-14 in July 1981 and deployed with its sister squadron aboard the USS *America* on their first cruise in May 1982. Despite its inexperience with the new aircraft, VF-102 received an award from Grumman for the best TARPS fighter squadron of 1983. In 1986 the squadron saw service in the Mediterranean during which its aircraft were fired on by Libyan SAMs during US air strikes on Operation *Prairie Fire* and flew cover for attacking aircraft in Operation *El Dorado Canyon*.

The squadron was in action during Operation *Desert Storm* and went on to win other awards for alert-ready status before it was left as the only F-14 squadron aboard the USS *America* after VF-33 was disbanded on 1 October 1993.

VF-103 'Sluggers'

Although the 'Sluggers' would partner with VF-74, they were not on board the USS *Saratoga* when the carrier sailed with that squadron for the first time in January 1984. For most of 1983 VF-103 had been converting to the Tomcat and joined Air Wing 17 when it sailed for the Mediterranean in April 1984, returning six months later. For the next three years its sailings were the same as VF-74's and the 'Sluggers' participated in the air operations against Libya during 1986 and in co-operative exercises with the French Navy in 1987.

Leaving its sister squadron for a while, VF-103 deployed with the USS *Independence* from 15 August 1988 to mid October during which it moved to the Pacific via Cape Horn. After having re-equipped with the F-14B, the 'Sluggers' were back on the *Saratoga* for a sailing to the Mediterranean and the Red Sea on 7 August 1990 and participation in *Desert Storm*, after which they returned to the US on 28 March 1991. VF-103 had the misfortune to lose a Tomcat over the desert to a SA-2 Guideline SAM. The pilot was rescued but the NFO was captured by the Iraqis.

Specializing in ground attack, VF-103 supported Operation *Provide Relief* during a cruise with its sister squadron in 1992, but when the 'Sluggers' departed for another cruise on 12 January 1994 they were the only F-14 squadron on the *Saratoga*. VF-74 disbanded on 28 April 1994 and the *Saratoga* was retired from service in August after thirty-eight years of service. VF-103 was pulled from operations and assigned a special role working up as the first squadron of F-14s capable of delivering precision guided munitions. Equipped with a Lantirn pod each Tomcat would become a fully operational multi-role combat aircraft. VF-103 returned to sea on the *Enterprise* in June 1996.

VF-111 'Sundowners'

Established in January 1959 as an F-4 Phantom squadron, VF-111 converted to Tomcats in 1978. It joined VF-51 in Air Wing 15 aboard the USS *Kitty Hawk* for a shakedown cruise to the Indian Ocean and the Gulf region, where it remained on an extended cruise monitoring events in Afghanistan. Throughout their operational career the 'Sundowners' remained with VF-51 and shared the same sailing dates. When the paired squadrons temporarily shifted to the *Carl Vinson* in 1983 for a world cruise VF-111 was equipped with TARPS, the first time that carrier had operated with the system. Indelibly recorded in the squadron log is one embarrassing event which took place on 5 May 1986 when a VF-111 pilot accidentally landed on the wrong carrier, the *Constellation*, just twelve miles away from the *Carl Vinson*!

In 1988 VF-111 participated along with its sister squadron in Operation *Earnest Will*, flying tanker protection in the Gulf. Mundane and routine, it did, nevertheless, provide the opportunity for much flying and VF-111 performed in excess of a thousand sorties, filling more than 2,000 flying hours. During this period, and in support of *Earnest Will*, VF-111 performed tests with the new KS-135A telephoto-camera with 610mm lens for high-altitude photography. Along with VF-51, VF-111 was to have become the first operational F-14D squadron but this plan was dropped in response to reshaped objectives resulting from the collapse of the Soviet Union. The 1994 sailing aboard the *Kitty Hawk* was the last for VF-111 and the squadron disbanded in March 1995.

VF-114 'Aardvarks'

A veteran of Vietnam, VF-114 transitioned to the Tomcat between December 1975 and January 1977 and joined Air Wing 11 on the *Kitty Hawk* for a cruise to the west Pacific with its sister squadron VF-213, beginning on 25 October 1977 and returning on 14 May 1978. Untypically for Pacific-based units, VF-114 and VF-213 shifted to the USS *America* for a cruise to the Mediterranean that began on 13 March 1979 and ended six months later on 22 September. When next the 'Aardvarks' went to sea it was on 14 April 1981 to the Mediterranean and the Indian Ocean aboard *America*, the largest carrier to pass through the Suez Canal. As if to highlight the busy life of a naval aviator on carrier fleet defence duty, VF-111 logged 3,100 flying hours and 1,500 deck landings before returning home on 12 November 1981.

Picking up the USS *Enterprise* from its extensive refit, VF-114 and Air Wing 11 sailed for the Pacific and the Indian Ocean on 1 September 1982, returning to port on 28 May 1983. The cruise was repeated by the paired squadrons in 1984. When next they went to sea it was on 15 January 1986 for a cruise to the west Pacific, the Indian Ocean and the Mediterranean, then back home on 12 August in an uneventful trip that allowed time to carry out some trials with the F-14 electronic battle modes. A brief north Pacific sailing between 25 October and 24 November 1987 preceded a long cruise through the west Pacific and the Indian Ocean from 5 January to 3 July 1988.

Little more than a year later, Air Wing 11 departed on 17 September 1989 for a world cruise ending on 16 March 1990. Air Wing 11 and VF-114 deployed to the USS *Abraham Lincoln* for a cruise round Cape Horn, leaving Norfolk on 25 September 1990 and arriving at Alameda, which was to be its new home port, on 20 November. Between 28 May and 25 November 1991 VF-114 cruised to the west Pacific, the Indian Ocean and the Persian Gulf, during which the squadron participated in Operation *Fiery Vigil*. A victim of Navy cuts, VF-114 was disbanded on 30 April 1993, leaving its sister squadron, VF-213, as the F-14 unit aboard the *Abraham Lincoln*.

VF-124 'Gunfighters'

Gaining its reputation as a training squadron for the F-8 Crusader, VF-124 acquired a role as the West Coast Tomcat fleet replenishment squadron when it was assigned that task in 1970, receiving its first aircraft on 8 October 1972. The following year the 'Gunfighters' provided an F-14A for display at the Paris Air Show, the year in which the first F-14 squadrons (VF-1 and VF-2) received their aircraft. Primarily dedicated to training Pacific squadrons, VF-124 trained two more Atlantic units, VF-142 and VF-143, before VF-101 began training East Coast squadrons from 1977.

In 1980 VF-124 began training up the first TARPS squadrons and on 18 January 1983 a milestone was achieved when the 'Gunfighters' notched up 25,000 accident-free flying hours. Two months later they logged three years of operations devoid of major accidents, a period during which they made 18,150 sorties and 2,700 arrested landings. On 16 November 1990 the unit received its first F-14D and the following year took charge of a few Beech T-34C aircraft for range spotting. Established on 16 August 1948, VF-124 was disbanded on 30 September 1994 from which date all F-14 crews and personnel replenishment were the responsibility of VF-101.

VF-142 'Ghostriders'

A noted Phantom-flyer, VF-142 had achieved an impressive record in south-east Asia flying F-4Bs and F-4Js and several credited victories over MiGs. They traded for F-14s in 1974 and went to sea with their new aircraft to join Air Wing 6 on the USS *America*, teamed with VF-143 and cruised to the Mediterranean on a trip lasting from 15 April to 25 October 1976. While there they covered the evacuation of civilian personnel from war-torn Beirut under Operation *Fluid Drive*. Then it was a cruise to the south Atlantic from 10 June to 19 July 1977, followed by a return to the Mediterranean from 29 September 1977 to 25 April 1978. VF-142 stood down for the next cruise of the *America* and transferred to the USS *Dwight D. Eisenhower* when it sailed for the Mediterranean and assignment to the Sixth Fleet on 16 January 1979; the sister squadron VF-143 had already transferred to the *Eisenhower* for two cruises in 1978. The 'Ghostriders' were back in the USA on 13 July 1979.

In 1980 an Indian Ocean/Arabian Sea cruise between 15 April and 22 December was extended as trouble brewed in the Middle East. The carrier *Eisenhower* did not return to port until 22 December 1980 during which time it had been in port for only five days, in Singapore, logged 3,673 flying hours and made 1,813 deck landings. The carrier achieved another record when it completed 153 days at sea between ports. VF-142 was back at sea on 17 August 1981 when it cruised to the Mediterranean aboard the *Eisenhower* in support of a NATO exercise that ended on 7 October. Three months later another cruise to the Mediterranean from 5 January to 13 July 1982 had the 'Ghostriders' at high readiness when Israel attacked Lebanon raising tension in the region.. Again, from 27 April to 30 November 1983, Air Wing 7 was

back again supprting US peacekeeping operations in Beirut.

Ever busy with Mediterranean matters, VF-142 sailed to that area again between 11 October 1984 and 8 May 1985 and departed on 8 July for a cruise through the north Atlantic as part of Exercise *Ocean Safari*, returning to port on 8 September 1985. For more than twenty-one months the squadron remained ashore and then returned to patrols when it sailed for the Caribbean and the south Atlantic on 16 June 1987 and returned on 28 July. A major Mediterranean appointment kept the squadron occupied between 29 February and 29 August 1988 and then various detachments of aircraft moved to Key West and Roosevelt Roads for electronic warfare training and missile firing tests.

After accepting new F-14B Tomcats, VF-142 embarked upon another Mediterranean jaunt between 8 March and 12 September 1990, the first carrier deployment with aircraft of this type. Access to the Gulf region was made through the Suez Canal on 1 May 1991. The squadron returned to the Persian Gulf via the Mediterranean and the Red Sea in a cruise lasting from 26 September 1991 to 2 April 1992, taking time to participate in the NATO Exercise *Teamwork 92*. Along with its sister squadron VF-143, the 'Ghostriders' accompanied the USS *George Washington* on a shakedown cruise between 3 September and 23 October 1992 after which they stood down for two years, their aircraft undergoing upgrades. On 20 May 1994 they returned to a cruise when the *Washington* sailed in support of the D-Day commemorations and went on to participate in Operation *Deny Flight* from the Mediterranean. VF-142 was disestablished in April 1995 leaving VF-143 as the only F-14 squadron aboard the carrier.

VF-143 'Pukin Dogs'

A veteran Phantom squadron, VF-143 became one of the first Tomcat units when it exchanged F-4s for F-14s in 1974 and switched from the Pacific to the Atlantic Fleet. Deployed to Air Wing 6 and the carrier *America*, the 'Pukin Dogs' sailed on their first Tomcat cruise on 15 April 1976. Its sailings are the same as VF-142's up to 29 September 1977. After that VF-143 switched to Air Wing 7 aboard the USS

Dwight D. Eisenhower and made two cruises without its sister squadron: to the Caribbean between 18 September and 26 October 1978 and to the Gulf region between 14 November and 4 December 1978. From 16 January 1979 it was rejoined by VF-142 when the two squadrons sailed for the Mediterranean, returning on 13 July.

During the Mediterranean cruise between January and July 1982 the 'Pukin Dogs' supported Operation *Peace for Galilee* and deployed three TARPS aircraft in support of intelligence gathering for Air Wing 7. From April to December 1983 the 'Dogs' took part in Exercise *Bright Star 83*, demonstrating long-range intercepts against fighters and bombers as varied as the F-16 and the B-52. In a multi-purpose role, VF-143 F-14s flew simulated strikes against Egyptian targets while simultaneously picking up reconnaissance data through their TARPS equipment. In October 1984 both VF-143 and its sister squadron VF-142 returned to the USS *Eisenhower* for a cruise to the Mediterranean.

After a Caribbean cruise between 8 July and 8 September 1985, the squadron remained on shore for almost thirty months until it rejoined the *Eisenhower* for a cruise to the Mediterranean from 29 February to 29 August 1988, where aircraft took detailed reconnaissance imagery of the Soviet warship *Baku*, one of the new *Kiev* class carriers. The first of the new F-14B TARPS Tomcats arrived with VF-143 on 26 May 1989 and the squadron was reunited with its sister for a Persian Gulf assignment sailing on 8 March 1990. In the year that saw the *Eisenhower* withdrawn from possible involvement in *Desert Shield*, VF-143 received an award for high maintenance standards. In May of the following year VF-143 became the first F-14B unit to drop live bombs, but from April 1995 it was the only Tomcat squadron on the *George Washington*, its sister squadron having been disbanded.

VF-154 'Black Knights'

The last of the Tomcat squadrons to deploy, the 'Black Knights' became operational in 1984 with three of their twelve F-14s equipped for TARPS. Paired with VF-21, as they had been when flying F-4 Phantoms, the 'Black Knights' went to sea with Air Wing 14 aboard the USS

Constellation on 18 October 1984 and returned on 15 November following a short exercise. Another brief excursion followed between 6 and 16 December that year. Further sailings matched those for VF-21 and in 1987 the squadron intercepted Iranian aircraft close to the Gulf of Oman during a cruise to the region that began on 11 April. The paired squadrons remained a team until VF-21 was disestablished in 1996, leaving VF-154 as the remaining F-14 unit.

VF-191 'Satan's Kittens'

A legend in its time, 'Satan's Kittens' formed up in 1942 and operated Grumman Hellcats for a time aboard the USS *Lexington* recording 155 air victories and twenty-five ships destroyed, reason enough for its adopted name. In Korea they operated another Grumman cat, the F8F Bearcat, and then the F11F Tiger before adopting the F-8 Crusader for service in Vietnam. Only briefly did the squadron get F-4 Phantoms before VF-191 was retired, only to rise again on 4 December 1986 to be one of two paired squadrons operating with Air Wing 10 aboard the USS *Independence*. Qualification trials were conducted aboard the *Enterprise* from 24 July to 5 August 1987 but plans for operational deployment ran foul of cuts and VF-191 was disbanded on 30 April 1988. The Navy toyed with the idea of making VF-191 the third F-14D squadron after VF-51 and VF-111 but these plans too were shelved.

VF-194 'Red Lightnings'

The 'Red Lightnings' had a history similar to that of their Tomcat sister squadron VF-191. Formed in 1942, they operated Hellcats and had Grumman F9F Panthers in the Korean War. For Vietnam they operated F-8 Crusaders but made only one tour with F-4 Phantoms before being disestablished on 1 March 1978. More than eight years later, on 1 December 1986, VF-194 was given life again in a plan to pair it with VF-191 for Air Wing 10 and service aboard the *Independence*. Along with its sister squadron, the 'Red Lightnings' conducted a brief cruise on the *Enterprise* between 24 July and 5 August 1987 but the unit was disestablished a second time on 30 April 1988; plans to

make it the fourth F-14D squadron being abandoned.

VF-201 'Hunters'

The second of two Naval Air Reserve Tomcat squadrons, VF-201 formed up on 25 July 1970 and was assigned to Reserve Air Wing 20 and deployed aboard the USS *Forrestal* on 14 June 1987 for a twelve-days cruise for training. A second training cruise in the Atlantic was conducted between 24 July and 3 August 1987 on the *Eisenhower*. Based at Naval Air Station Dallas, VF-201 was the only surviving F-14 Reserve Air Squadron when VF-202 was disestablished in October 1994.

VF-202 'Superheats'

The first of two Naval Air Reserve squadrons to replace its F-4 Phantoms with the Tomcat, VF-202 had formed on 1 July 1970 and received its first swing-wing fighter on 10 April 1987. By May 1988 it was up to full strength on the type. Based in Dallas, Texas, VF-202 conducted a brief shakedown aboard the carrier *America* off the eastern seaboard, qualifying as a TARPS unit in Reserve Air Wing 20. Later in 1988 the squadron visited Bergstrom Air Force Base for a gathering of reconnaissance units. The following year, between 24 July and 3 August, VF-202 joined its sister squadron VF-201 aboard the USS *Eisenhower* for a north Atlantic patrol. Success as a squadron was insufficient to save it from the axe and the 'Superheats' were disbanded in October 1994.

VF-211 'Fighting Checkmates'

Teamed for the Tomcat era with its sister squadron VF-24, the 'Fighting Checkmates' date back to World War II, having been formed on 1 May 1945 and relinquished F-8 Crusaders for F-14s during 1975. It was with VF-24 that the squadron sailed for the west Pacific aboard the USS *Constellation* on 12 April 1977. Its sailings were the same as those of VF-24. In 1979 the 'Fighting Checkmates' stood off the port of Aden when fighting broke out between North and South Yemen after the Shah of Iran had been deposed. Tomcats faced the prospect of fighting exported Tomcats then in the hands of the

Islamic Revolutionary Council of Iran. But that interesting possibility was not to be. VF-211 was around in the Gulf region when the Tehran hostage rescue went so badly wrong in 1980.

From 15 October 1980 VF-211 was assigned the TARPS role for Air Wing 9, three of its twelve aircraft having that role. The 'Fighting Checkmates' became the first F-14 TARPS operators on the West Coast. In 1982 the unit received a special award for combat readiness afloat and ashore and in 1984, while operating from the *Ranger*, VF-211 performed TARPS reconnaissance and surveillance missions in Central America. Beginning in April 1989 the squadron began exchanging its F-14As for F-14Bs Tomcats, but when contracts for the new fighter were cut the 'Fighting Checkmates' reverted to the earlier version. In June 1992 VF-211 became the first West Coast squadron operating Tomcats to pass the Advanced Attack Readiness Program, highlighting the multi-mission role of the aircraft. From 1996 VF-211 has operated as the only Tomcat unit with Air Wing 9.

VF-213 'Black Lions'

Formerly assigned to fly F-4B Phantoms, the 'Black Lions' date back to June 1955 but in September 1976 they began to receive Tomcats with an assignment to pair with their sister squadron VF-114 in Air Wing 11 aboard the USS *Kitty Hawk*. The first cruise began on 25 October 1977 and the sailings followed those described for the 'Aardvarks'. During 1982 the 'Black Lions' acquired the Air Wing 11 TARPS role and exploited their technology to photograph a large number of surface ships and submarines operated by the Soviets in the Pacific during a patrol that began on 1 September 1982 and ended on 28 May 1983.

By March 1983 the unit had logged 17,000 flying hours without a major accident and in early 1988 a VF-213 pilot became the first Tomcat pilot to complete 2,000 flying hours on the aircraft. In 1986 Tomcats from VF-213 were repainted in disruptive colours of brown and green but reverted to the standard finish in the following year. VF-213 was accompanied by its sister squadron when it sailed with the USS *Abraham Lincoln* on 24 September 1990, in a shakedown cruise into the south Atlantic, round the Horn and up to the

West Coast during which it deployed some aircraft in exercises with Chile and Argentina. In the second half of 1991 the 'Black Lions' were in the Persian Gulf and operated with aircraft from the Omani Air Force, including Jaguars and some very dated 'adversaries' such as the Hawker Hunter. In a more determined role, VF-213 flew reconnaissance and surveillance flights over Iraq and participated in Operation *Fiery Vigil*.

In early 1992 the squadron received word that it was to extend its multi-mission role and take on Bombcat duties, beginning the training for that activity in May. Adapting to survive, VF-213 lost its sister squadron when VF-114 was disestablished on 30 April 1993 but sailed with the *Abraham Lincoln* to the west Pacific, the Indian Ocean and the Persian Gulf region in a patrol flexing its new capability; this ended on 15 December. In the Gulf area the 'Black Lions' supported US operations in Somalia and took turns with neighbouring squadrons at policing the no-fly zones in southern Iraq.

VF-301 'Devil's Disciples'

Based at Naval Air Station Miramar, the 'Devil's Disciples' were established as part of Reserve Air Wing 30 on 1 October 1970 and formally began replacing their F-4S Phantoms with Tomcats in 1985, although some had been delivered from the US Navy as early as 1983. On 21 April 1985 five Tomcats from VF-301 flew to a weapons range at Yuma, Arizona, for

training in air-to-air combat and on 4 August the full squadron arrived at Naval Air Station Fallon for more extensive training. The first two-weeks active fleet training cruise took place between 15 and 26 January 1986 aboard the USS *Ranger*, subsequent cruises taking place from 10 to 22 August 1988 aboard the *Enterprise*, from 6 to 16 August 1990 aboard the *Nimitz* and from 15 to 24 August 1992 again aboard the *Nimitz*. The squadron was axed by Navy cuts in October 1994.

VF-302 'Stallions'

Formed in 1970 at Miramar with F-8 Crusaders, the 'Stallions' received F-4 Phantoms from November 1973, the first Reserve Air Squadron to get the type. In 1985 it began to work up on Tomcats, receiving old aircraft from the Navy and achieved readiness in 1986. Paired with VF-301, the 'Stallions' played the TARPS role whereby three of the twelve aircraft in complement were assigned to the tactical reconnaissance and surveillance role. Assignments and activities were the same as those described for VF-301 and, like its sister squadron, the 'Stallions' were disestablished in October 1994, leaving VF-201 as the only surviving Reserve Tomcat unit.

VX-4 'The Evaluators'

Living up to their name, the 'Evaluators' came into establishment at Point Mugu, California, on 15 September 1952 for the

purpose of testing air-launched guided weapons. Conversion to the Tomcat came via the Naval Air Test Center at Patuxent River, Maryland, from where the F-14s were delivered. It became the role of VX-4 to evaluate the AIM-54 Phoenix as well as participate in the development of the AIM-9L Sidewinder. During late 1970 the Navy joined with the Air Force to undertake the preparation of the specification leading to the AMRAAM missile concept and VX-4 was the unit primarily responsible for the Television Camera System.

By normal standards, the squadron is large and has an interservice mix of a few Marine and Air Force officers on exchange. During the early 1990s VX-4 played an instrumental part in the development of the Bombcat capability, using F-14D aircraft in these evaluations of the multi-mission role using Tomcats and Hornets in a variety of ways to determine the optimum spread of types. The squadron has carried more than usual irregular markings, most notably associated with the black Playboy bunny which on several occasions carried forward to an extramural licence! In 1994 the unit went through a transformation when on 29 April it was merged with VX-5 to become VX-9. Operating from China Lake, it has been tasked with testing a wide variety of ordnance and tactical applications.

Index